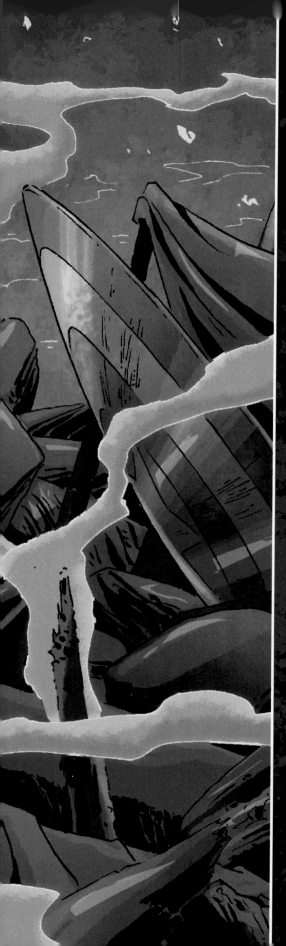

S0-BAU-773

WRITER
CULLEN **BUNN**
ARTIST
DALIBOR **TALAJIĆ**
COLORIST
LEE **LOUGHRIDGE**
LETTERER
VC'S JOE **SABINO**
COVER ARTIST
KAARE **ANDREWS**
EDITOR
JORDAN D. **WHITE**
SENIOR EDITOR
NICK **LOWE**

COLLECTION EDITOR & DESIGN
CORY LEVINE
ASSISTANT EDITORS
ALEX STARBUCK
& NELSON RIBEIRO
EDITORS, SPECIAL PROJECTS
JENNIFER GRÜNWALD
& MARK D. BEAZLEY
SENIOR EDITOR, SPECIAL PROJECTS
JEFF YOUNGQUIST
SENIOR VICE PRESIDENT OF SALES
DAVID GABRIEL
SVP OF BRAND PLANNING
& COMMUNICATIONS
MICHAEL PASCIULLO

EDITOR IN CHIEF
AXEL ALONSO
CHIEF CREATIVE OFFICER
JOE QUESADA
PUBLISHER
DAN BUCKLEY
EXECUTIVE PRODUCER
ALAN FINE

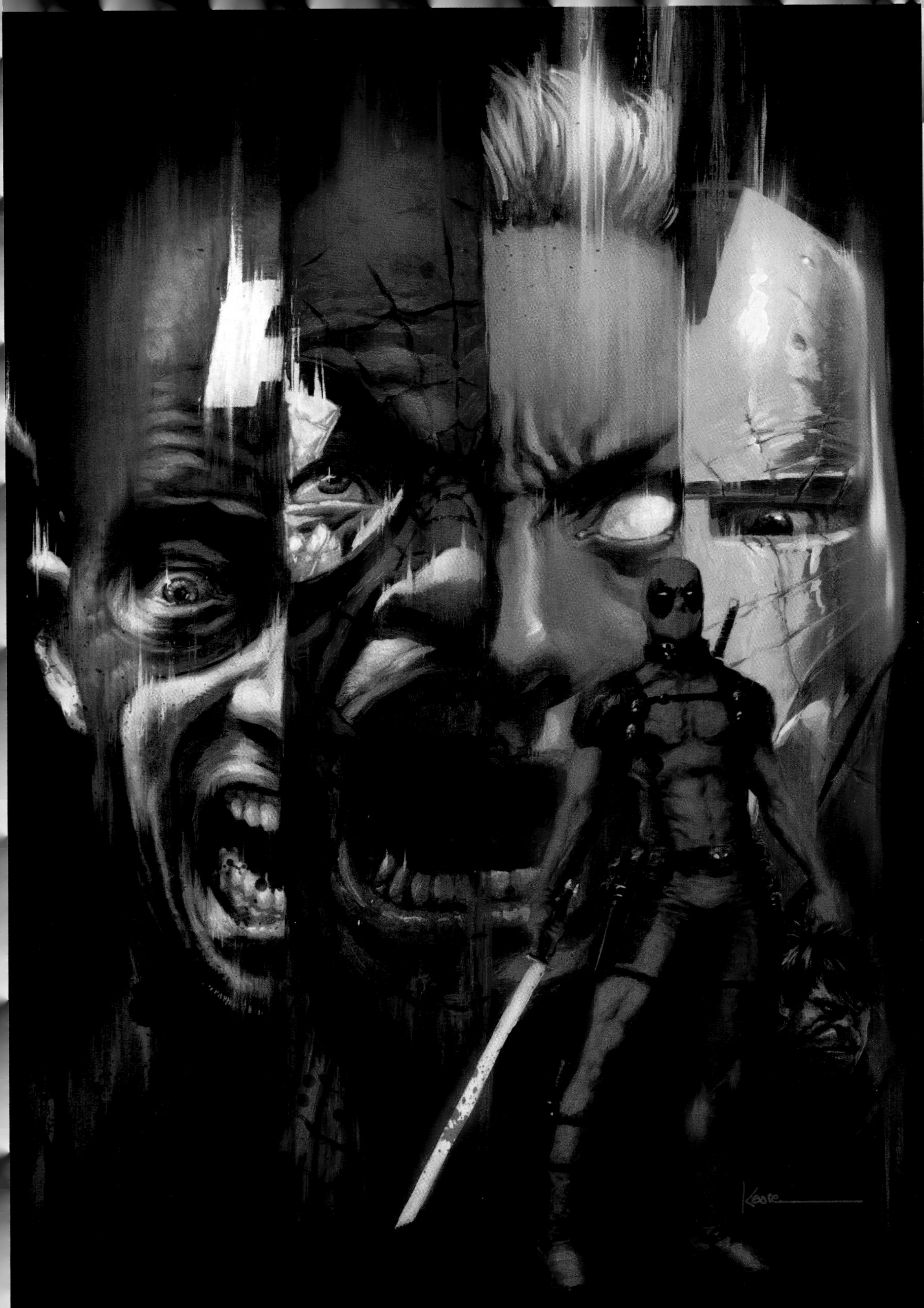

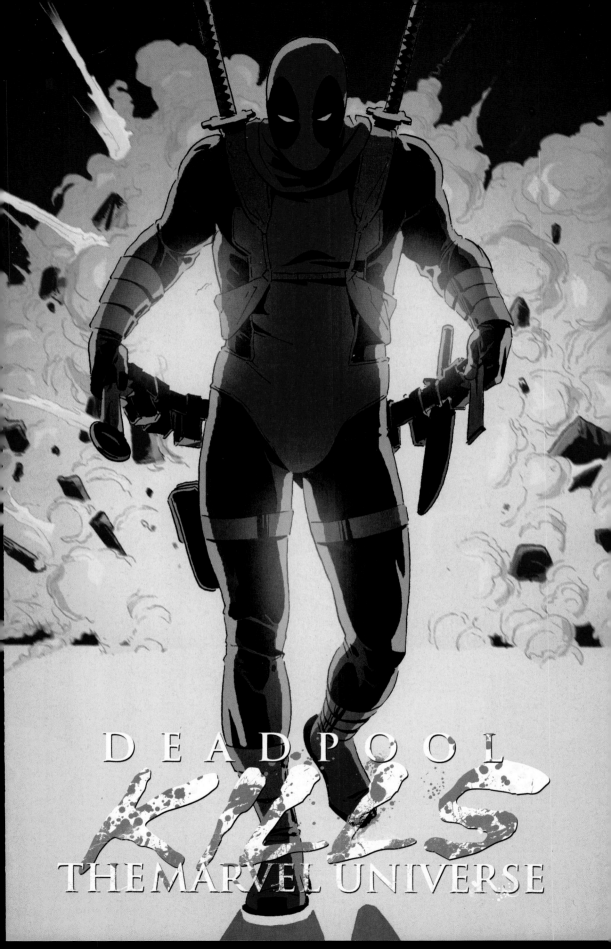

DEADPOOL KILLS
THE MARVEL UNIVERSE

DEADPOOL KILLS THE MARVEL UNIVERSE. Contains material originally published in magazine form as DEADPOOL KILLS THE MARVEL UNIVERSE #1-4. Second printing 2013. ISBN# 978-0-7851-6403-6. Published by MARVEL WORLDWIDE, INC., a subsidiary of MARVEL ENTERTAINMENT, LLC. OFFICE OF PUBLICATION: 135 West 50th Street, New York, NY 10020. Copyright © 2012 Marvel Characters, Inc. All rights reserved. All characters featured in this issue and the distinctive names and likenesses thereof, and all related indicia are trademarks of Marvel Characters, Inc. No similarity between any of the names, characters, persons, and/or institutions in this magazine with those of any living or dead person or institution is intended, and any such similarity which may exist is purely coincidental. **Printed in the U.S.A.** ALAN FINE, EVP - Office of the President, Marvel Worldwide, Inc. and EVP & CMO Marvel Characters B.V.; DAN BUCKLEY, Publisher & President - Print, Animation & Digital Divisions; JOE QUESADA, Chief Creative Officer; TOM BREVOORT, SVP of Publishing; DAVID BOGART, SVP of Operations & Procurement, Publishing; RUWAN JAYATILLEKE, SVP & Associate Publisher, Publishing; C.B. CEBULSKI, SVP of Creator & Content Development; DAVID GABRIEL, SVP of Print & Digital Publishing Sales; JIM O'KEEFE, VP of Operations & Logistics; DAN CARR, Executive Director of Publishing Technology; SUSAN CRESPI, Editorial Operations Manager; ALEX MORALES, Publishing Operations Manager; STAN LEE, Chairman Emeritus. For information regarding advertising in Marvel Comics or on Marvel.com, please contact Niza Disla, Director of Marvel Partnerships, at ndisla@marvel.com. For Marvel subscription inquiries, please call 800-217-9158. **Manufactured between 1/16/2013 and 2/19/2013 by QUAD/GRAPHICS, DUBUQUE, IA, USA.**

10 9 8 7 6 5 4 3 2

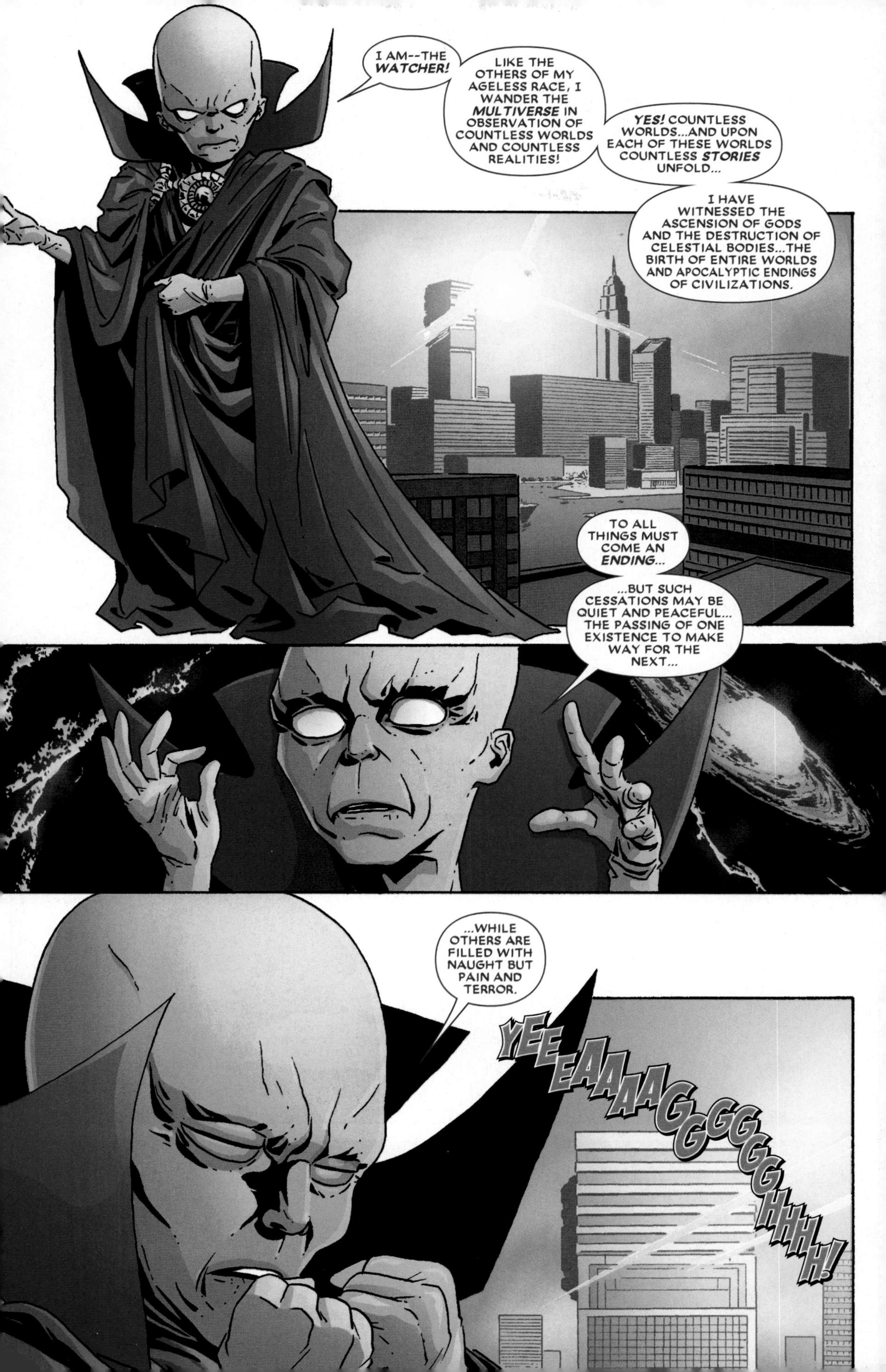
I AM--THE WATCHER!
LIKE THE OTHERS OF MY AGELESS RACE, I WANDER THE MULTIVERSE IN OBSERVATION OF COUNTLESS WORLDS AND COUNTLESS REALITIES!
YES! COUNTLESS WORLDS...AND UPON EACH OF THESE WORLDS COUNTLESS STORIES UNFOLD...
I HAVE WITNESSED THE ASCENSION OF GODS AND THE DESTRUCTION OF CELESTIAL BODIES...THE BIRTH OF ENTIRE WORLDS AND APOCALYPTIC ENDINGS OF CIVILIZATIONS.
TO ALL THINGS MUST COME AN ENDING...
...BUT SUCH CESSATIONS MAY BE QUIET AND PEACEFUL... THE PASSING OF ONE EXISTENCE TO MAKE WAY FOR THE NEXT...
...WHILE OTHERS ARE FILLED WITH NAUGHT BUT PAIN AND TERROR.
YEEEAAAAAGGGGGGHHHH!

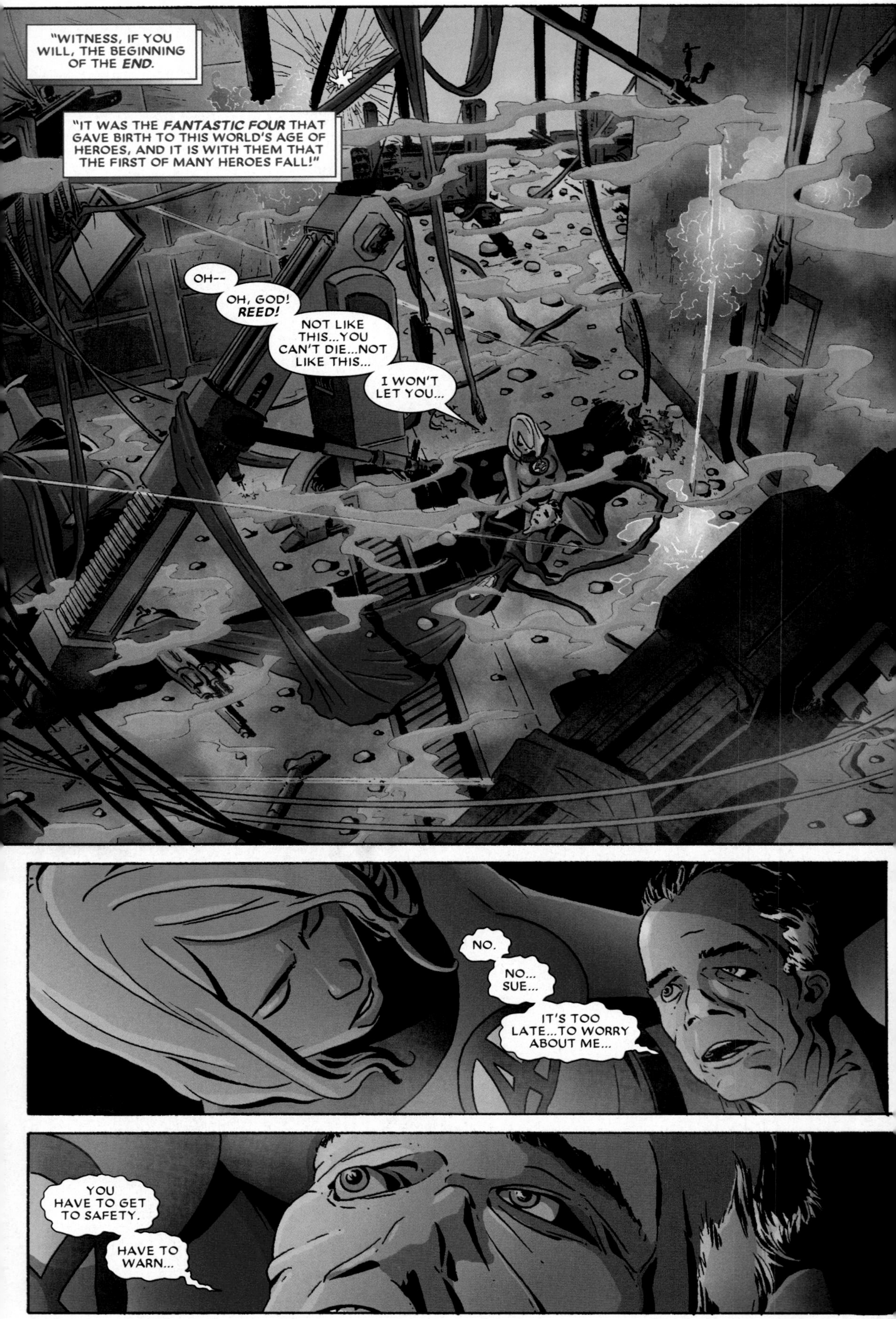
"WITNESS, IF YOU WILL, THE BEGINNING OF THE *END*.
"IT WAS THE *FANTASTIC FOUR* THAT GAVE BIRTH TO THIS WORLD'S AGE OF HEROES, AND IT IS WITH THEM THAT THE FIRST OF MANY HEROES FALL!"
OH--
OH, GOD! *REED!*
NOT LIKE THIS...YOU CAN'T DIE...NOT LIKE THIS...
I WON'T LET YOU...
NO.
NO... SUE...
IT'S TOO LATE...TO WORRY ABOUT ME...
YOU HAVE TO GET TO SAFETY.
HAVE TO WARN...

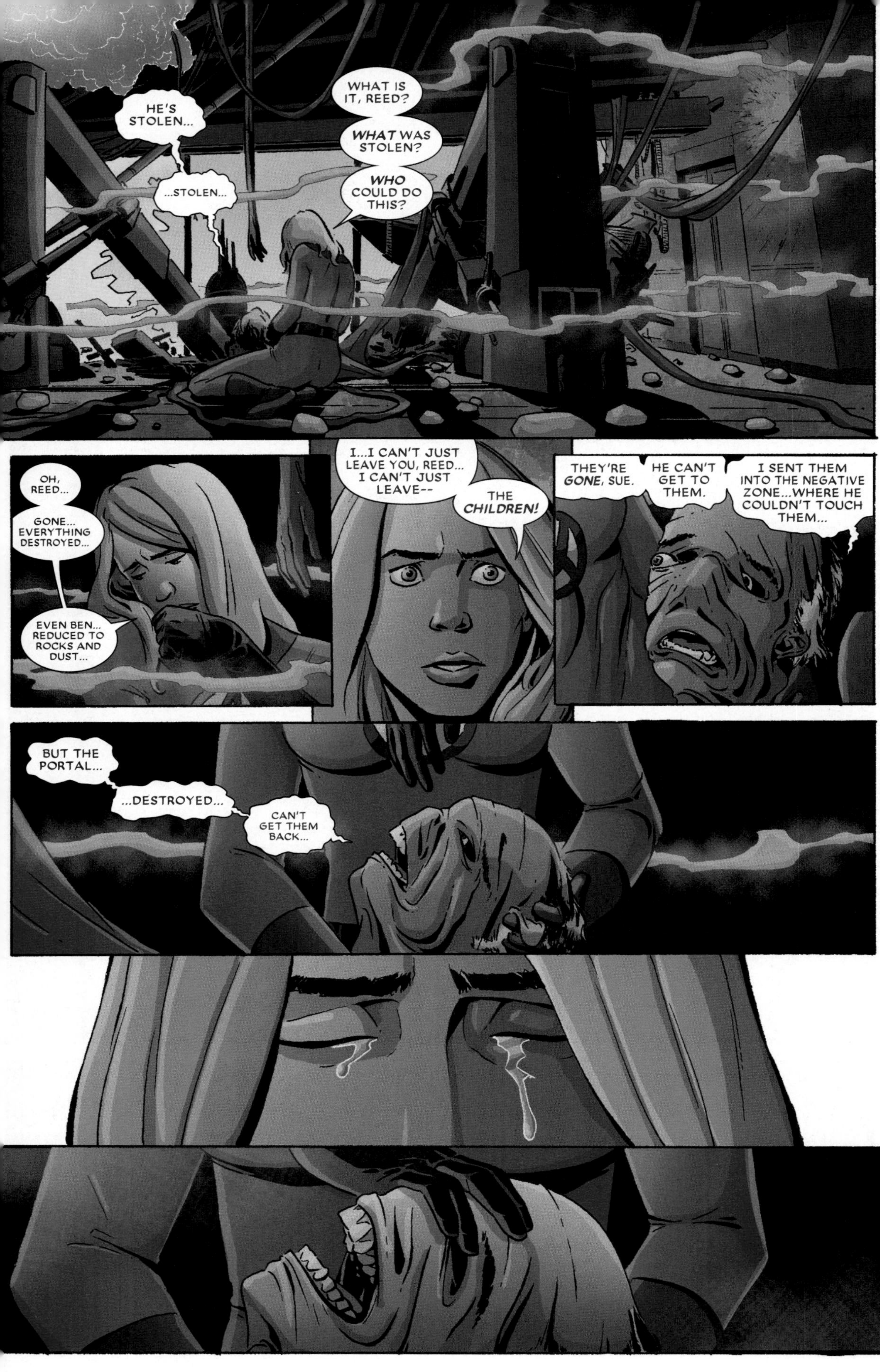

HE'S STOLEN...
...STOLEN...
WHAT IS IT, REED?
WHAT WAS STOLEN?
WHO COULD DO THIS?
OH, REED...
GONE... EVERYTHING DESTROYED...
EVEN BEN... REDUCED TO ROCKS AND DUST...
I...I CAN'T JUST LEAVE YOU, REED... I CAN'T JUST LEAVE--
THE CHILDREN!
THEY'RE GONE, SUE.
HE CAN'T GET TO THEM.
I SENT THEM INTO THE NEGATIVE ZONE...WHERE HE COULDN'T TOUCH THEM...
BUT THE PORTAL...
...DESTROYED...
CAN'T GET THEM BACK...

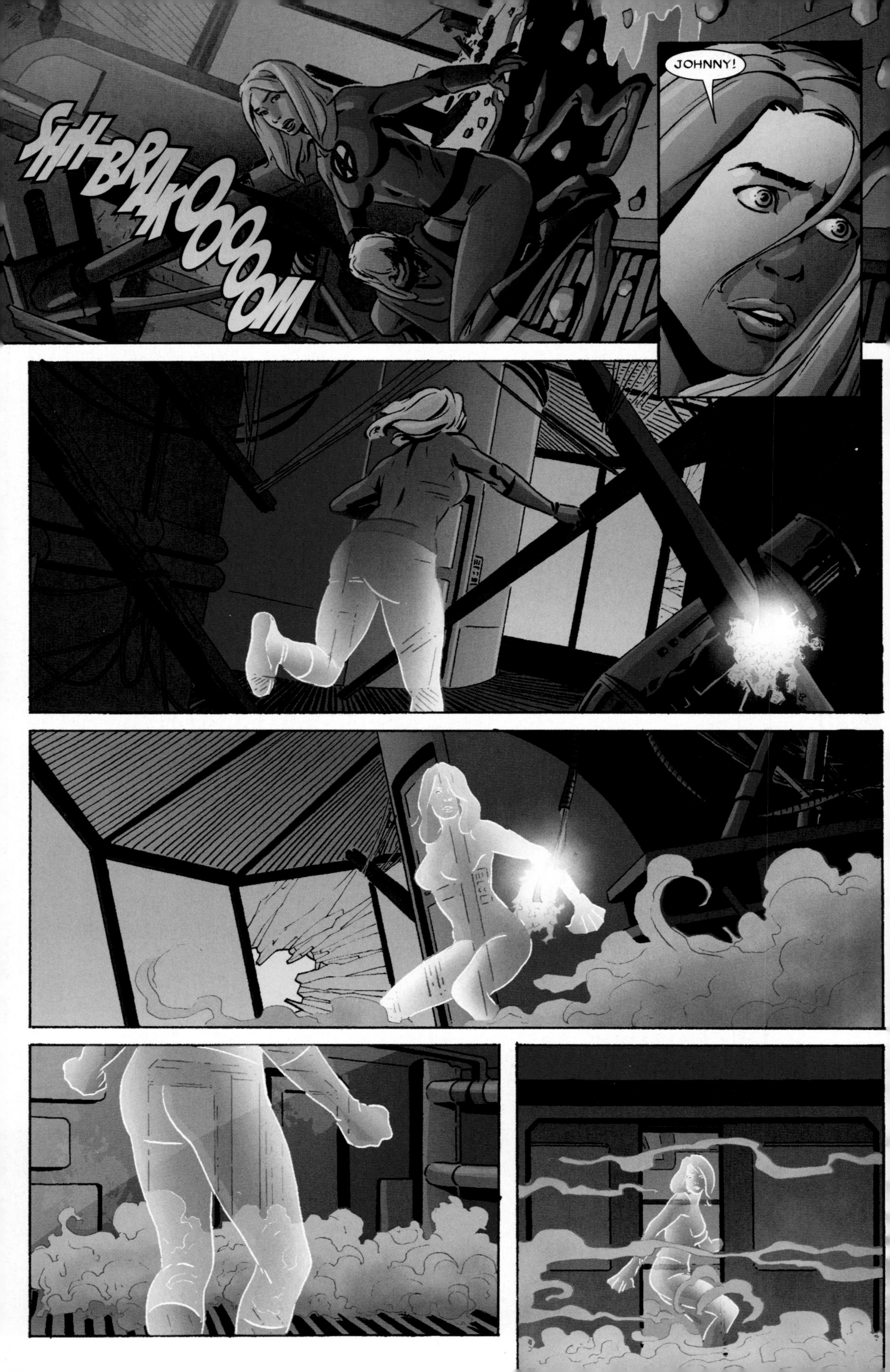
SHHBRAKOOOOOM
JOHNNY!

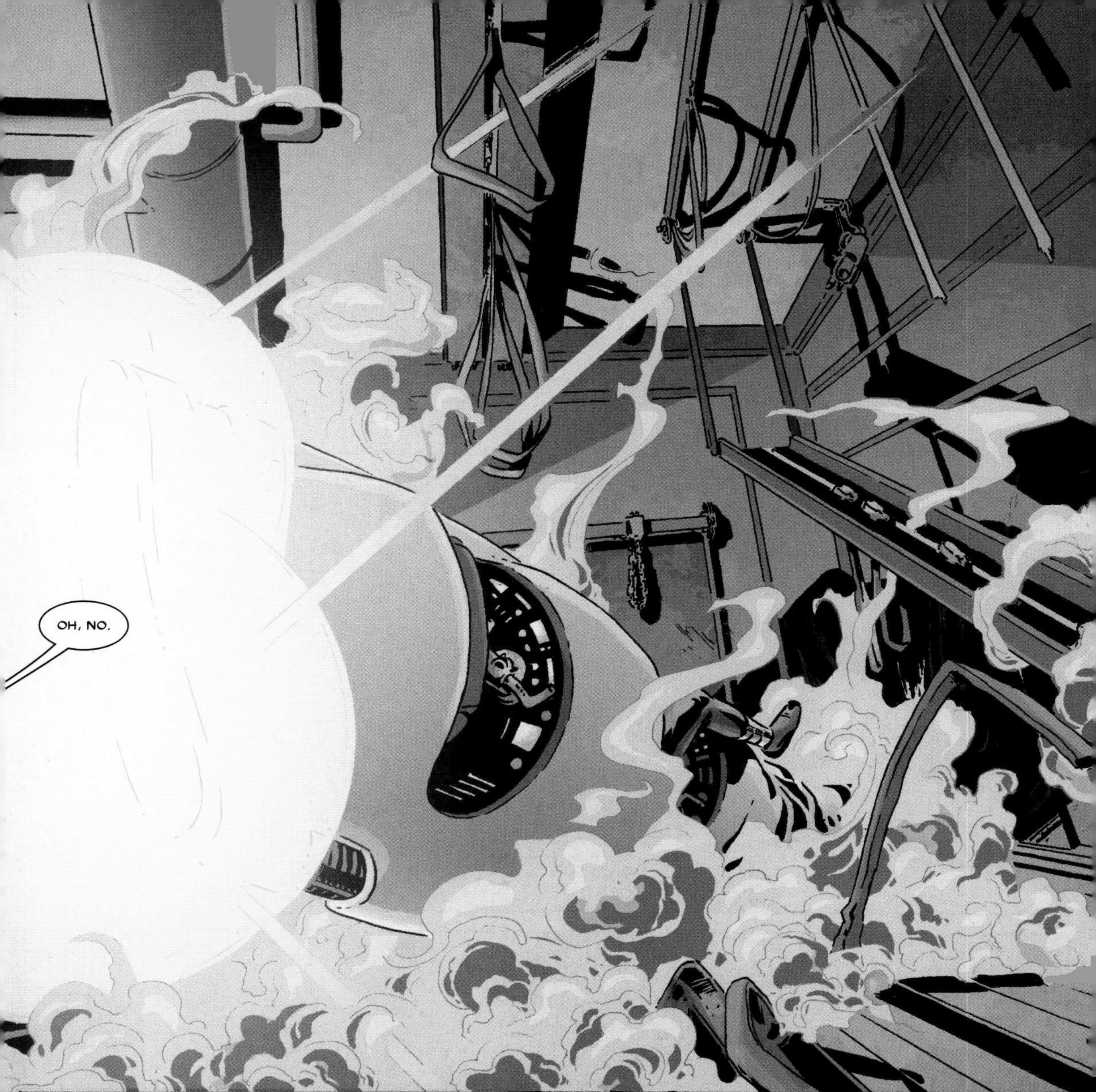
OH, NO.

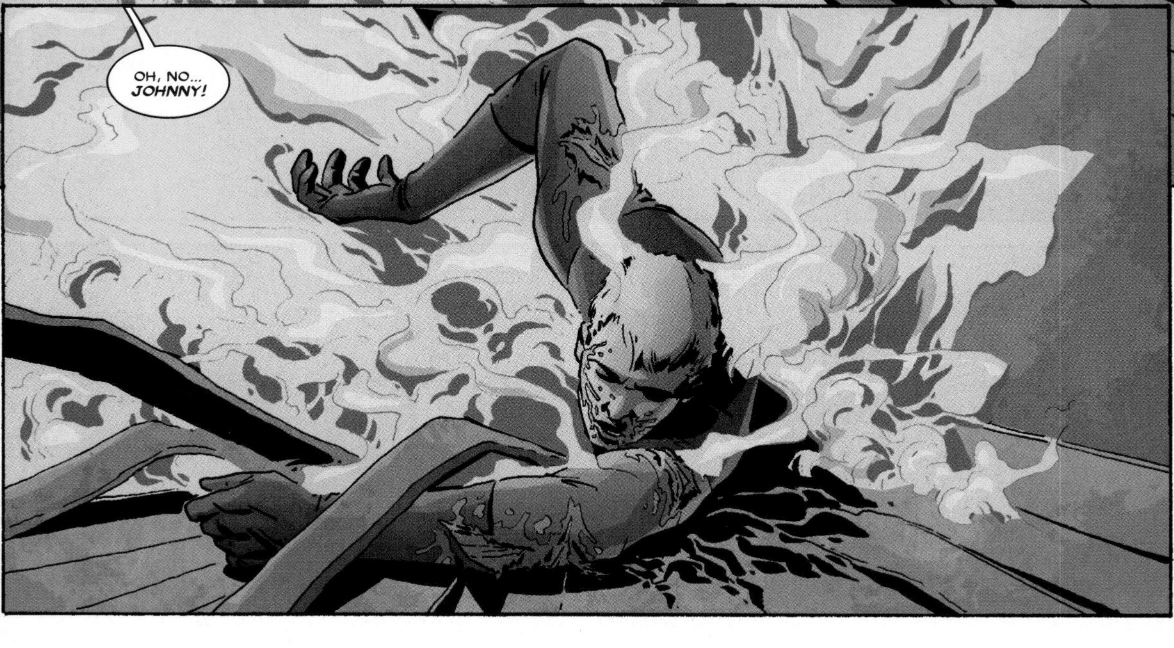
OH, NO...
JOHNNY!

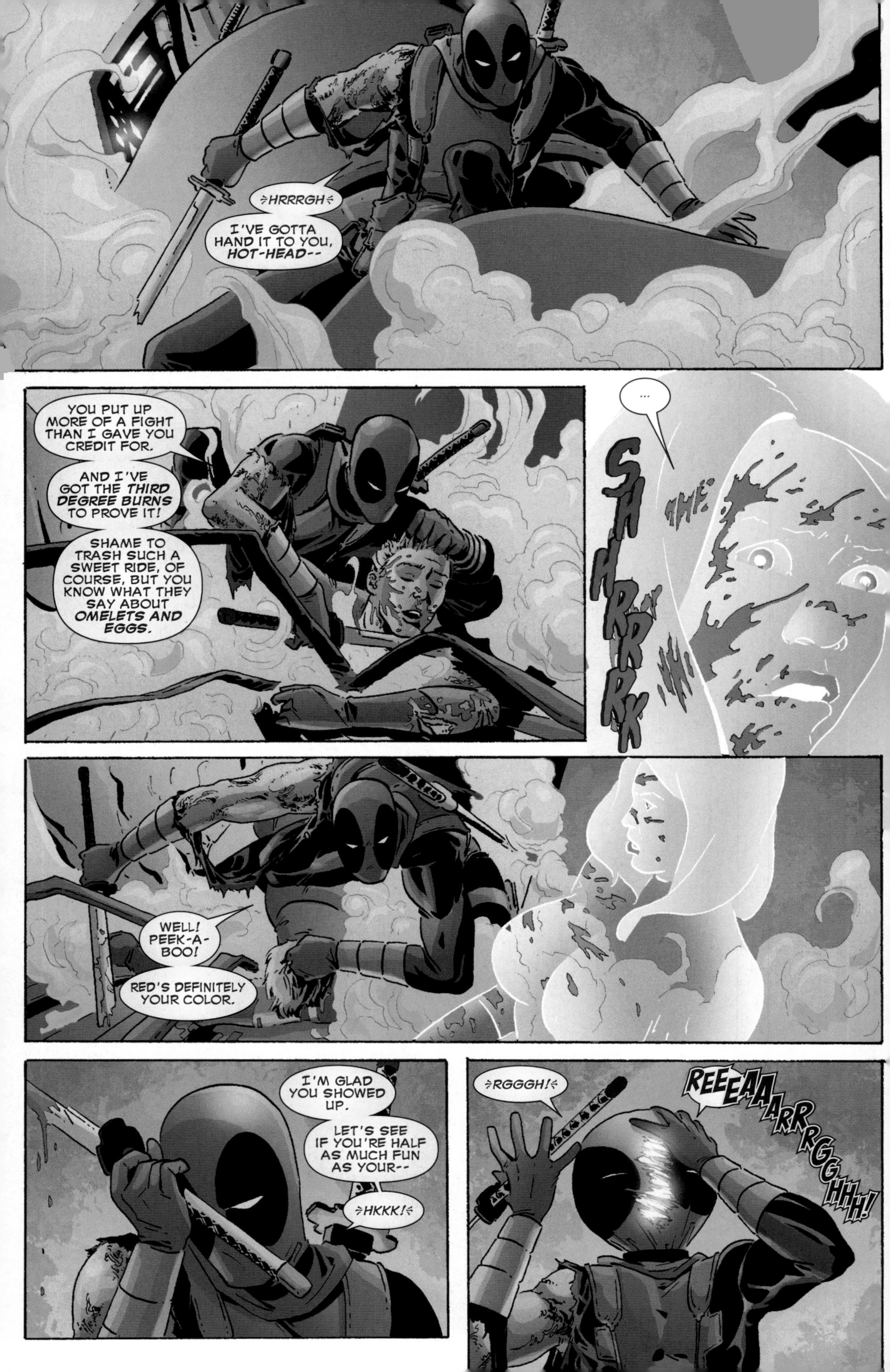

HRRRGH
I'VE GOTTA HAND IT TO YOU, HOT-HEAD--
YOU PUT UP MORE OF A FIGHT THAN I GAVE YOU CREDIT FOR.
AND I'VE GOT THE THIRD DEGREE BURNS TO PROVE IT!
SHAME TO TRASH SUCH A SWEET RIDE, OF COURSE, BUT YOU KNOW WHAT THEY SAY ABOUT OMELETS AND EGGS.
...
SHHRRRK
WELL! PEEK-A-BOO!
RED'S DEFINITELY YOUR COLOR.
I'M GLAD YOU SHOWED UP.
LET'S SEE IF YOU'RE HALF AS MUCH FUN AS YOUR--
HKKK!
RGGGH!
REEEAAARRRGGHHH!

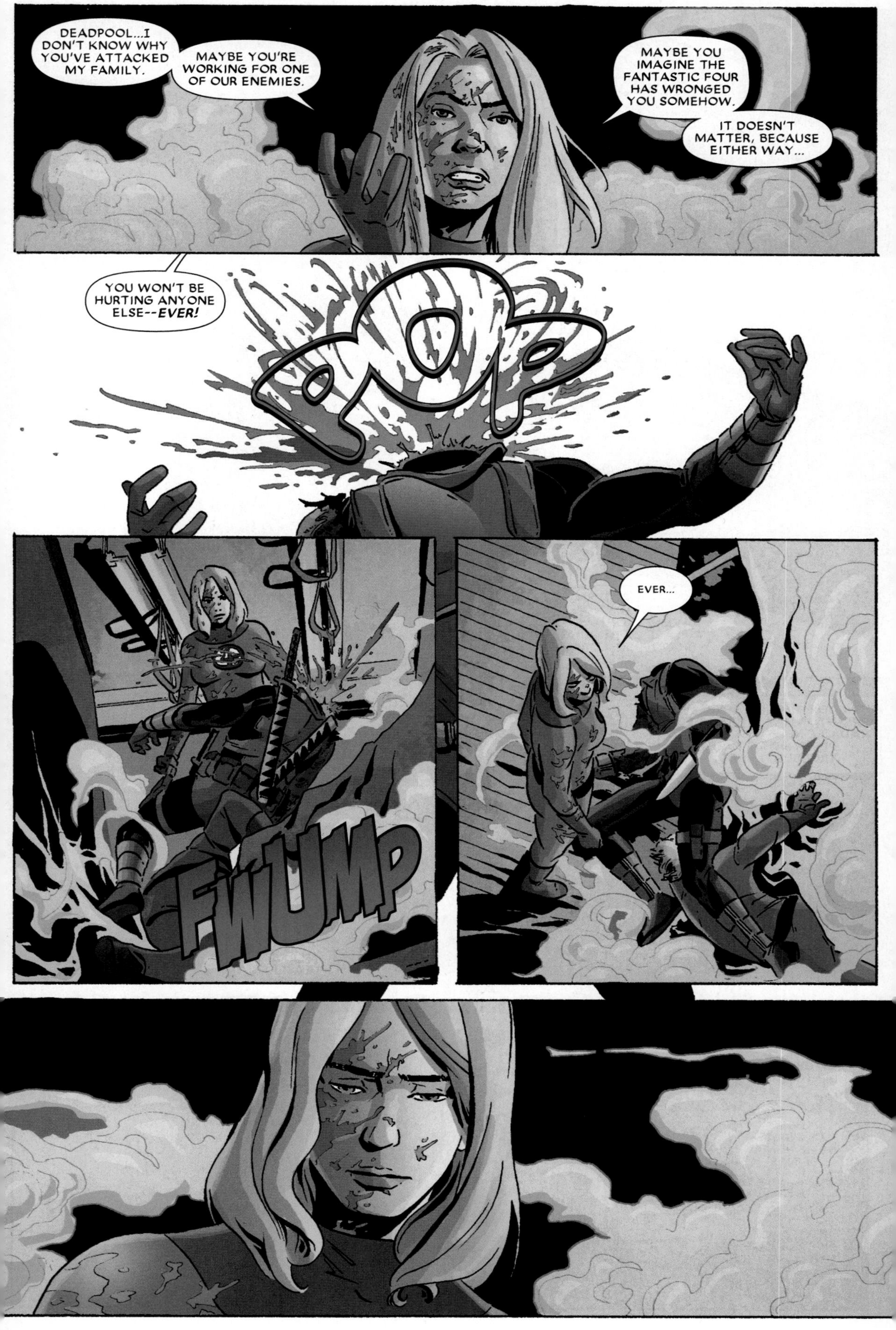
DEADPOOL...I DON'T KNOW WHY YOU'VE ATTACKED MY FAMILY.
MAYBE YOU'RE WORKING FOR ONE OF OUR ENEMIES.
MAYBE YOU IMAGINE THE FANTASTIC FOUR HAS WRONGED YOU SOMEHOW.
IT DOESN'T MATTER, BECAUSE EITHER WAY...
YOU WON'T BE HURTING ANYONE ELSE--EVER!
POP
FWUMP
EVER...

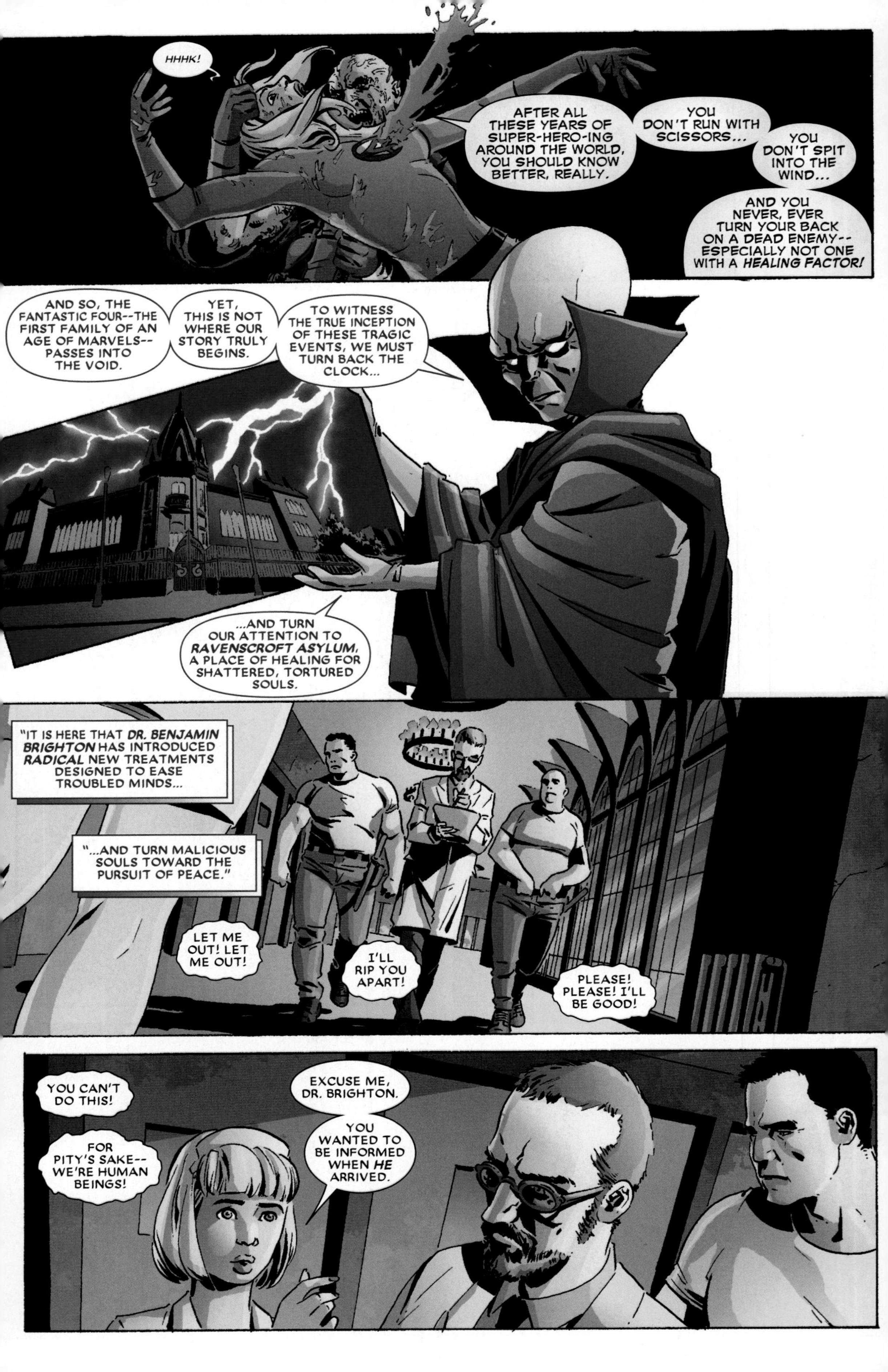
HHHK!
AFTER ALL THESE YEARS OF SUPER-HERO-ING AROUND THE WORLD, YOU SHOULD KNOW BETTER, REALLY.
YOU DON'T RUN WITH SCISSORS...
YOU DON'T SPIT INTO THE WIND...
AND YOU NEVER, EVER TURN YOUR BACK ON A DEAD ENEMY--ESPECIALLY NOT ONE WITH A HEALING FACTOR!
AND SO, THE FANTASTIC FOUR--THE FIRST FAMILY OF AN AGE OF MARVELS--PASSES INTO THE VOID.
YET, THIS IS NOT WHERE OUR STORY TRULY BEGINS.
TO WITNESS THE TRUE INCEPTION OF THESE TRAGIC EVENTS, WE MUST TURN BACK THE CLOCK...
...AND TURN OUR ATTENTION TO RAVENSCROFT ASYLUM, A PLACE OF HEALING FOR SHATTERED, TORTURED SOULS.
"IT IS HERE THAT DR. BENJAMIN BRIGHTON HAS INTRODUCED RADICAL NEW TREATMENTS DESIGNED TO EASE TROUBLED MINDS...
"...AND TURN MALICIOUS SOULS TOWARD THE PURSUIT OF PEACE."
LET ME OUT! LET ME OUT!
I'LL RIP YOU APART!
PLEASE! PLEASE! I'LL BE GOOD!
YOU CAN'T DO THIS!
FOR PITY'S SAKE--WE'RE HUMAN BEINGS!
EXCUSE ME, DR. BRIGHTON.
YOU WANTED TO BE INFORMED WHEN HE ARRIVED.

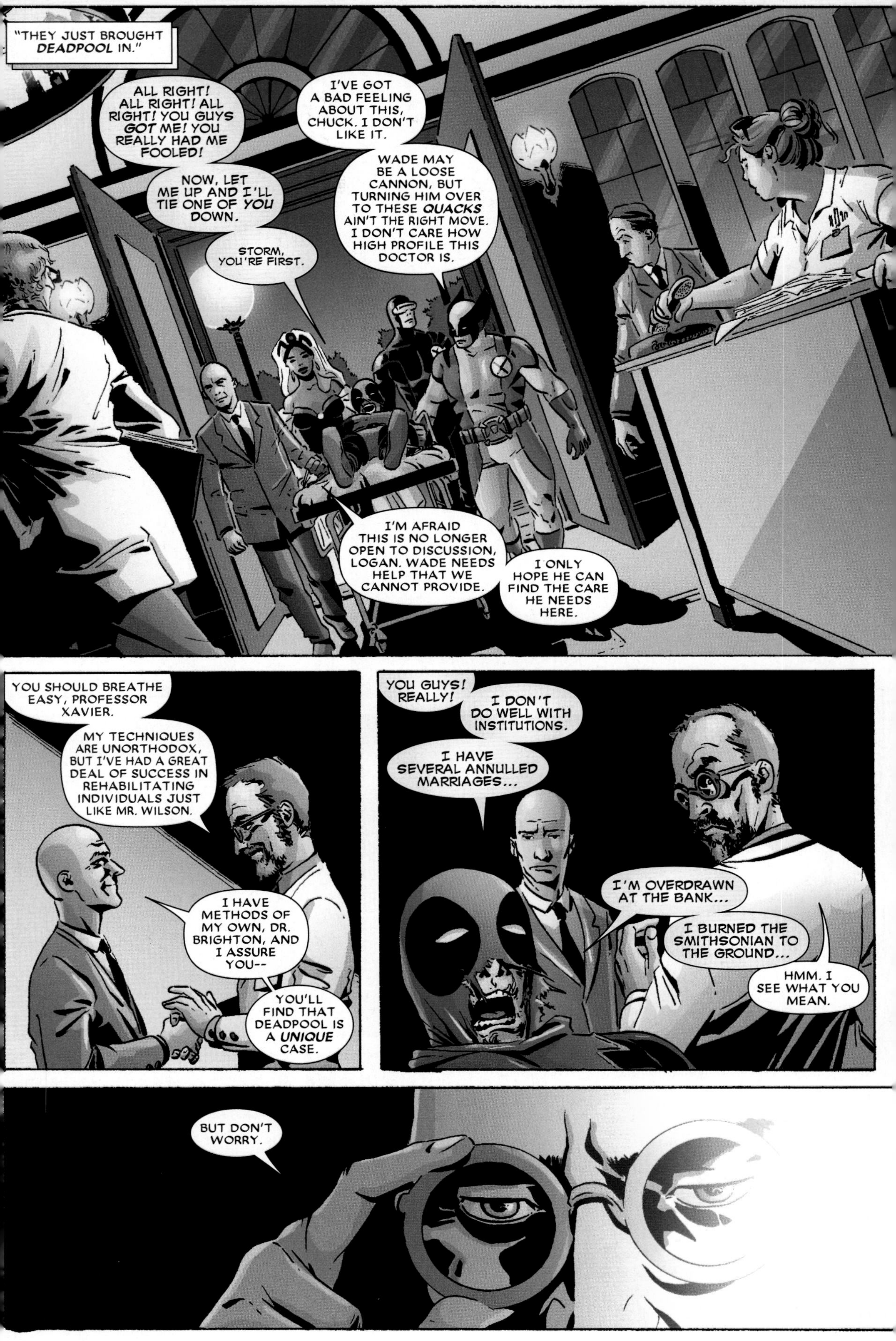
"THEY JUST BROUGHT DEADPOOL IN."
ALL RIGHT! ALL RIGHT! ALL RIGHT! YOU GUYS GOT ME! YOU REALLY HAD ME FOOLED!
NOW, LET ME UP AND I'LL TIE ONE OF YOU DOWN.
STORM, YOU'RE FIRST.
I'VE GOT A BAD FEELING ABOUT THIS, CHUCK. I DON'T LIKE IT.
WADE MAY BE A LOOSE CANNON, BUT TURNING HIM OVER TO THESE QUACKS AIN'T THE RIGHT MOVE. I DON'T CARE HOW HIGH PROFILE THIS DOCTOR IS.
I'M AFRAID THIS IS NO LONGER OPEN TO DISCUSSION, LOGAN. WADE NEEDS HELP THAT WE CANNOT PROVIDE.
I ONLY HOPE HE CAN FIND THE CARE HE NEEDS HERE.
YOU SHOULD BREATHE EASY, PROFESSOR XAVIER.
MY TECHNIQUES ARE UNORTHODOX, BUT I'VE HAD A GREAT DEAL OF SUCCESS IN REHABILITATING INDIVIDUALS JUST LIKE MR. WILSON.
I HAVE METHODS OF MY OWN, DR. BRIGHTON, AND I ASSURE YOU--
YOU'LL FIND THAT DEADPOOL IS A UNIQUE CASE.
YOU GUYS! REALLY!
I DON'T DO WELL WITH INSTITUTIONS.
I HAVE SEVERAL ANNULLED MARRIAGES...
I'M OVERDRAWN AT THE BANK...
I BURNED THE SMITHSONIAN TO THE GROUND...
HMM. I SEE WHAT YOU MEAN.
BUT DON'T WORRY.

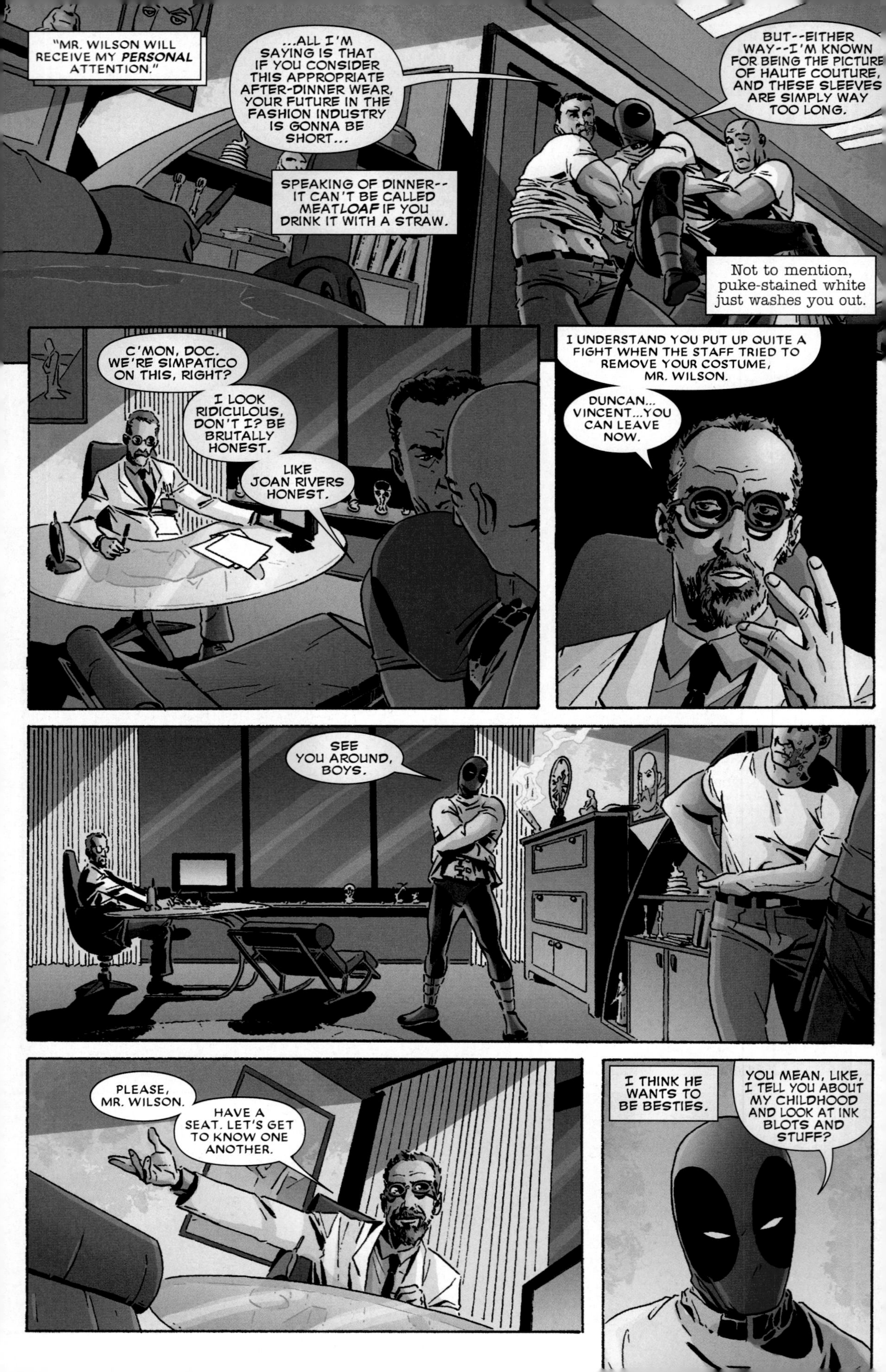
"MR. WILSON WILL RECEIVE MY PERSONAL ATTENTION."
...ALL I'M SAYING IS THAT IF YOU CONSIDER THIS APPROPRIATE AFTER-DINNER WEAR, YOUR FUTURE IN THE FASHION INDUSTRY IS GONNA BE SHORT...
SPEAKING OF DINNER--IT CAN'T BE CALLED MEATLOAF IF YOU DRINK IT WITH A STRAW.
BUT--EITHER WAY--I'M KNOWN FOR BEING THE PICTURE OF HAUTE COUTURE, AND THESE SLEEVES ARE SIMPLY WAY TOO LONG.
Not to mention, puke-stained white just washes you out.
C'MON, DOC. WE'RE SIMPATICO ON THIS, RIGHT?
I LOOK RIDICULOUS, DON'T I? BE BRUTALLY HONEST.
LIKE JOAN RIVERS HONEST.
I UNDERSTAND YOU PUT UP QUITE A FIGHT WHEN THE STAFF TRIED TO REMOVE YOUR COSTUME, MR. WILSON.
DUNCAN... VINCENT...YOU CAN LEAVE NOW.
SEE YOU AROUND, BOYS.
PLEASE, MR. WILSON.
HAVE A SEAT. LET'S GET TO KNOW ONE ANOTHER.
I THINK HE WANTS TO BE BESTIES.
YOU MEAN, LIKE, I TELL YOU ABOUT MY CHILDHOOD AND LOOK AT INK BLOTS AND STUFF?

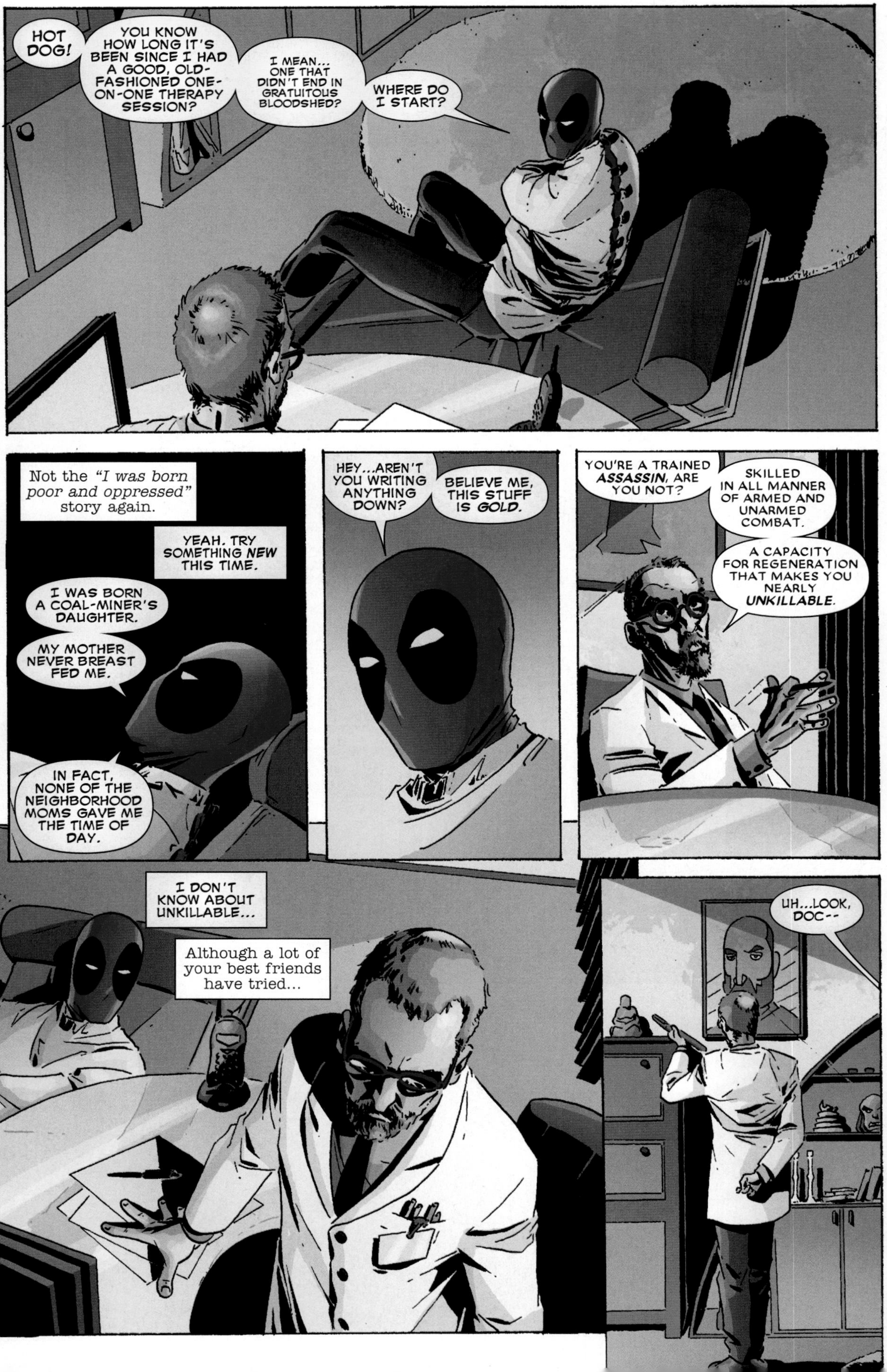
HOT DOG!
YOU KNOW HOW LONG IT'S BEEN SINCE I HAD A GOOD, OLD-FASHIONED ONE-ON-ONE THERAPY SESSION?
I MEAN... ONE THAT DIDN'T END IN GRATUITOUS BLOODSHED?
WHERE DO I START?
Not the "I was born poor and oppressed" story again.
YEAH. TRY SOMETHING NEW THIS TIME.
I WAS BORN A COAL-MINER'S DAUGHTER.
MY MOTHER NEVER BREAST FED ME.
IN FACT, NONE OF THE NEIGHBORHOOD MOMS GAVE ME THE TIME OF DAY.
HEY...AREN'T YOU WRITING ANYTHING DOWN?
BELIEVE ME, THIS STUFF IS GOLD.
YOU'RE A TRAINED ASSASSIN, ARE YOU NOT?
SKILLED IN ALL MANNER OF ARMED AND UNARMED COMBAT.
A CAPACITY FOR REGENERATION THAT MAKES YOU NEARLY UNKILLABLE.
I DON'T KNOW ABOUT UNKILLABLE...
Although a lot of your best friends have tried...
UH...LOOK, DOC--

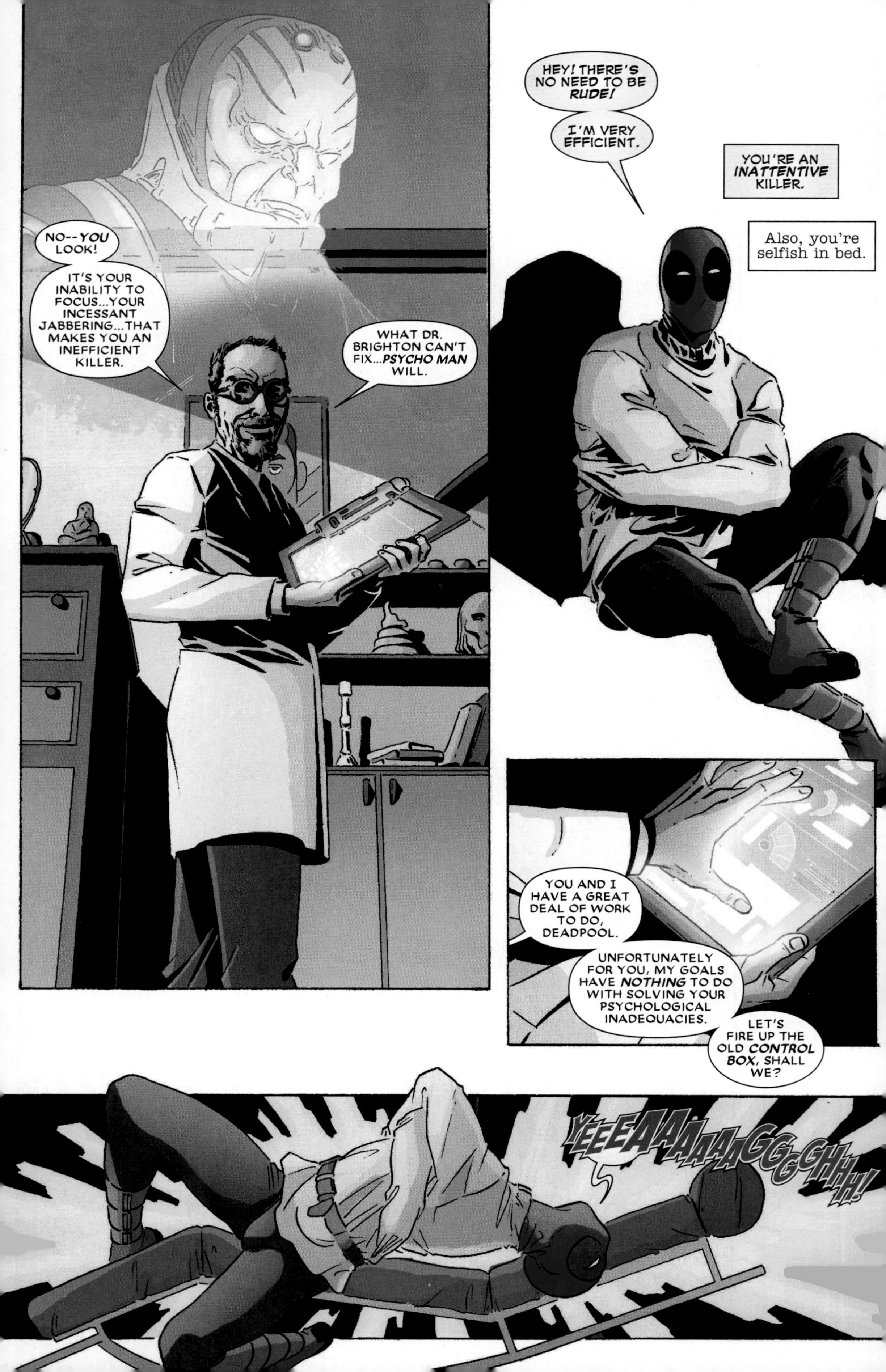
NO--YOU LOOK!
IT'S YOUR INABILITY TO FOCUS...YOUR INCESSANT JABBERING...THAT MAKES YOU AN INEFFICIENT KILLER.
WHAT DR. BRIGHTON CAN'T FIX...PSYCHO MAN WILL.
HEY! THERE'S NO NEED TO BE RUDE!
I'M VERY EFFICIENT.
YOU'RE AN INATTENTIVE KILLER.
Also, you're selfish in bed.
YOU AND I HAVE A GREAT DEAL OF WORK TO DO, DEADPOOL.
UNFORTUNATELY FOR YOU, MY GOALS HAVE NOTHING TO DO WITH SOLVING YOUR PSYCHOLOGICAL INADEQUACIES.
LET'S FIRE UP THE OLD CONTROL BOX, SHALL WE?
YEEEAAAAAAGGGGHHH!

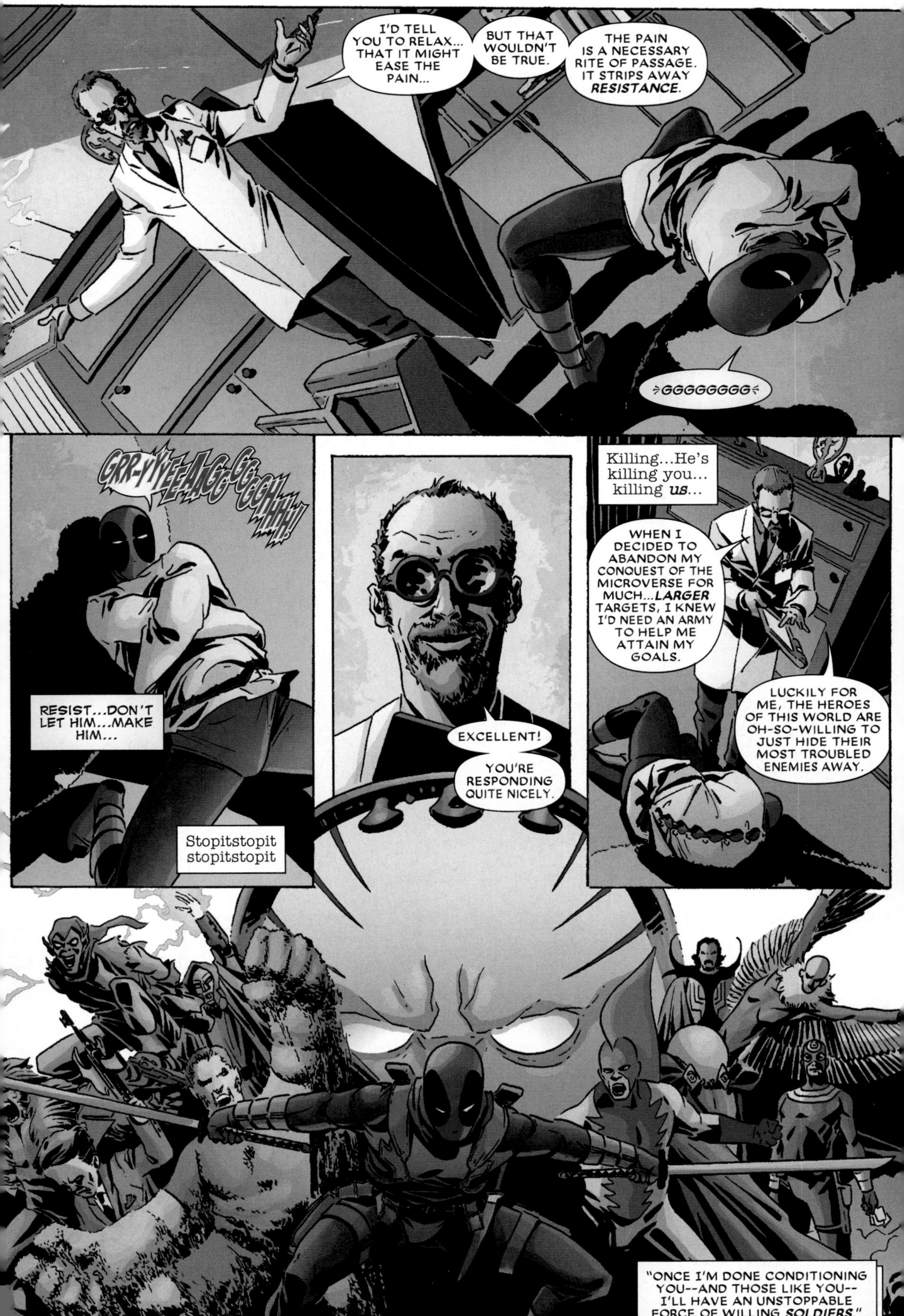
I'D TELL YOU TO RELAX... THAT IT MIGHT EASE THE PAIN...
BUT THAT WOULDN'T BE TRUE.
THE PAIN IS A NECESSARY RITE OF PASSAGE. IT STRIPS AWAY RESISTANCE.
GGGGGGGG
GRR-YYYEEAAGGGGGHHH!
RESIST...DON'T LET HIM...MAKE HIM...
Stopitstopit stopitstopit
EXCELLENT!
YOU'RE RESPONDING QUITE NICELY.
Killing...He's killing you... killing us...
WHEN I DECIDED TO ABANDON MY CONQUEST OF THE MICROVERSE FOR MUCH...LARGER TARGETS, I KNEW I'D NEED AN ARMY TO HELP ME ATTAIN MY GOALS.
LUCKILY FOR ME, THE HEROES OF THIS WORLD ARE OH-SO-WILLING TO JUST HIDE THEIR MOST TROUBLED ENEMIES AWAY.
"ONCE I'M DONE CONDITIONING YOU--AND THOSE LIKE YOU--I'LL HAVE AN UNSTOPPABLE FORCE OF WILLING SOLDIERS."

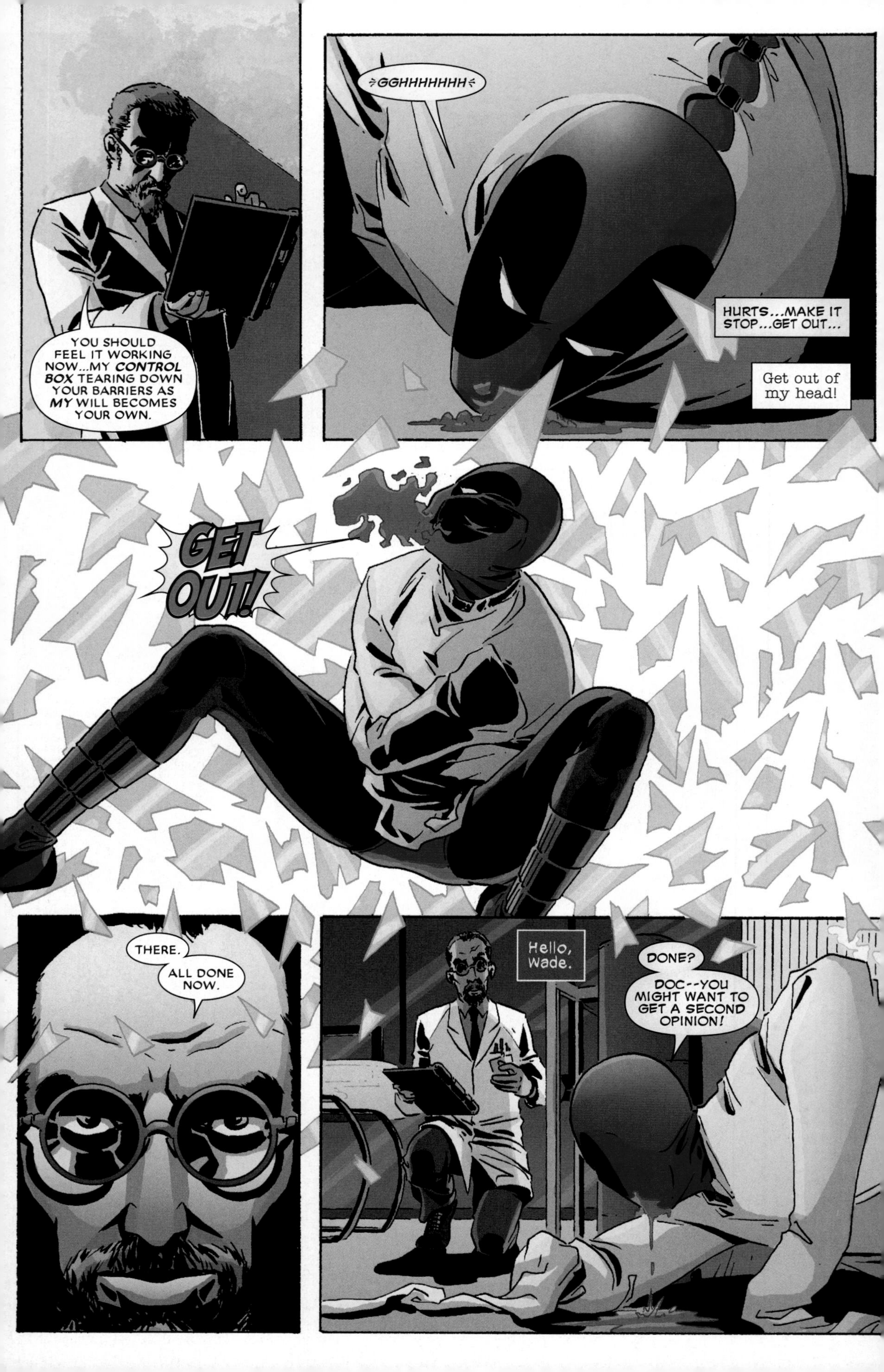
YOU SHOULD FEEL IT WORKING NOW...MY CONTROL BOX TEARING DOWN YOUR BARRIERS AS MY WILL BECOMES YOUR OWN.
GGHHHHHHH
HURTS...MAKE IT STOP...GET OUT...
Get out of my head!
GET OUT!
THERE.
ALL DONE NOW.
Hello, Wade.
DONE?
DOC--YOU MIGHT WANT TO GET A SECOND OPINION!

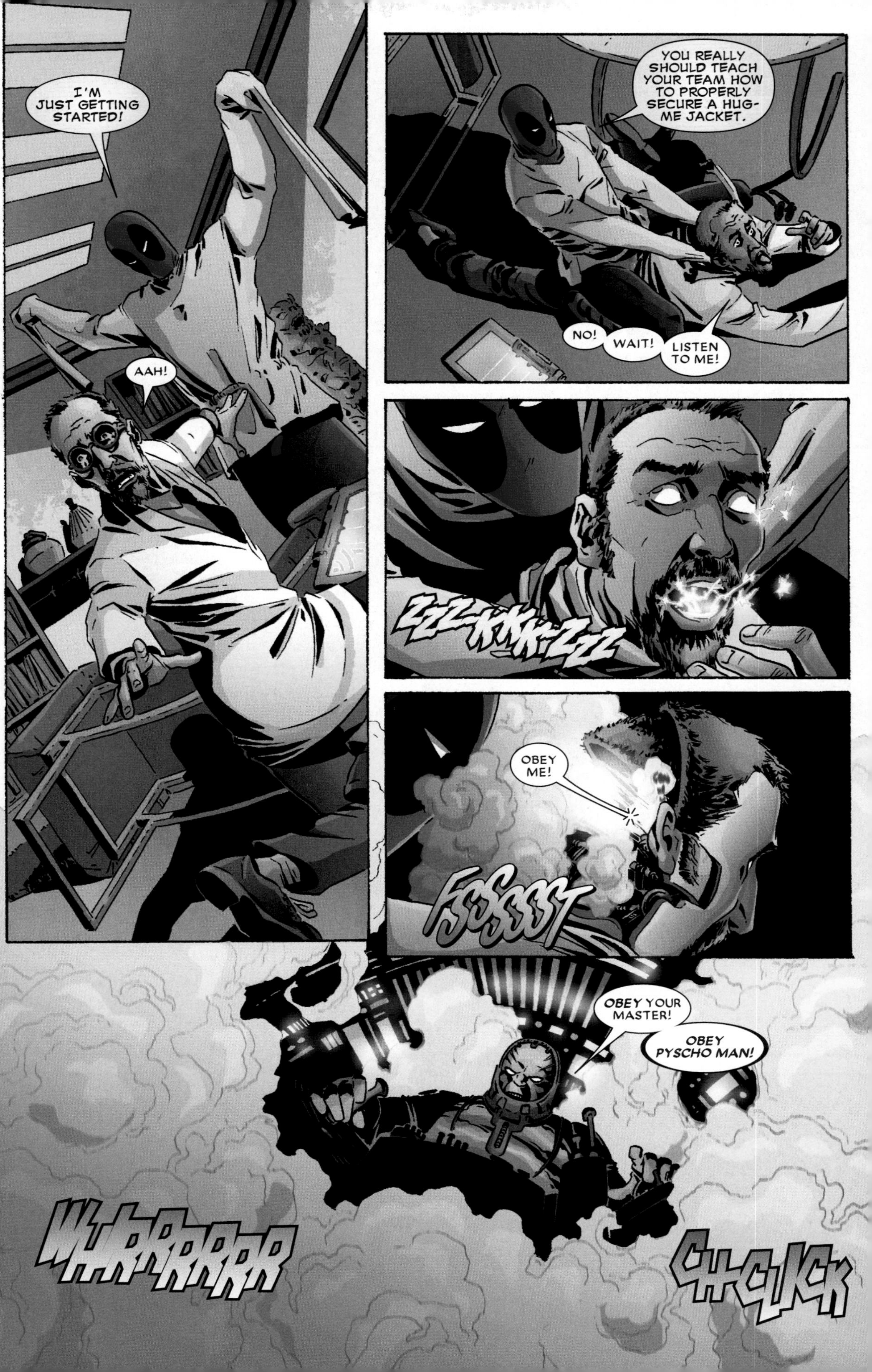

I'M JUST GETTING STARTED!
AAH!
YOU REALLY SHOULD TEACH YOUR TEAM HOW TO PROPERLY SECURE A HUG-ME JACKET.
NO!
WAIT!
LISTEN TO ME!
ZZZ-KKK-ZZZ
OBEY ME!
FSSSSST
OBEY YOUR MASTER!
OBEY PYSCHO MAN!
WHRRRRR
CHCLICK

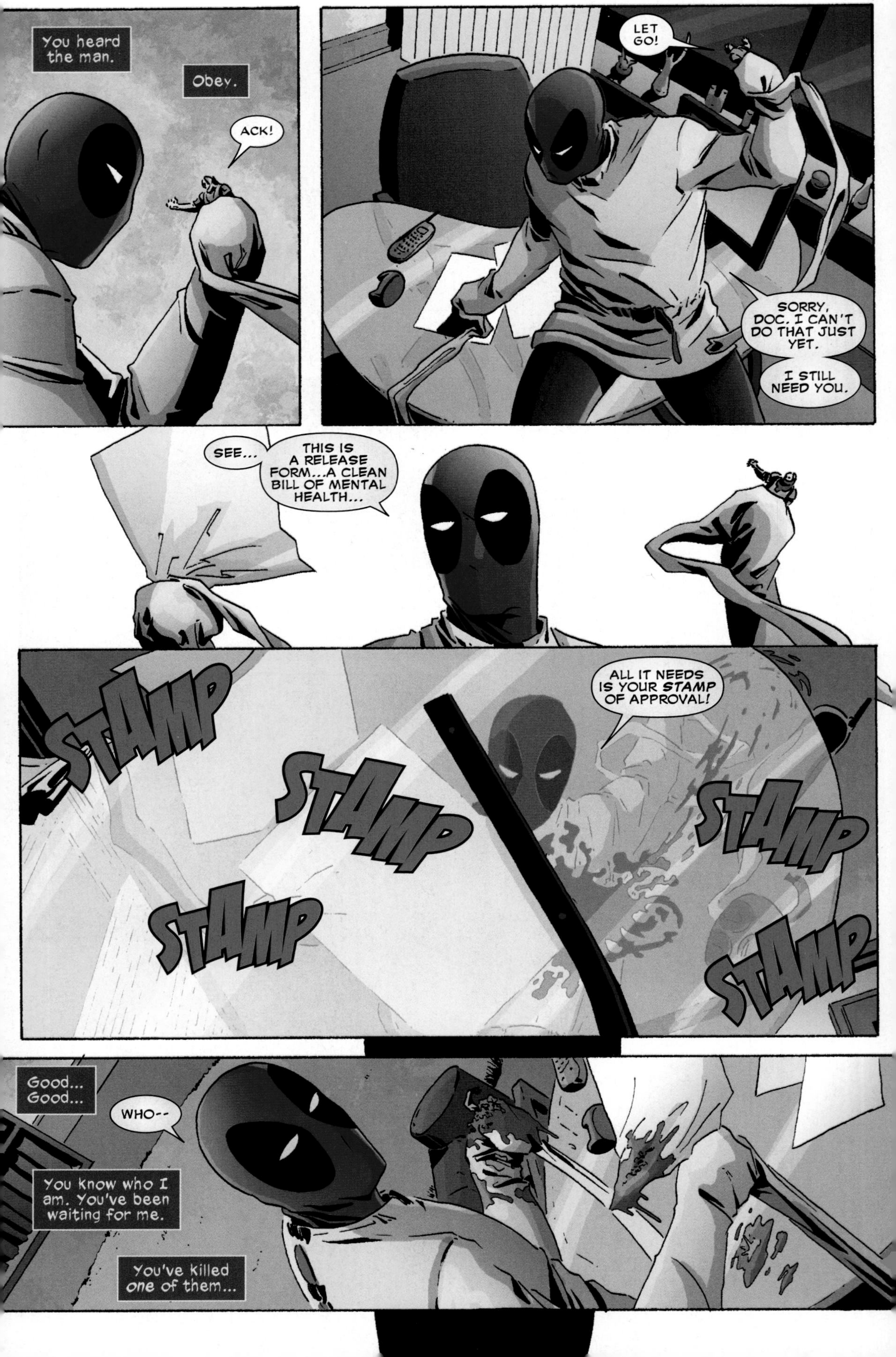
You heard the man.
Obey.
ACK!
LET GO!
SORRY, DOC. I CAN'T DO THAT JUST YET.
I STILL NEED YOU.
SEE...
THIS IS A RELEASE FORM...A CLEAN BILL OF MENTAL HEALTH...
STAMP
STAMP
STAMP
ALL IT NEEDS IS YOUR STAMP OF APPROVAL!
STAMP
STAMP
Good... Good...
WHO--
You know who I am. You've been waiting for me.
You've killed one of them...

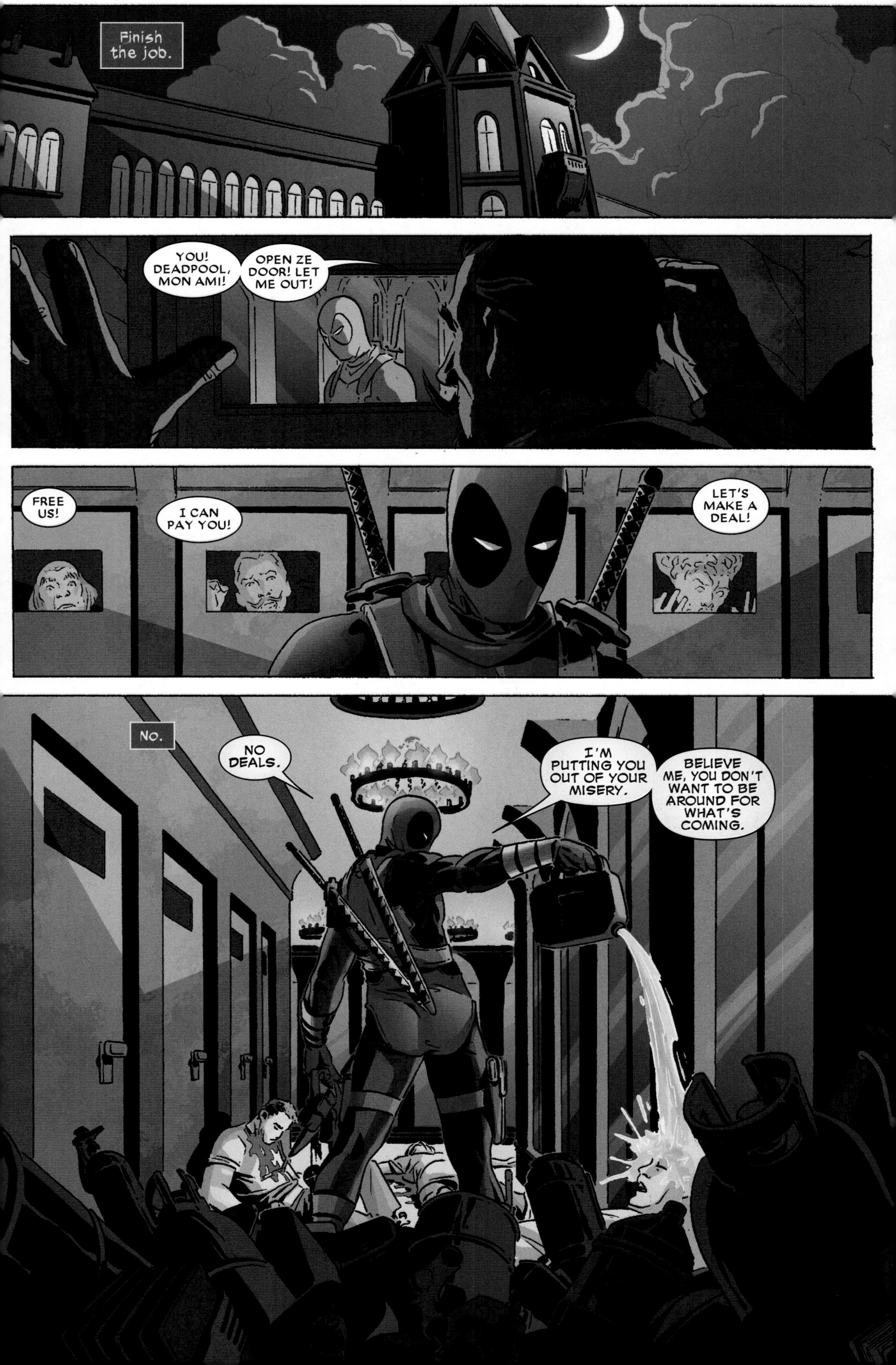
Finish the job.
YOU! DEADPOOL, MON AMI!
OPEN ZE DOOR! LET ME OUT!
FREE US!
I CAN PAY YOU!
LET'S MAKE A DEAL!
No.
NO DEALS.
I'M PUTTING YOU OUT OF YOUR MISERY.
BELIEVE ME, YOU DON'T WANT TO BE AROUND FOR WHAT'S COMING.

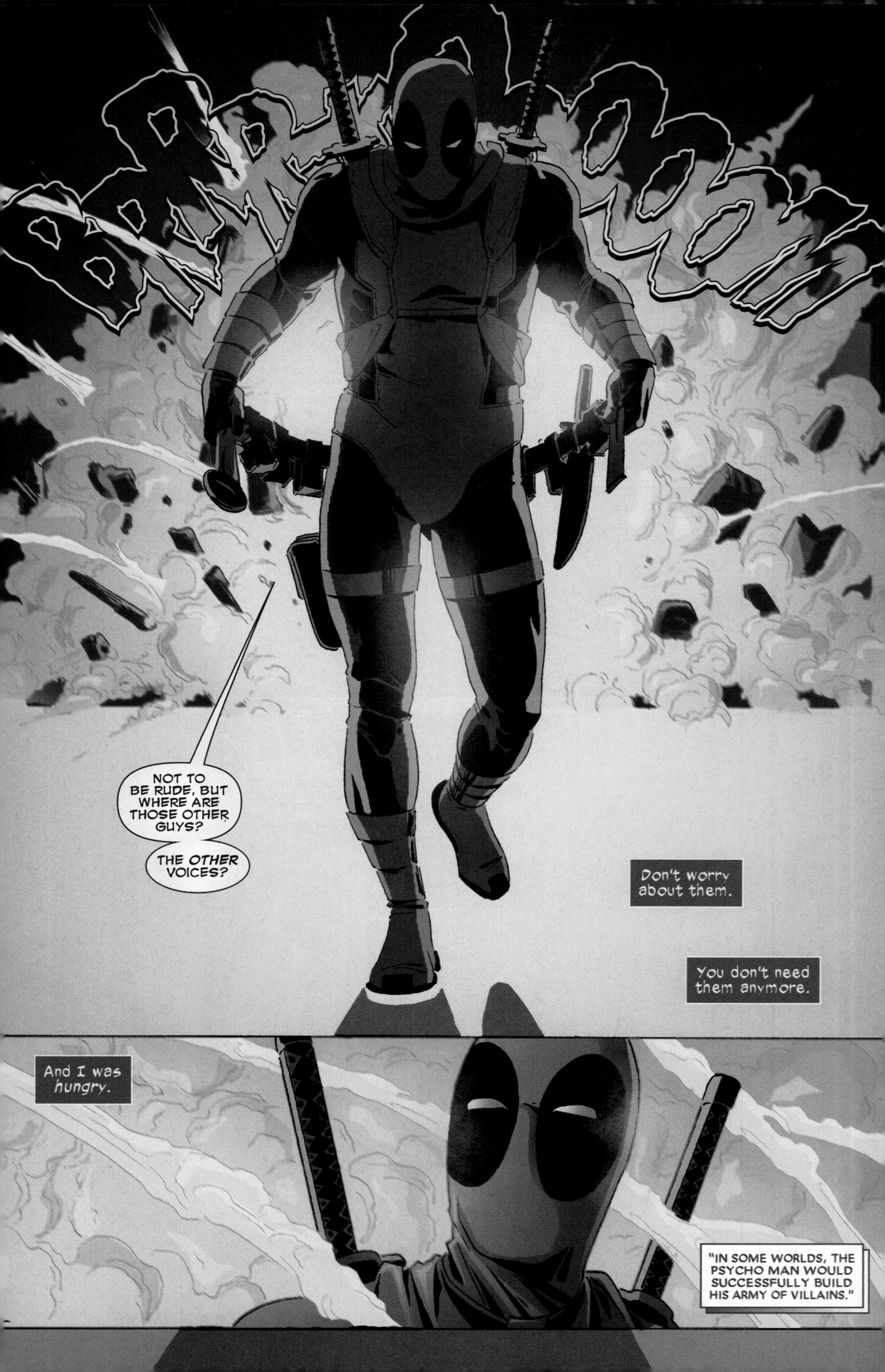
BRRRAKOOOM
NOT TO BE RUDE, BUT WHERE ARE THOSE OTHER GUYS?
THE *OTHER* VOICES?
Don't worry about them.
You don't need them anymore.
And I was *hungry*.
"IN SOME WORLDS, THE PSYCHO MAN WOULD SUCCESSFULLY BUILD HIS ARMY OF VILLAINS."

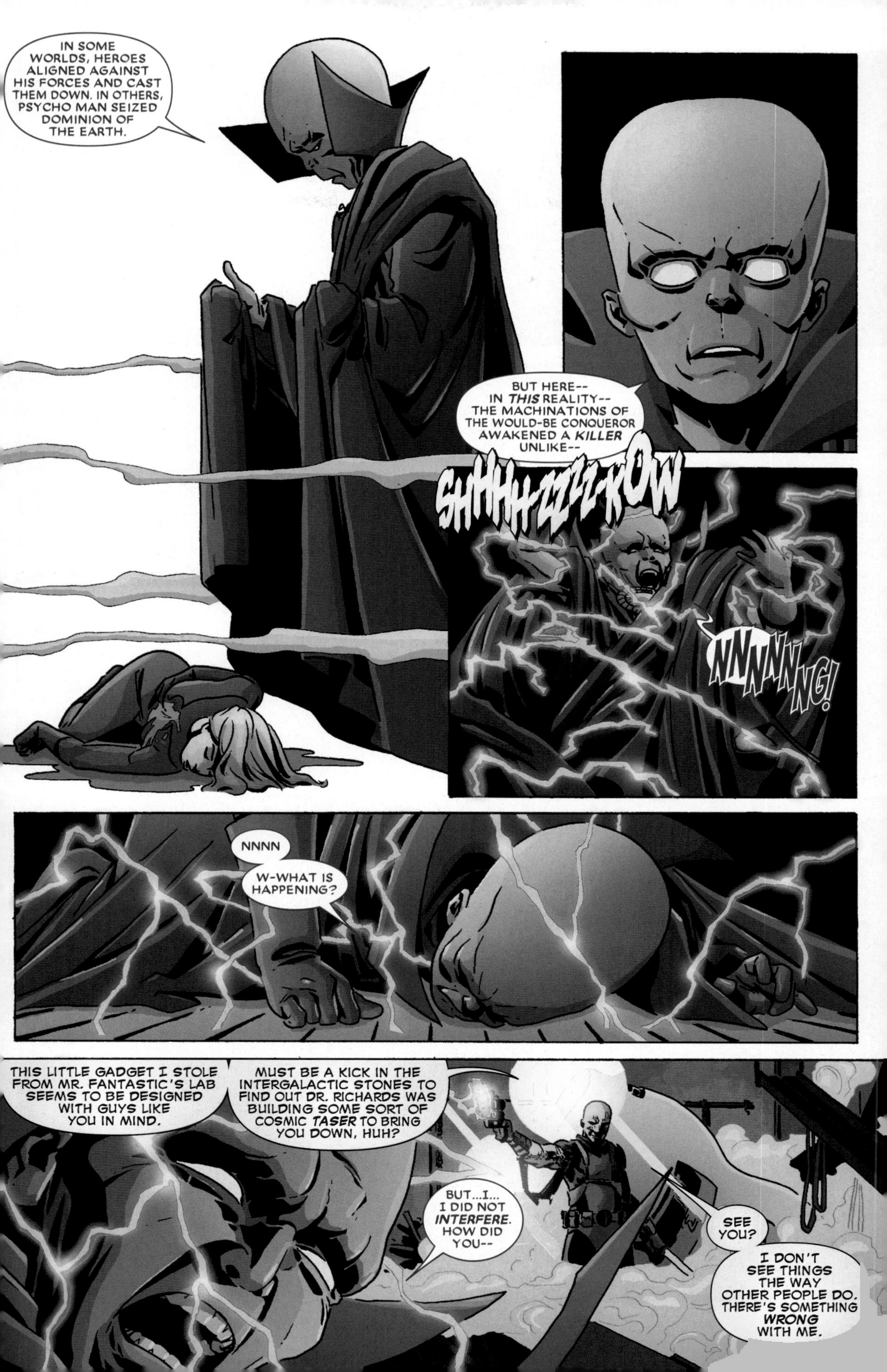
IN SOME WORLDS, HEROES ALIGNED AGAINST HIS FORCES AND CAST THEM DOWN. IN OTHERS, PSYCHO MAN SEIZED DOMINION OF THE EARTH.
BUT HERE-- IN THIS REALITY-- THE MACHINATIONS OF THE WOULD-BE CONQUEROR AWAKENED A KILLER UNLIKE--
SHHHH-ZZZZ-KOW
NNNNNNG!
NNNN
W-WHAT IS HAPPENING?
THIS LITTLE GADGET I STOLE FROM MR. FANTASTIC'S LAB SEEMS TO BE DESIGNED WITH GUYS LIKE YOU IN MIND.
MUST BE A KICK IN THE INTERGALACTIC STONES TO FIND OUT DR. RICHARDS WAS BUILDING SOME SORT OF COSMIC TASER TO BRING YOU DOWN, HUH?
BUT...I... I DID NOT INTERFERE. HOW DID YOU--
SEE YOU?
I DON'T SEE THINGS THE WAY OTHER PEOPLE DO. THERE'S SOMETHING WRONG WITH ME.

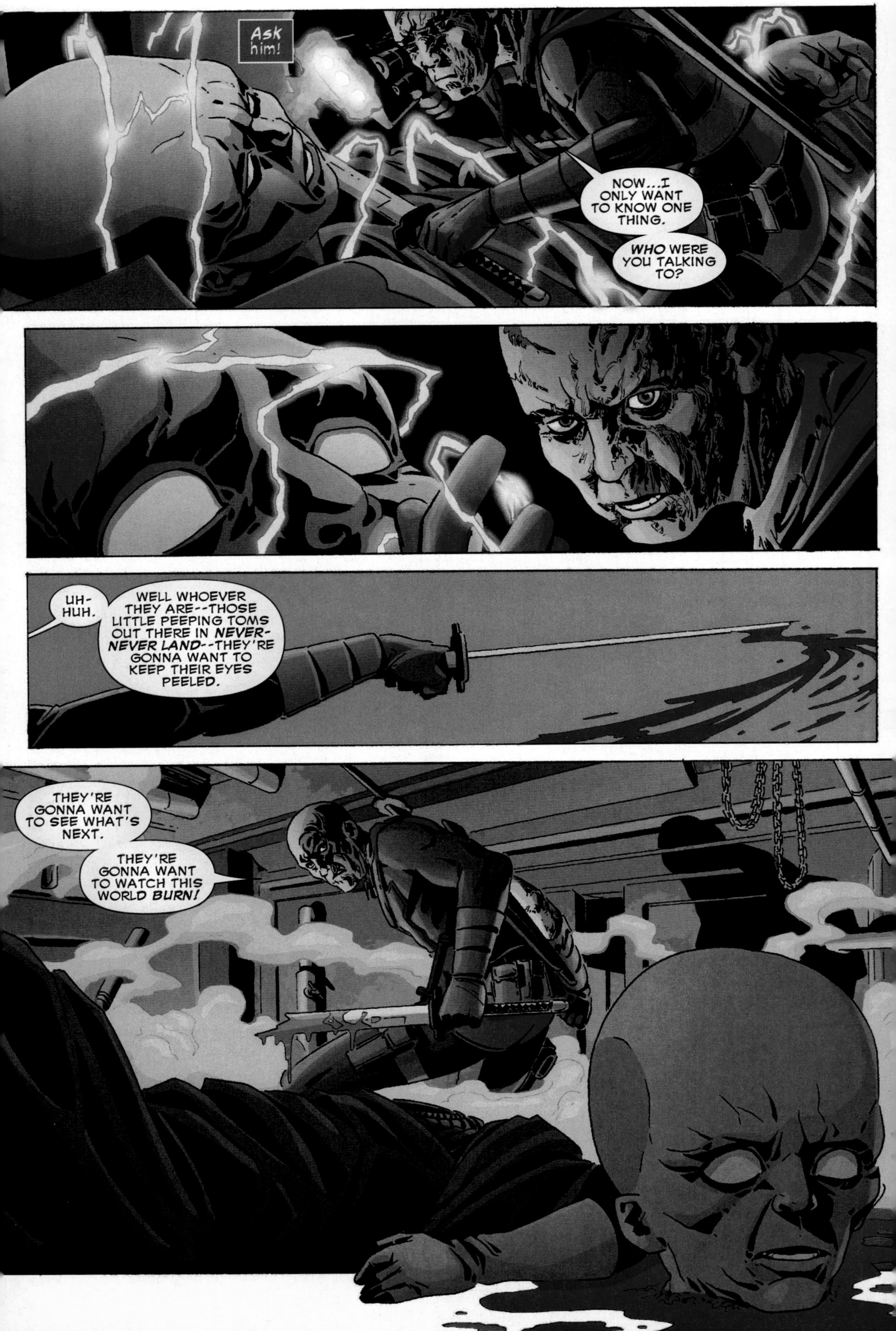

Ask him!
NOW...I ONLY WANT TO KNOW ONE THING.
WHO WERE YOU TALKING TO?
UH-HUH.
WELL WHOEVER THEY ARE--THOSE LITTLE PEEPING TOMS OUT THERE IN NEVER-NEVER LAND--THEY'RE GONNA WANT TO KEEP THEIR EYES PEELED.
THEY'RE GONNA WANT TO SEE WHAT'S NEXT.
THEY'RE GONNA WANT TO WATCH THIS WORLD BURN!

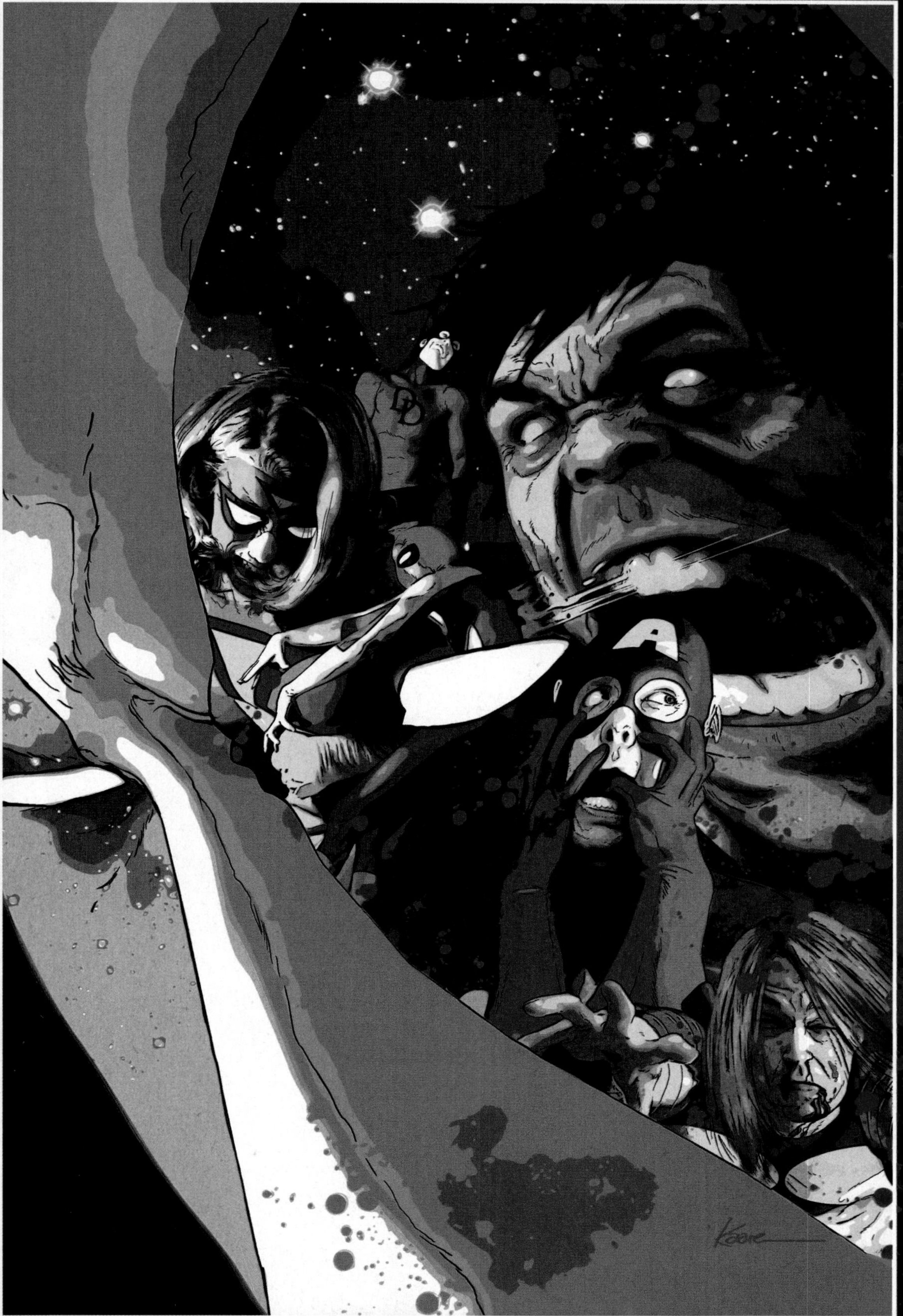

#2

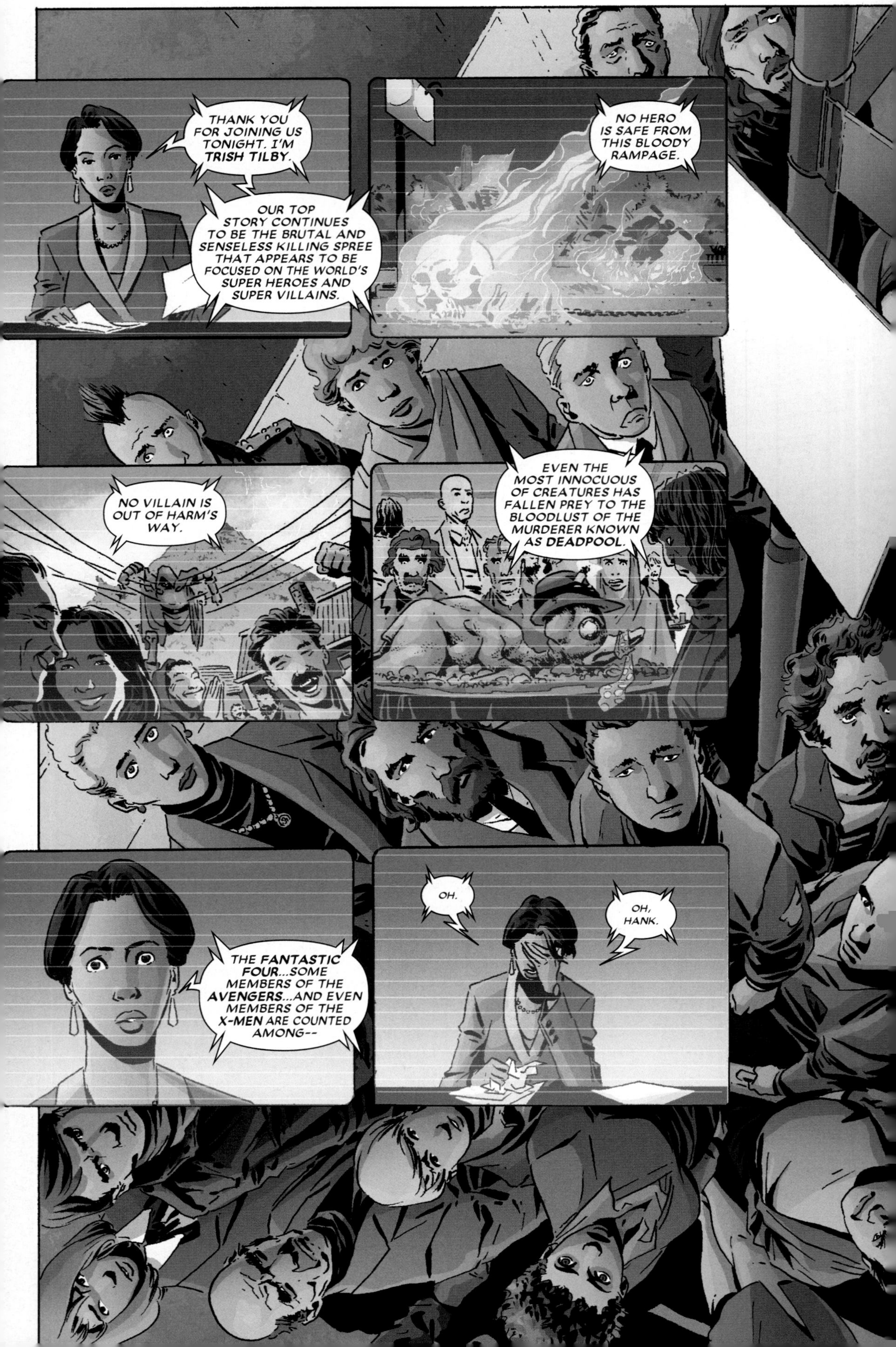
THANK YOU FOR JOINING US TONIGHT. I'M TRISH TILBY.
OUR TOP STORY CONTINUES TO BE THE BRUTAL AND SENSELESS KILLING SPREE THAT APPEARS TO BE FOCUSED ON THE WORLD'S SUPER HEROES AND SUPER VILLAINS.
NO HERO IS SAFE FROM THIS BLOODY RAMPAGE.
NO VILLAIN IS OUT OF HARM'S WAY.
EVEN THE MOST INNOCUOUS OF CREATURES HAS FALLEN PREY TO THE BLOODLUST OF THE MURDERER KNOWN AS DEADPOOL.
THE FANTASTIC FOUR...SOME MEMBERS OF THE AVENGERS...AND EVEN MEMBERS OF THE X-MEN ARE COUNTED AMONG--
OH.
OH, HANK.

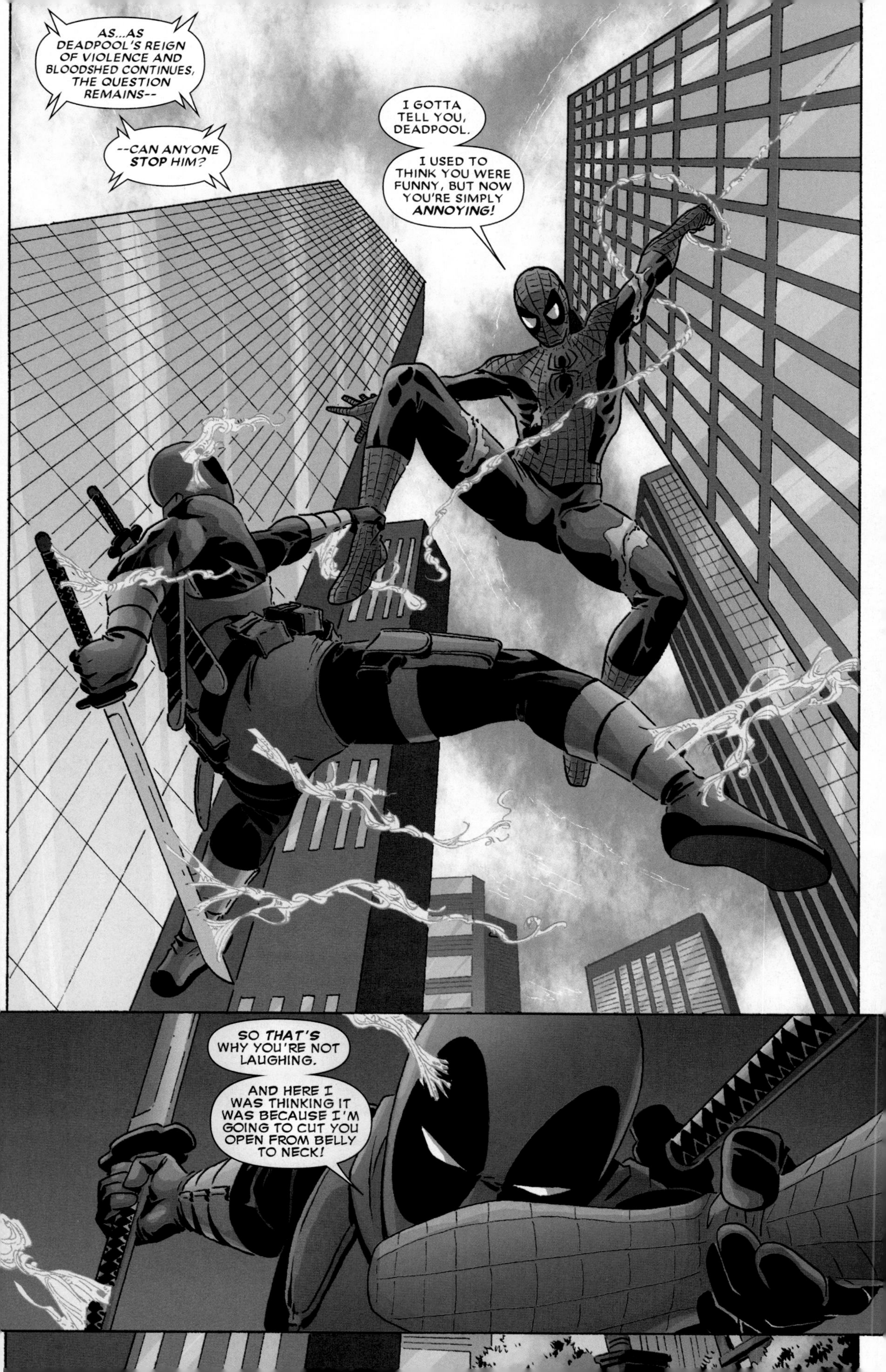
AS...AS DEADPOOL'S REIGN OF VIOLENCE AND BLOODSHED CONTINUES, THE QUESTION REMAINS--
--CAN ANYONE STOP HIM?
I GOTTA TELL YOU, DEADPOOL.
I USED TO THINK YOU WERE FUNNY, BUT NOW YOU'RE SIMPLY ANNOYING!
SO THAT'S WHY YOU'RE NOT LAUGHING.
AND HERE I WAS THINKING IT WAS BECAUSE I'M GOING TO CUT YOU OPEN FROM BELLY TO NECK!

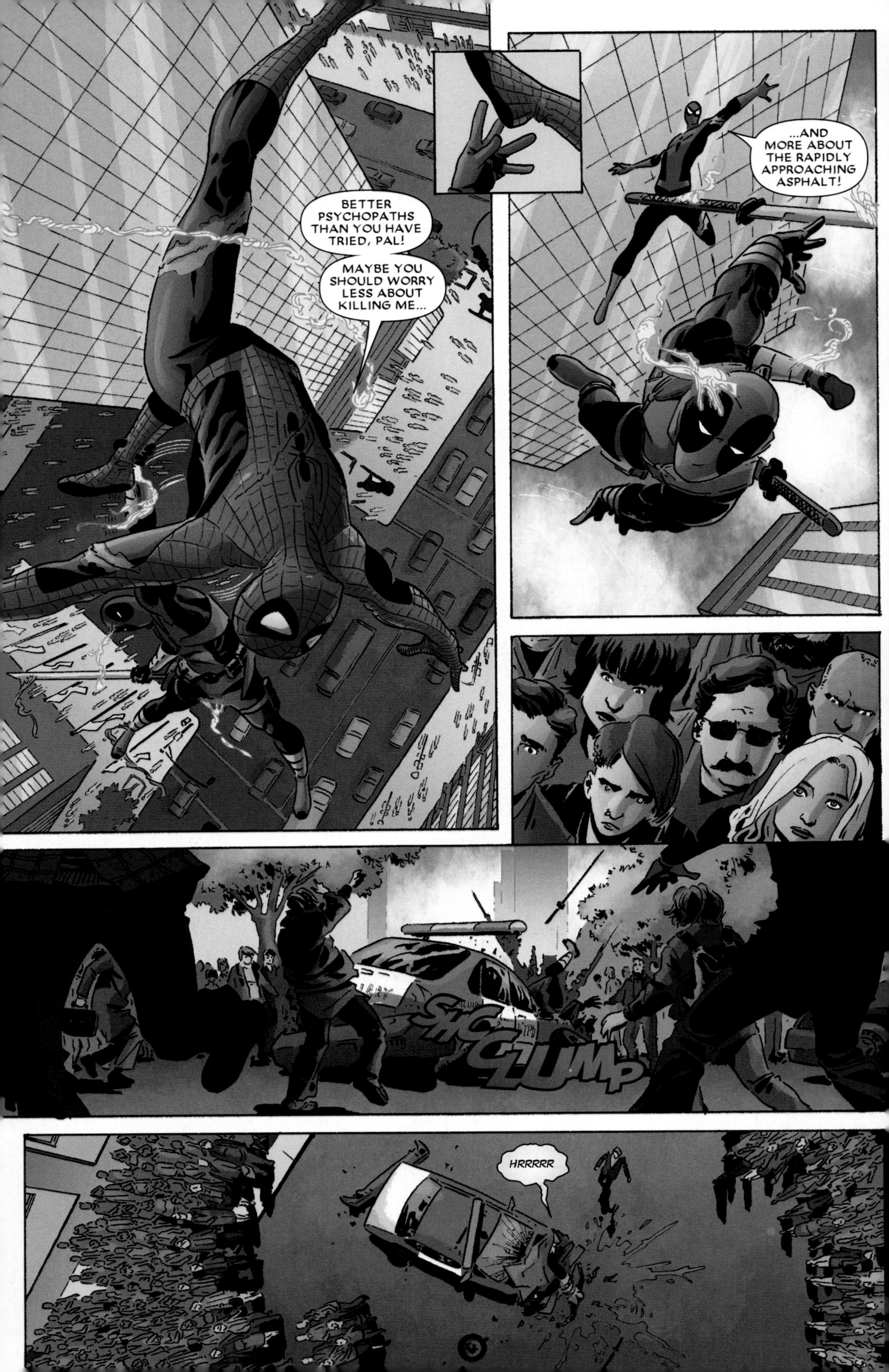
BETTER PSYCHOPATHS THAN YOU HAVE TRIED, PAL!
MAYBE YOU SHOULD WORRY LESS ABOUT KILLING ME...
...AND MORE ABOUT THE RAPIDLY APPROACHING ASPHALT!
SHC CLUMP
HRRRRR

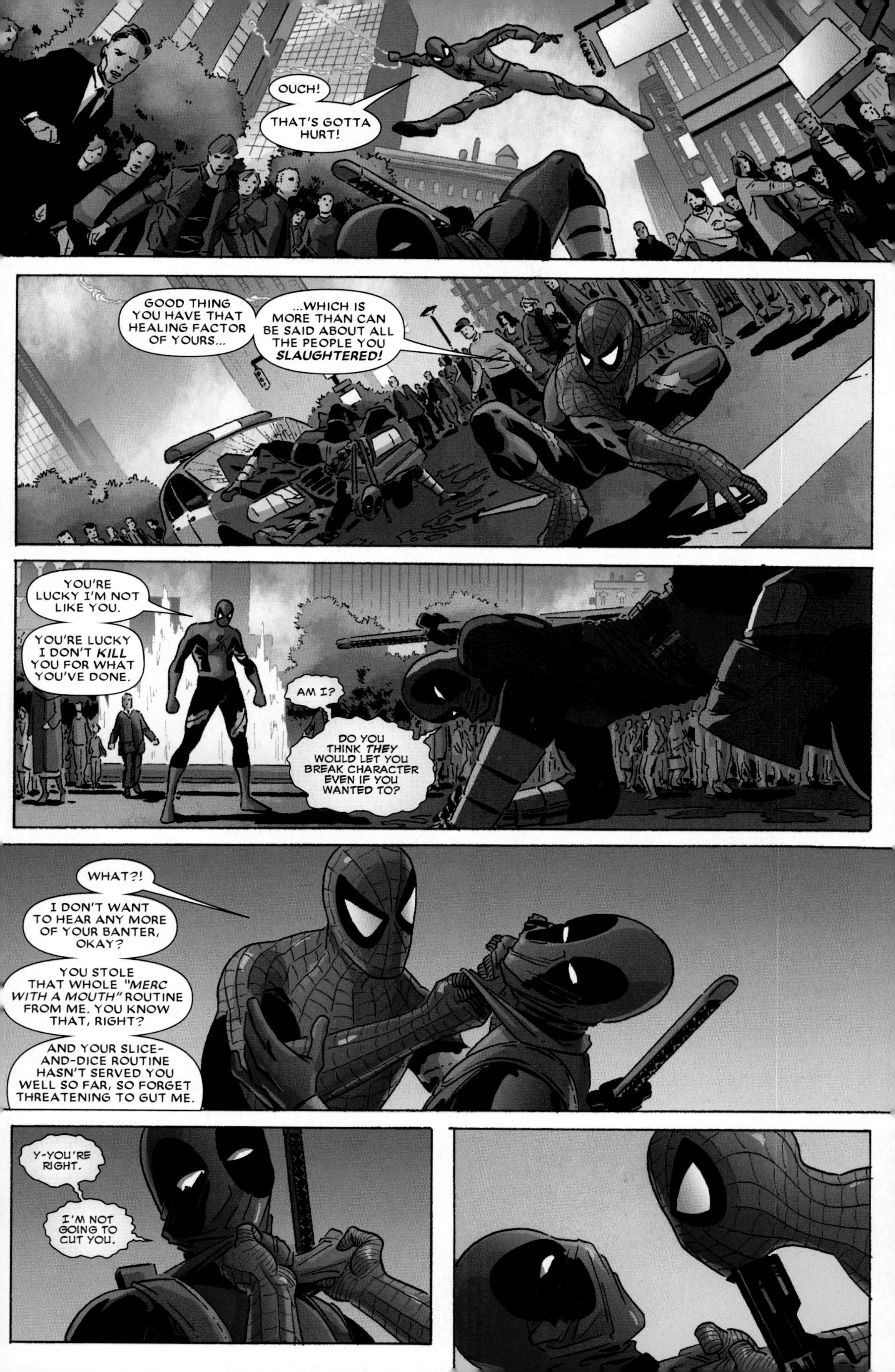
OUCH!
THAT'S GOTTA HURT!
GOOD THING YOU HAVE THAT HEALING FACTOR OF YOURS...
...WHICH IS MORE THAN CAN BE SAID ABOUT ALL THE PEOPLE YOU *SLAUGHTERED!*
YOU'RE LUCKY I'M NOT LIKE YOU.
YOU'RE LUCKY I DON'T *KILL* YOU FOR WHAT YOU'VE DONE.
AM I?
DO YOU THINK *THEY* WOULD LET YOU BREAK CHARACTER EVEN IF YOU WANTED TO?
WHAT?!
I DON'T WANT TO HEAR ANY MORE OF YOUR BANTER, OKAY?
YOU STOLE THAT WHOLE *"MERC WITH A MOUTH"* ROUTINE FROM ME. YOU KNOW THAT, RIGHT?
AND YOUR SLICE-AND-DICE ROUTINE HASN'T SERVED YOU WELL SO FAR, SO FORGET THREATENING TO GUT ME.
Y-YOU'RE RIGHT.
I'M NOT GOING TO CUT YOU.

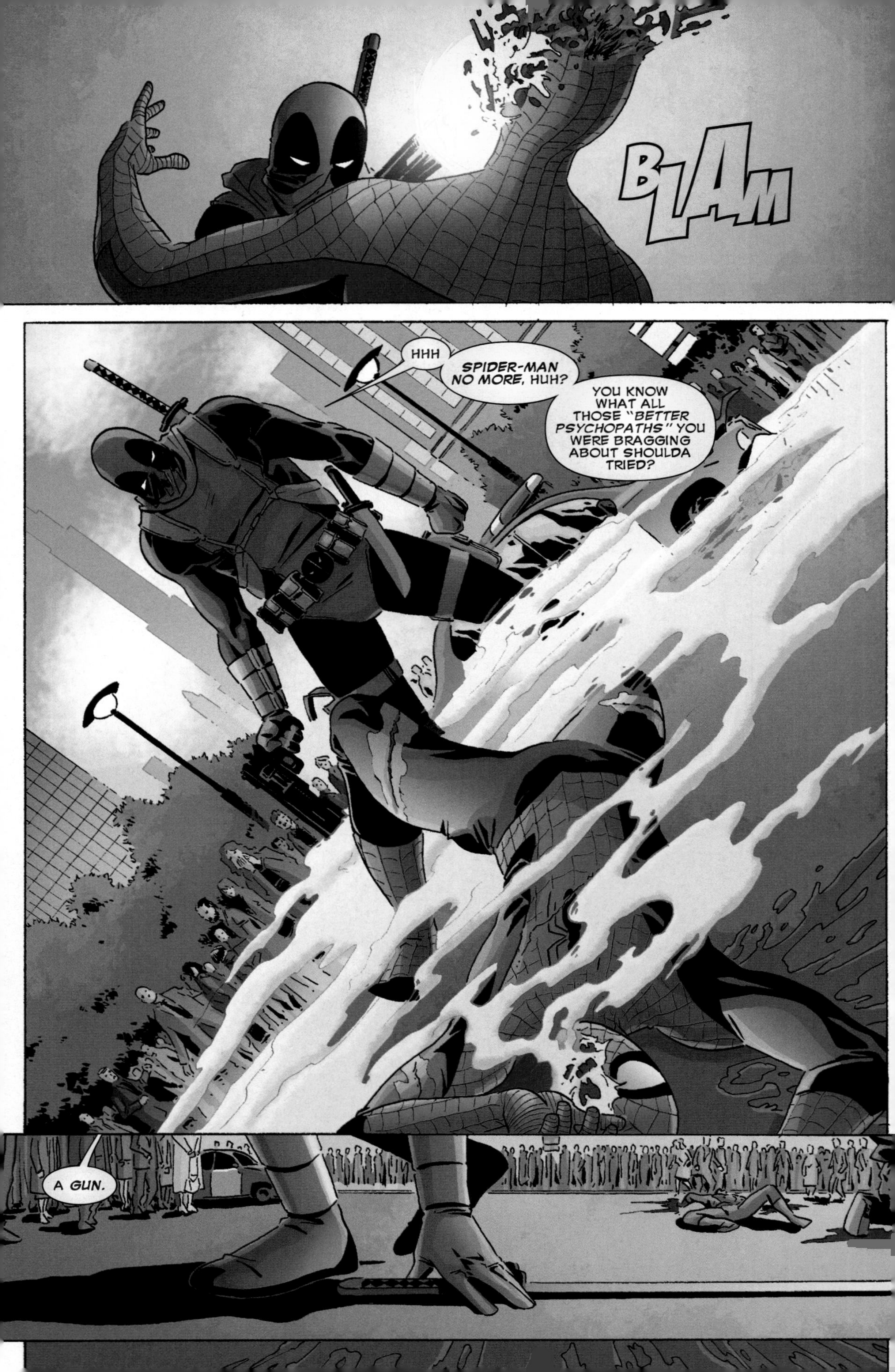
BLAM
HHH
SPIDER-MAN NO MORE, HUH?
YOU KNOW WHAT ALL THOSE "BETTER PSYCHOPATHS" YOU WERE BRAGGING ABOUT SHOULDA TRIED?
A GUN.

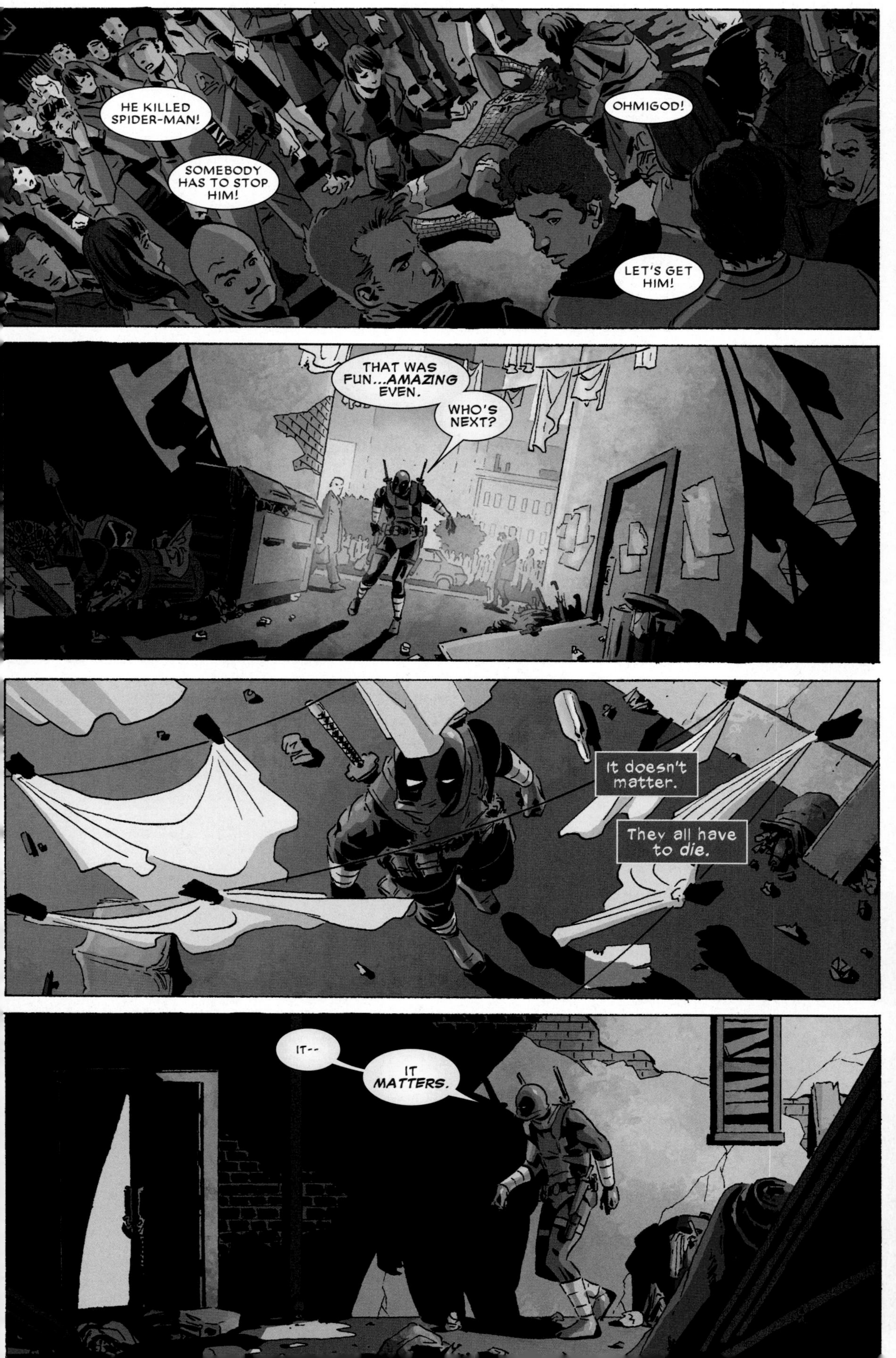
HE KILLED SPIDER-MAN!
OHMIGOD!
SOMEBODY HAS TO STOP HIM!
LET'S GET HIM!
THAT WAS FUN...AMAZING EVEN.
WHO'S NEXT?
It doesn't matter.
They all have to die.
IT--
IT MATTERS.

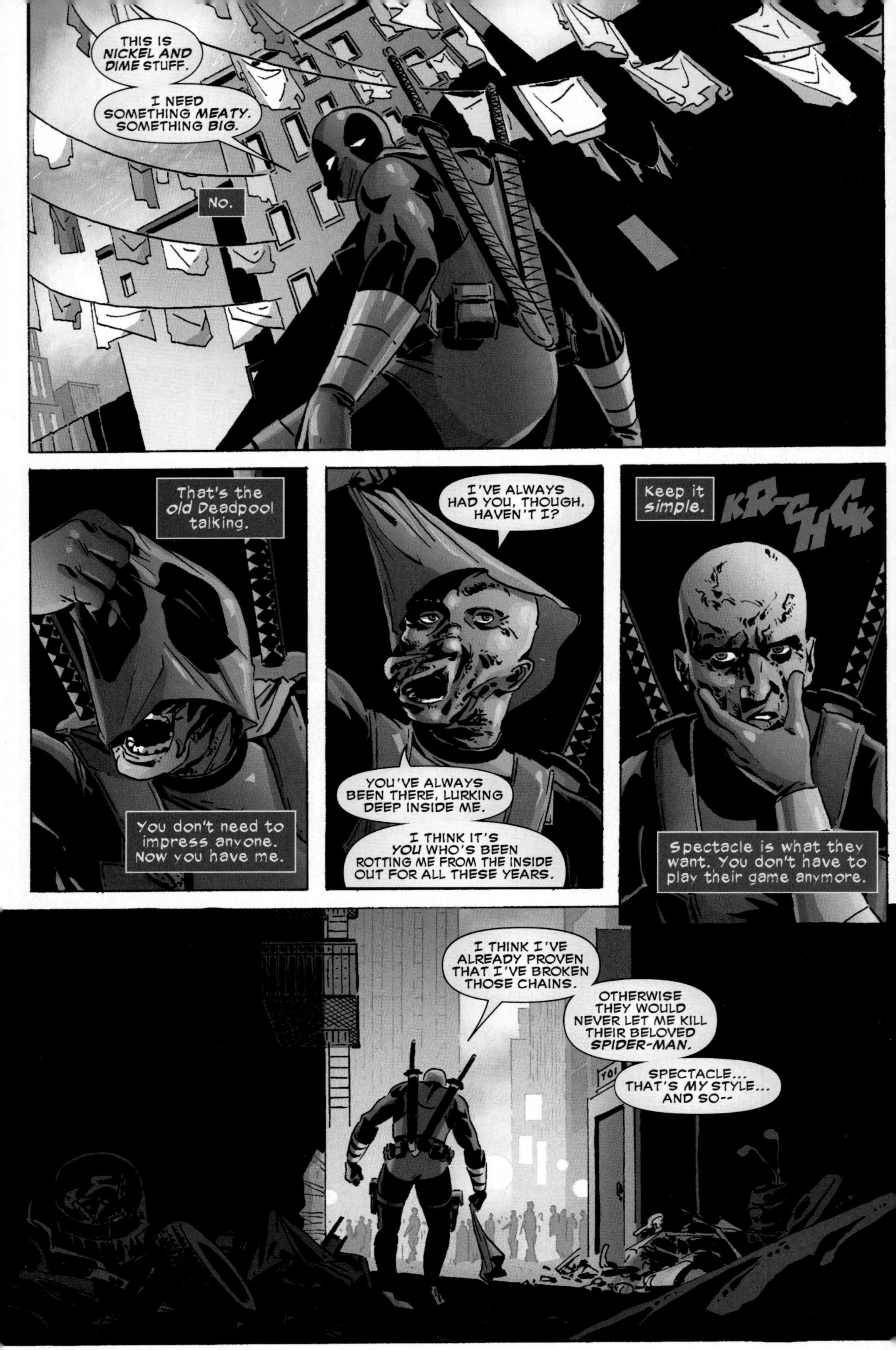

THIS IS NICKEL AND DIME STUFF.
I NEED SOMETHING MEATY. SOMETHING BIG.
No.
That's the old Deadpool talking.
You don't need to impress anyone. Now you have me.
I'VE ALWAYS HAD YOU, THOUGH, HAVEN'T I?
YOU'VE ALWAYS BEEN THERE, LURKING DEEP INSIDE ME.
I THINK IT'S YOU WHO'S BEEN ROTTING ME FROM THE INSIDE OUT FOR ALL THESE YEARS.
Keep it simple.
KR-CHGK
Spectacle is what they want. You don't have to play their game anymore.
I THINK I'VE ALREADY PROVEN THAT I'VE BROKEN THOSE CHAINS.
OTHERWISE THEY WOULD NEVER LET ME KILL THEIR BELOVED SPIDER-MAN.
SPECTACLE... THAT'S MY STYLE... AND SO--

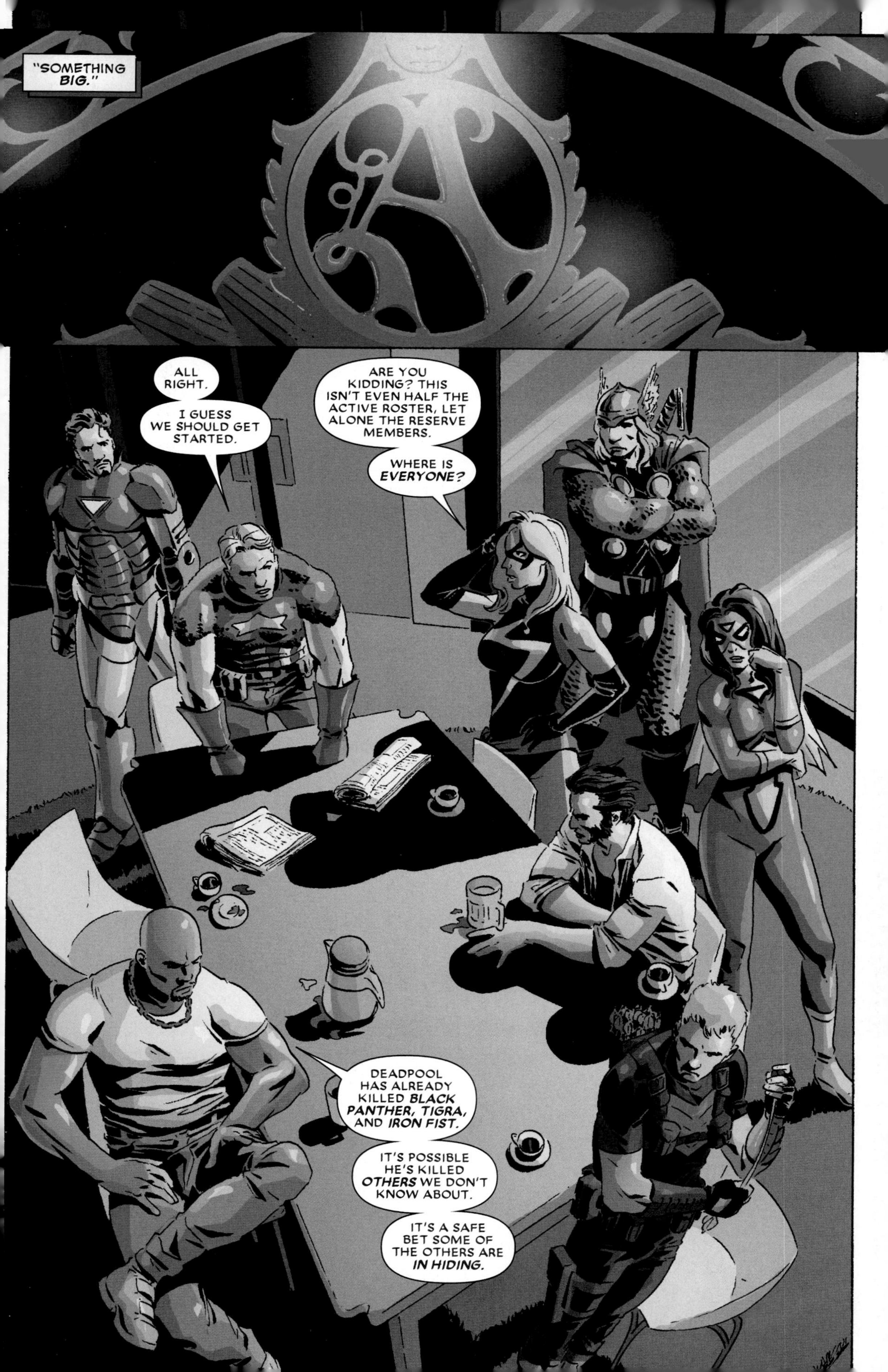
"SOMETHING BIG."
ALL RIGHT.
I GUESS WE SHOULD GET STARTED.
ARE YOU KIDDING? THIS ISN'T EVEN HALF THE ACTIVE ROSTER, LET ALONE THE RESERVE MEMBERS.
WHERE IS EVERYONE?
DEADPOOL HAS ALREADY KILLED BLACK PANTHER, TIGRA, AND IRON FIST.
IT'S POSSIBLE HE'S KILLED OTHERS WE DON'T KNOW ABOUT.
IT'S A SAFE BET SOME OF THE OTHERS ARE IN HIDING.

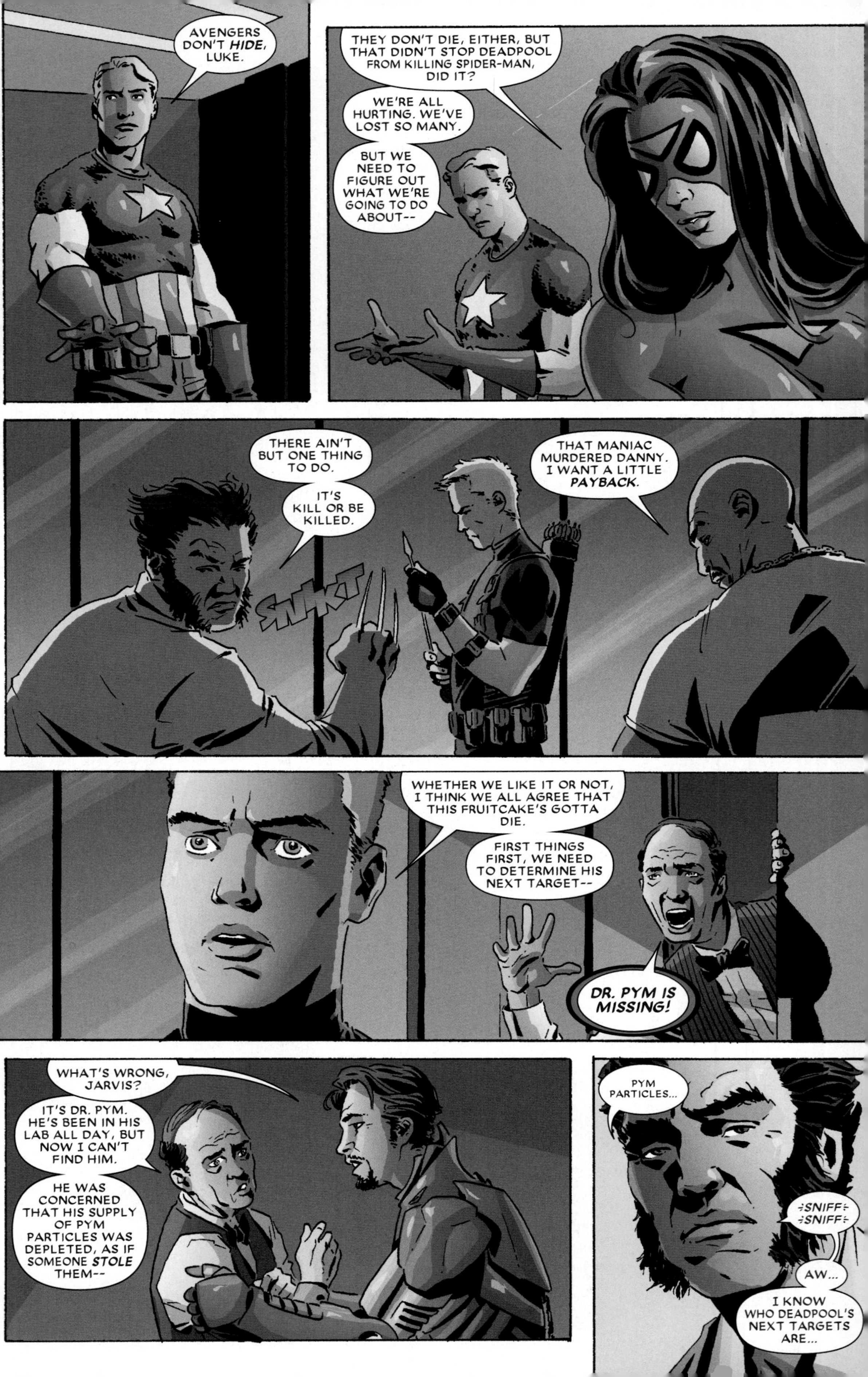
AVENGERS DON'T *HIDE*, LUKE.
THEY DON'T DIE, EITHER, BUT THAT DIDN'T STOP DEADPOOL FROM KILLING SPIDER-MAN, DID IT?
WE'RE ALL HURTING. WE'VE LOST SO MANY.
BUT WE NEED TO FIGURE OUT WHAT WE'RE GOING TO DO ABOUT--
THERE AIN'T BUT ONE THING TO DO.
IT'S KILL OR BE KILLED.
SNIKT
THAT MANIAC MURDERED DANNY. I WANT A LITTLE *PAYBACK*.
WHETHER WE LIKE IT OR NOT, I THINK WE ALL AGREE THAT THIS FRUITCAKE'S GOTTA DIE.
FIRST THINGS FIRST, WE NEED TO DETERMINE HIS NEXT TARGET--
DR. PYM IS MISSING!
WHAT'S WRONG, JARVIS?
IT'S DR. PYM. HE'S BEEN IN HIS LAB ALL DAY, BUT NOW I CAN'T FIND HIM.
HE WAS CONCERNED THAT HIS SUPPLY OF PYM PARTICLES WAS DEPLETED, AS IF SOMEONE *STOLE* THEM--
PYM PARTICLES...
SNIFF
SNIFF
AW...
I KNOW WHO DEADPOOL'S NEXT TARGETS ARE...

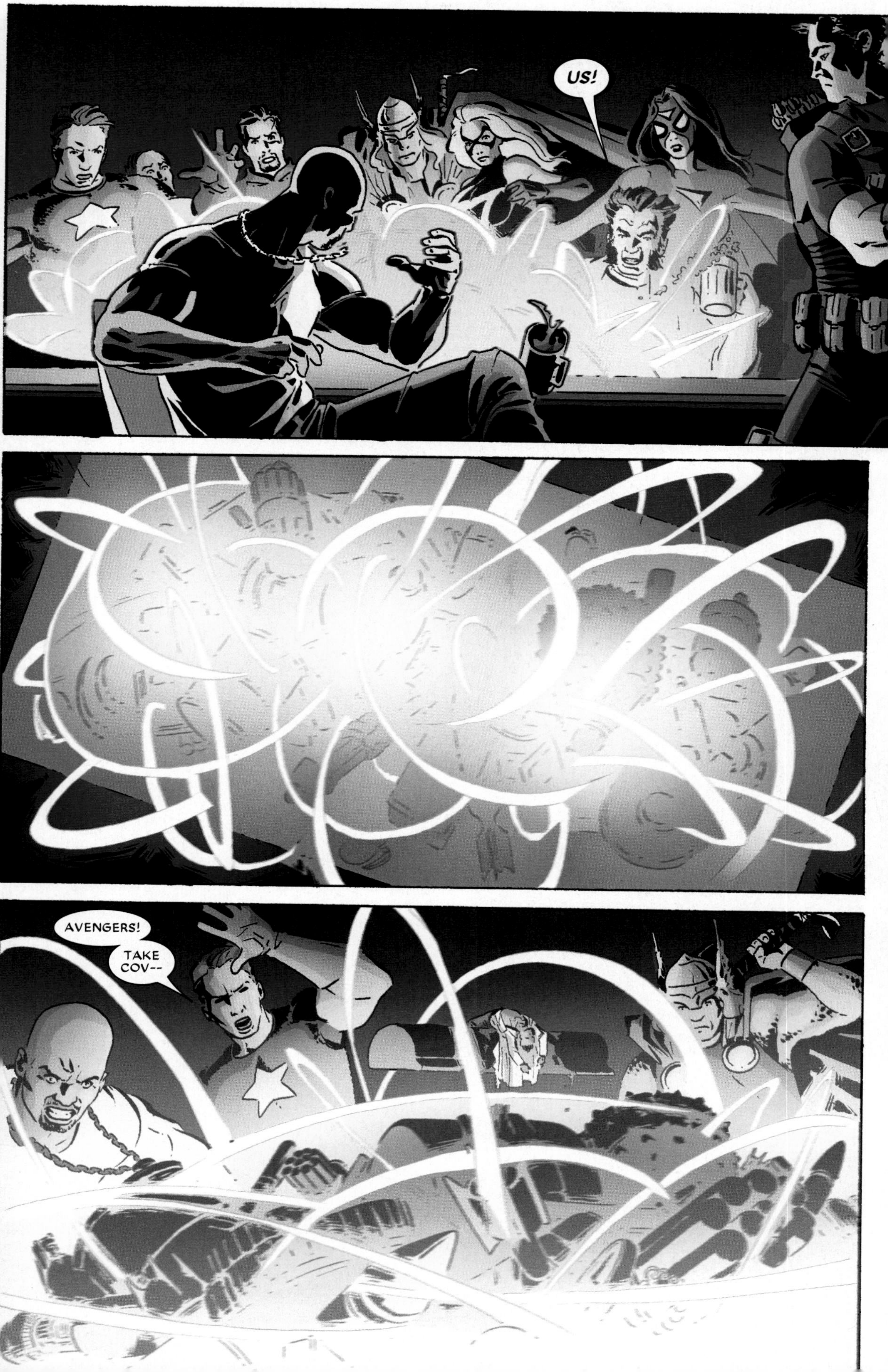
US!
AVENGERS!
TAKE COV--

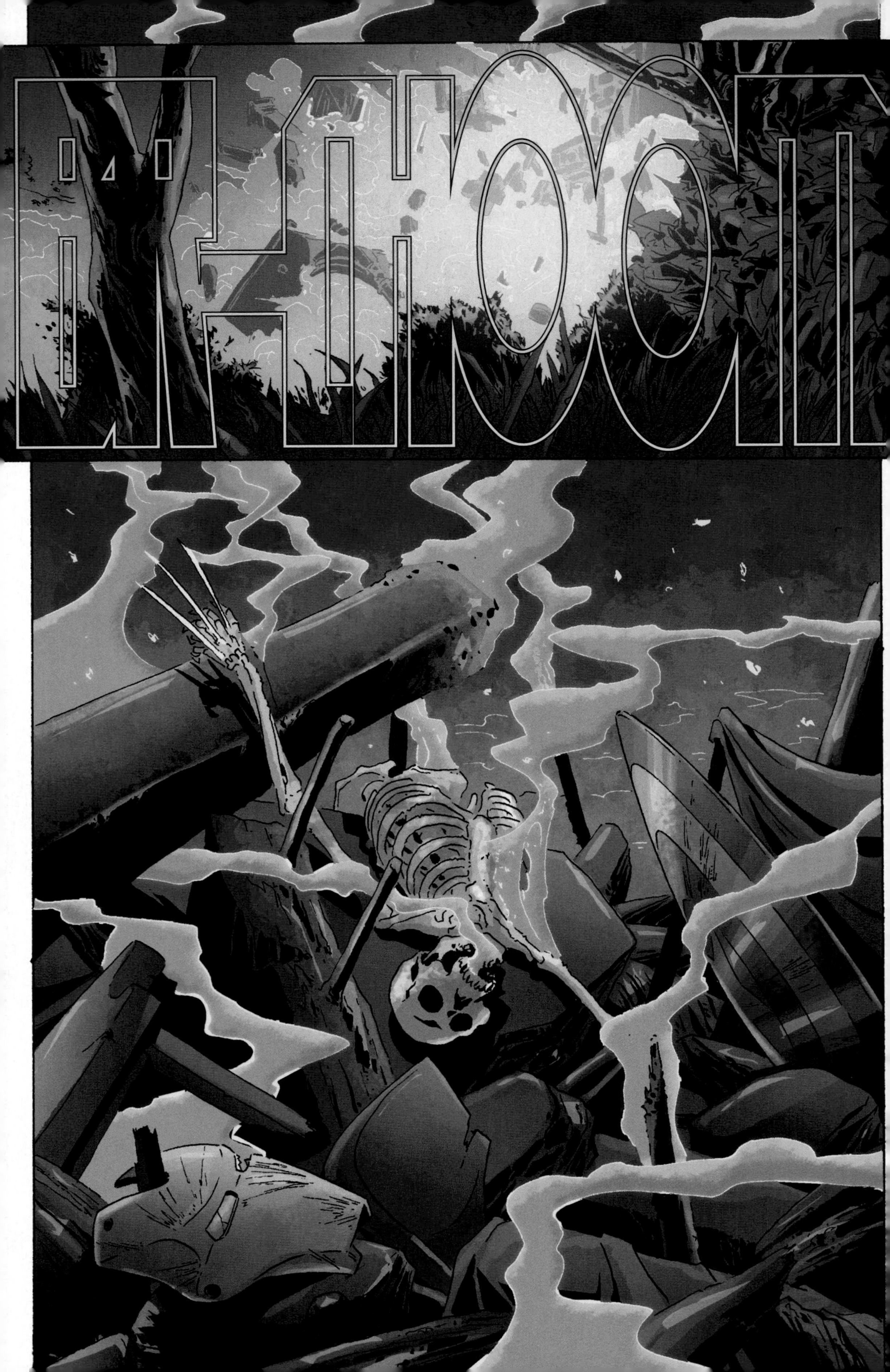

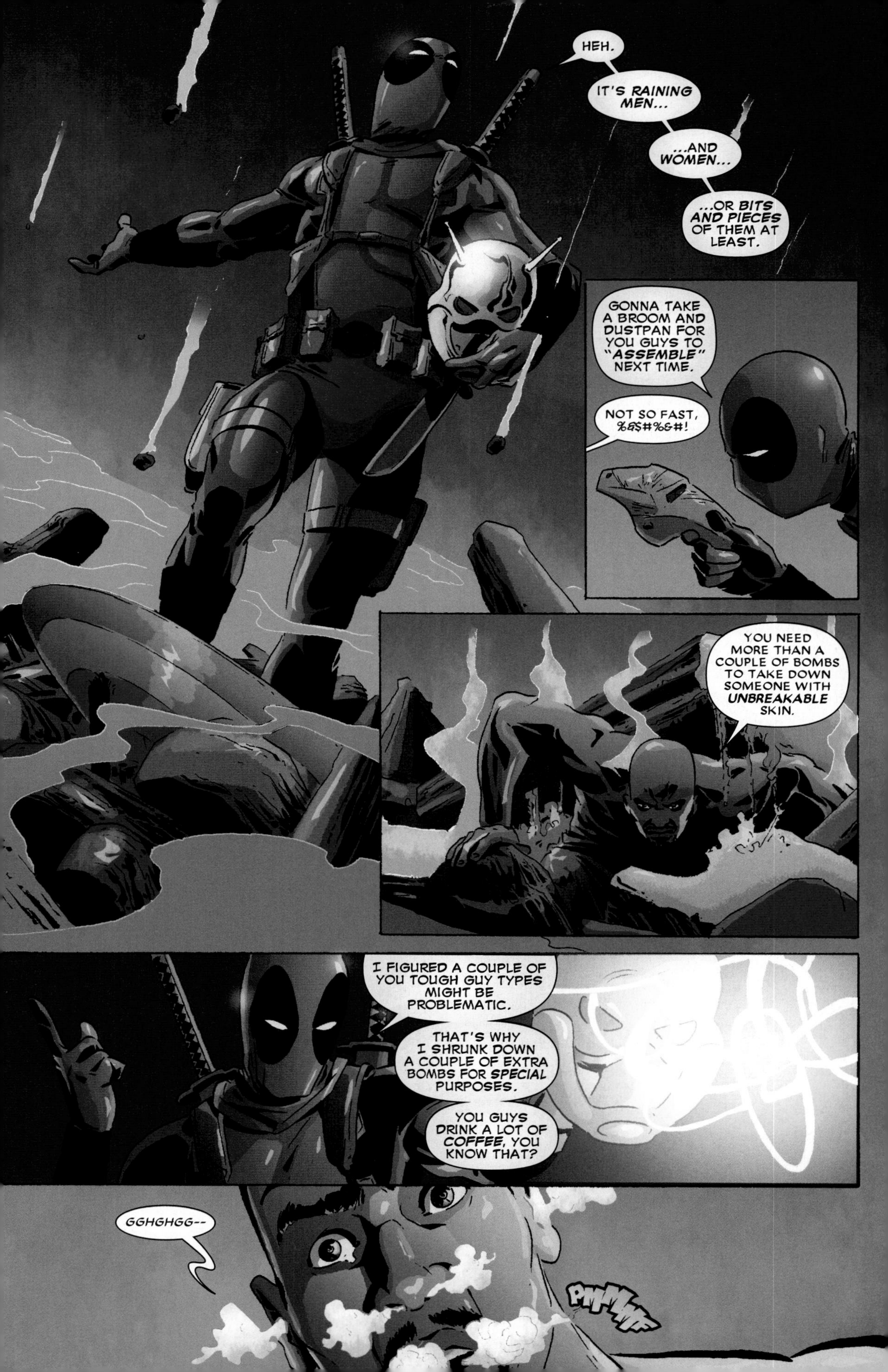
HEH.
IT'S RAINING MEN...
...AND WOMEN...
...OR BITS AND PIECES OF THEM AT LEAST.
GONNA TAKE A BROOM AND DUSTPAN FOR YOU GUYS TO "ASSEMBLE" NEXT TIME.
NOT SO FAST, %&$#%&#!
YOU NEED MORE THAN A COUPLE OF BOMBS TO TAKE DOWN SOMEONE WITH UNBREAKABLE SKIN.
I FIGURED A COUPLE OF YOU TOUGH GUY TYPES MIGHT BE PROBLEMATIC.
THAT'S WHY I SHRUNK DOWN A COUPLE OF EXTRA BOMBS FOR SPECIAL PURPOSES.
YOU GUYS DRINK A LOT OF COFFEE, YOU KNOW THAT?
GGHGHGG--
PMMMF

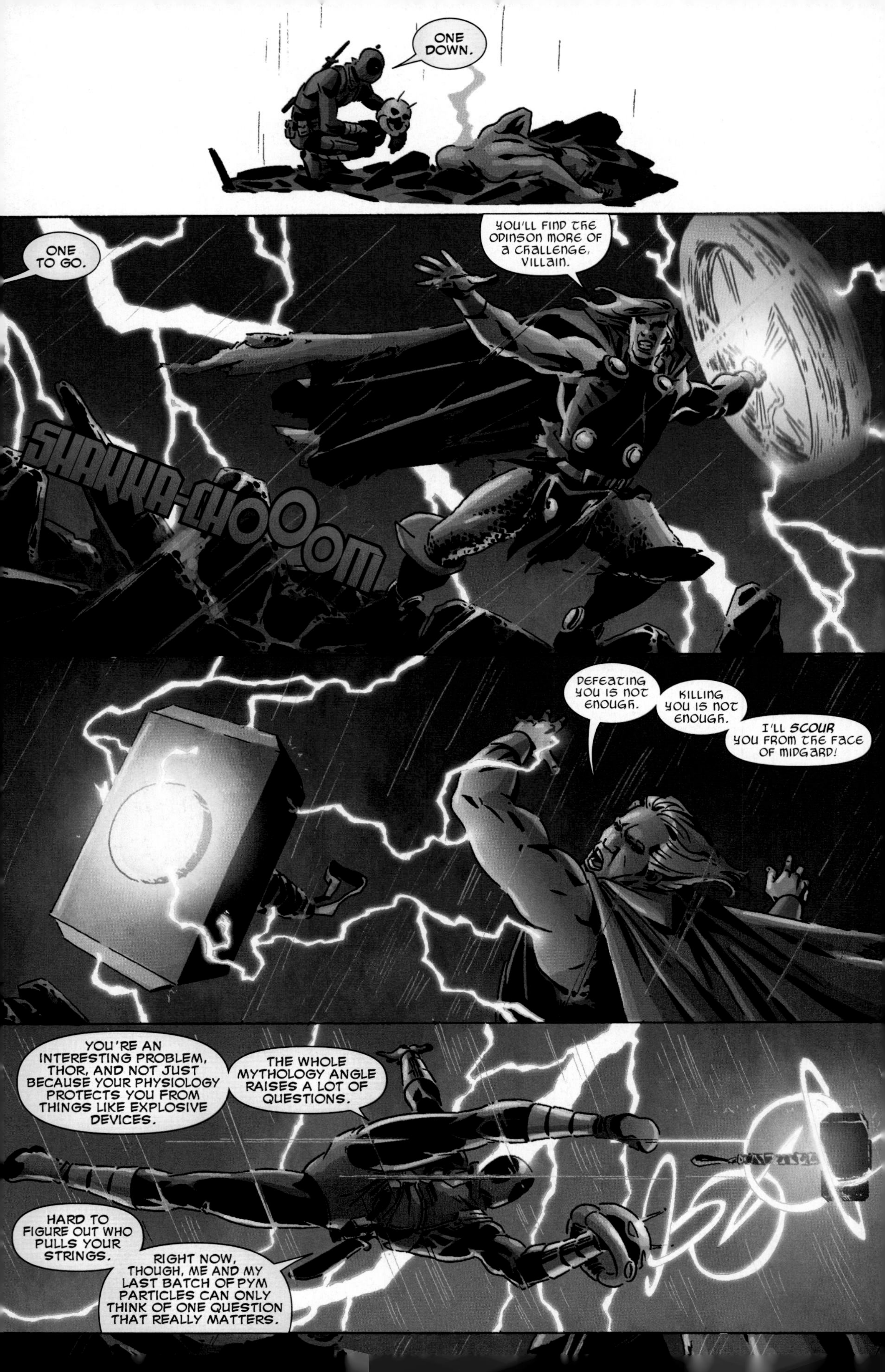
ONE DOWN.
ONE TO GO.
YOU'LL FIND THE ODINSON MORE OF A CHALLENGE, VILLAIN.
SHAKKA-CHOOOOM
DEFEATING YOU IS NOT ENOUGH.
KILLING YOU IS NOT ENOUGH.
I'LL SCOUR YOU FROM THE FACE OF MIDGARD!
YOU'RE AN INTERESTING PROBLEM, THOR, AND NOT JUST BECAUSE YOUR PHYSIOLOGY PROTECTS YOU FROM THINGS LIKE EXPLOSIVE DEVICES.
THE WHOLE MYTHOLOGY ANGLE RAISES A LOT OF QUESTIONS.
HARD TO FIGURE OUT WHO PULLS YOUR STRINGS.
RIGHT NOW, THOUGH, ME AND MY LAST BATCH OF PYM PARTICLES CAN ONLY THINK OF ONE QUESTION THAT REALLY MATTERS.

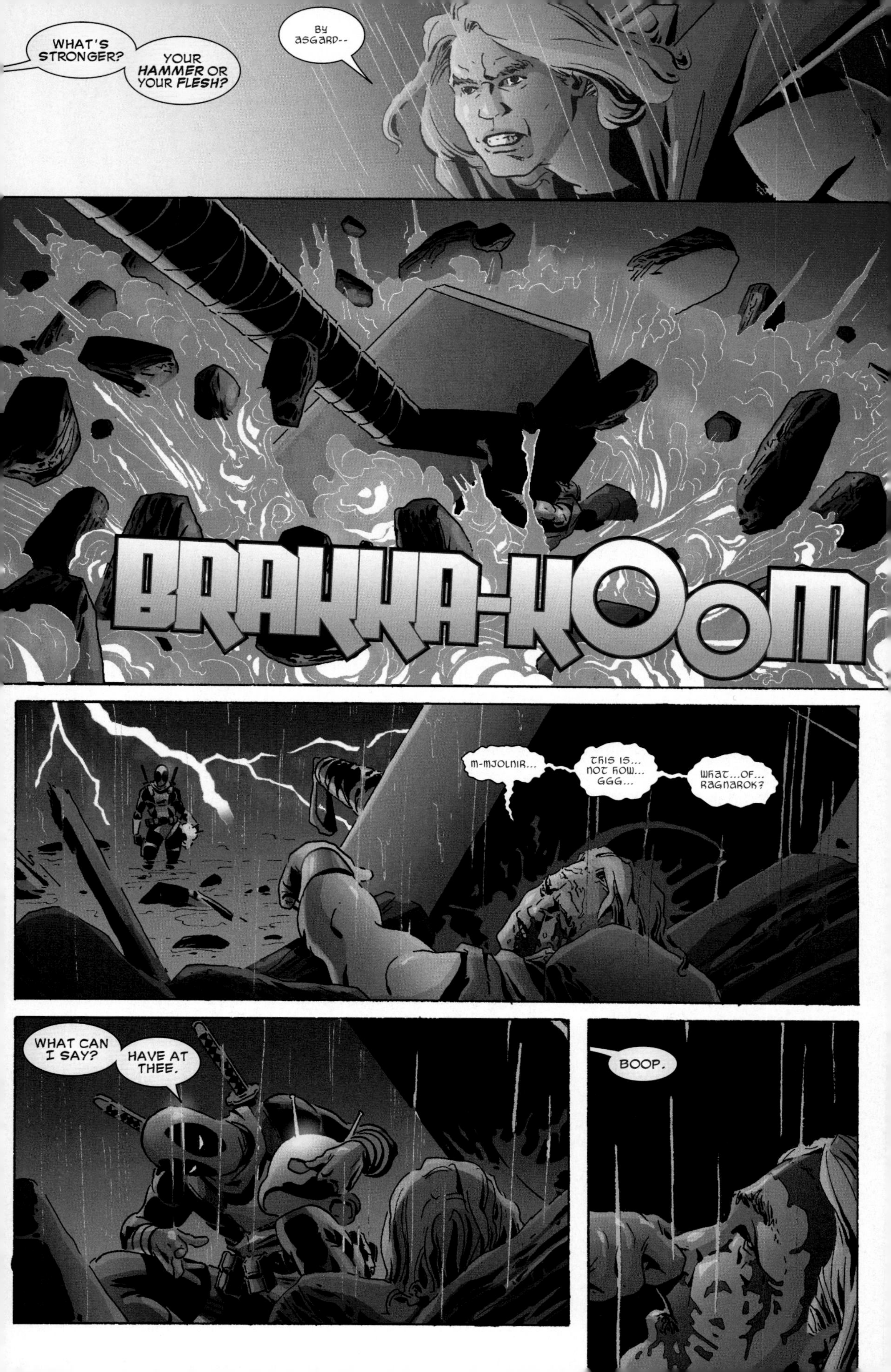
WHAT'S STRONGER?
YOUR HAMMER OR YOUR FLESH?
BY ASGARD--
BRAKKA-KOOOM
M-MJOLNIR...
THIS IS... NOT HOW... GGG...
WHAT...OF... RAGNAROK?
WHAT CAN I SAY?
HAVE AT THEE.
BOOP.

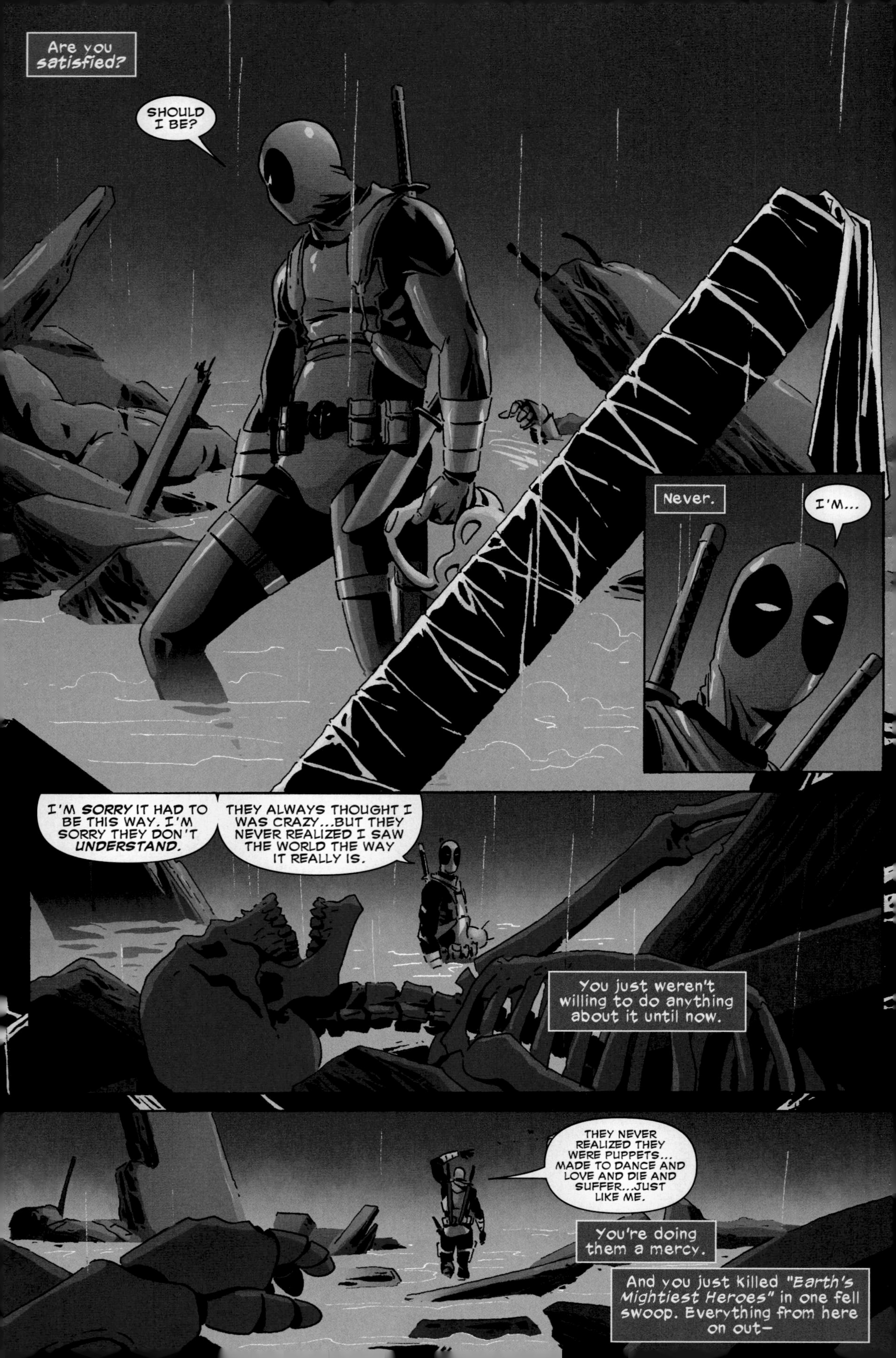
Are you satisfied?
SHOULD I BE?
Never.
I'M...
I'M SORRY IT HAD TO BE THIS WAY. I'M SORRY THEY DON'T UNDERSTAND.
THEY ALWAYS THOUGHT I WAS CRAZY...BUT THEY NEVER REALIZED I SAW THE WORLD THE WAY IT REALLY IS.
You just weren't willing to do anything about it until now.
THEY NEVER REALIZED THEY WERE PUPPETS... MADE TO DANCE AND LOVE AND DIE AND SUFFER...JUST LIKE ME.
You're doing them a mercy.
And you just killed "Earth's Mightiest Heroes" in one fell swoop. Everything from here on out—

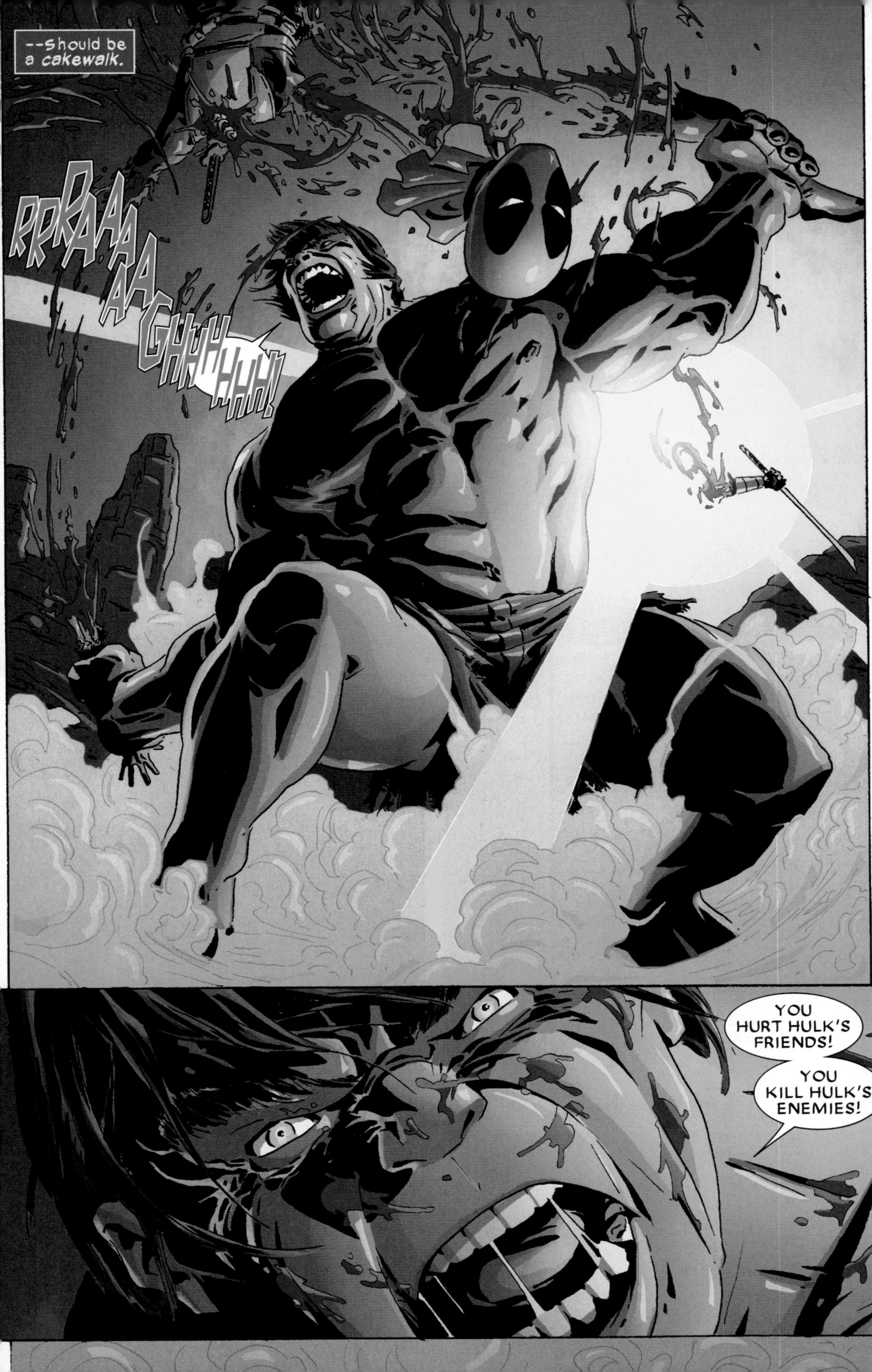
--Should be a cakewalk.
RRRAAAAAGHHHHHHHH!
YOU HURT HULK'S FRIENDS!
YOU KILL HULK'S ENEMIES!

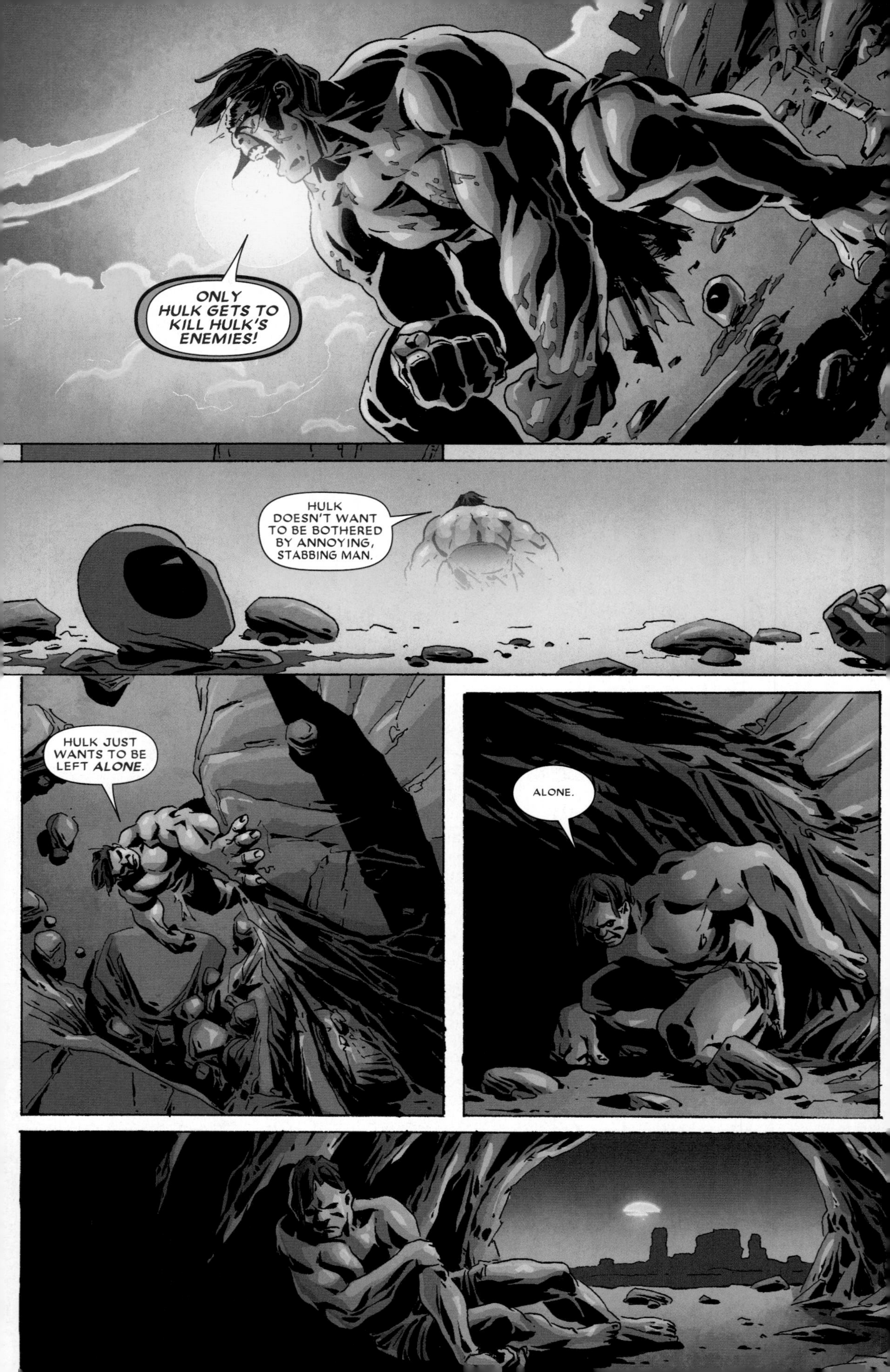
ONLY HULK GETS TO KILL HULK'S ENEMIES!
HULK DOESN'T WANT TO BE BOTHERED BY ANNOYING, STABBING MAN.
HULK JUST WANTS TO BE LEFT *ALONE*.
ALONE.

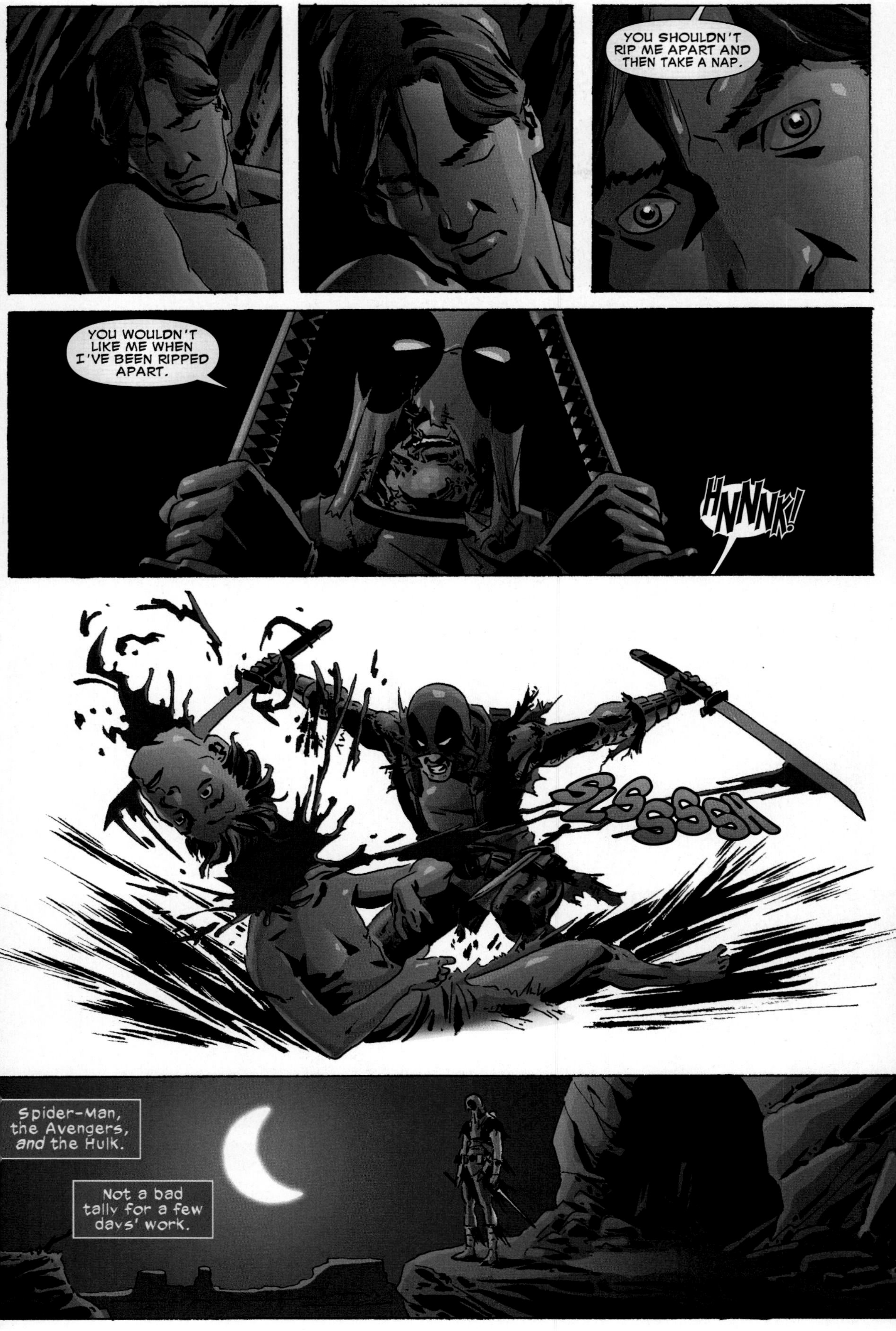
YOU SHOULDN'T RIP ME APART AND THEN TAKE A NAP.
YOU WOULDN'T LIKE ME WHEN I'VE BEEN RIPPED APART.
HNNNK!
SLSSSSH
Spider-Man, the Avengers, and the Hulk.
Not a bad tally for a few days' work.

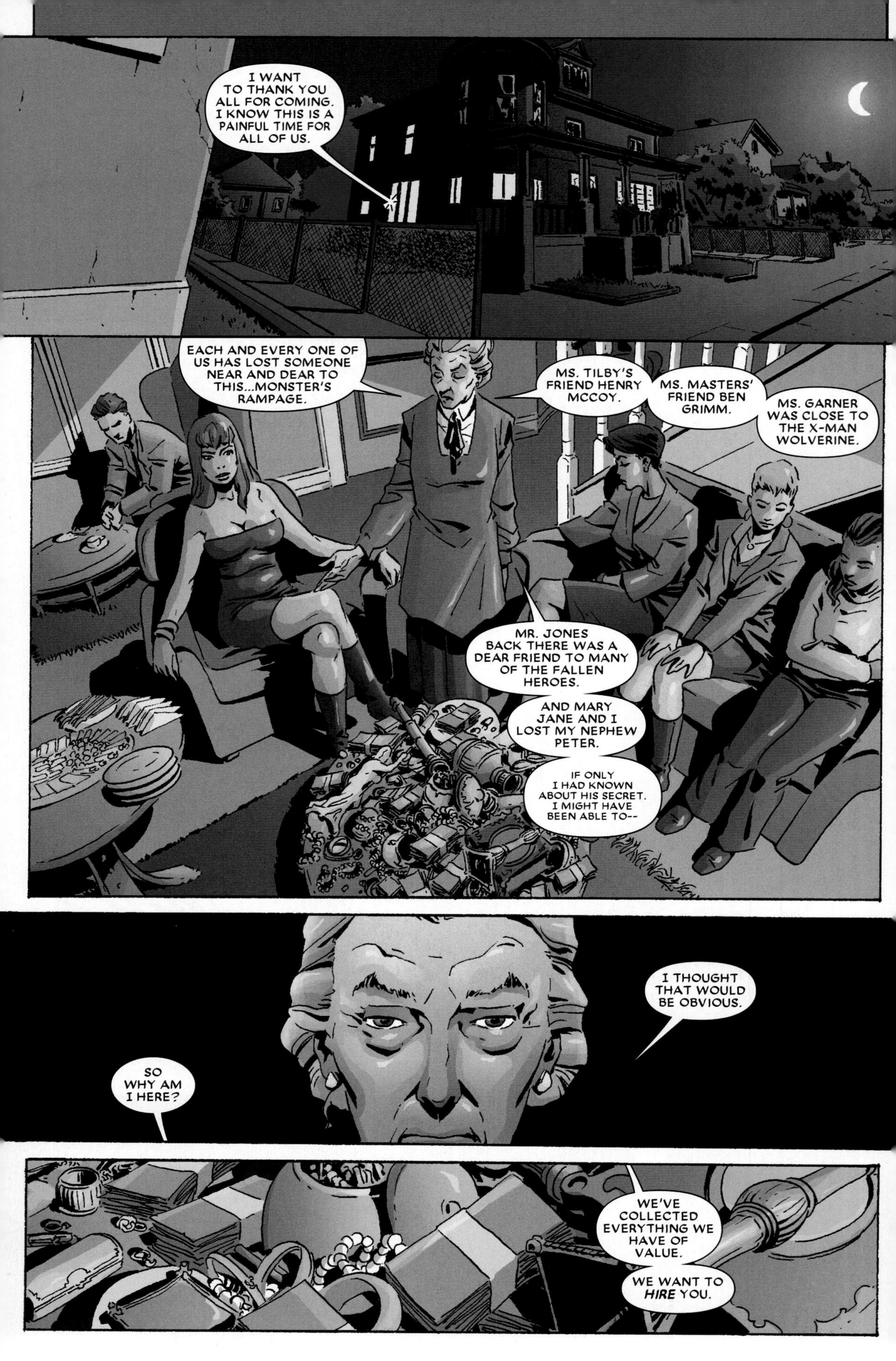
I WANT TO THANK YOU ALL FOR COMING. I KNOW THIS IS A PAINFUL TIME FOR ALL OF US.
EACH AND EVERY ONE OF US HAS LOST SOMEONE NEAR AND DEAR TO THIS...MONSTER'S RAMPAGE.
MS. TILBY'S FRIEND HENRY MCCOY.
MS. MASTERS' FRIEND BEN GRIMM.
MS. GARNER WAS CLOSE TO THE X-MAN WOLVERINE.
MR. JONES BACK THERE WAS A DEAR FRIEND TO MANY OF THE FALLEN HEROES.
AND MARY JANE AND I LOST MY NEPHEW PETER.
IF ONLY I HAD KNOWN ABOUT HIS SECRET. I MIGHT HAVE BEEN ABLE TO--
SO WHY AM I HERE?
I THOUGHT THAT WOULD BE OBVIOUS.
WE'VE COLLECTED EVERYTHING WE HAVE OF VALUE.
WE WANT TO *HIRE* YOU.

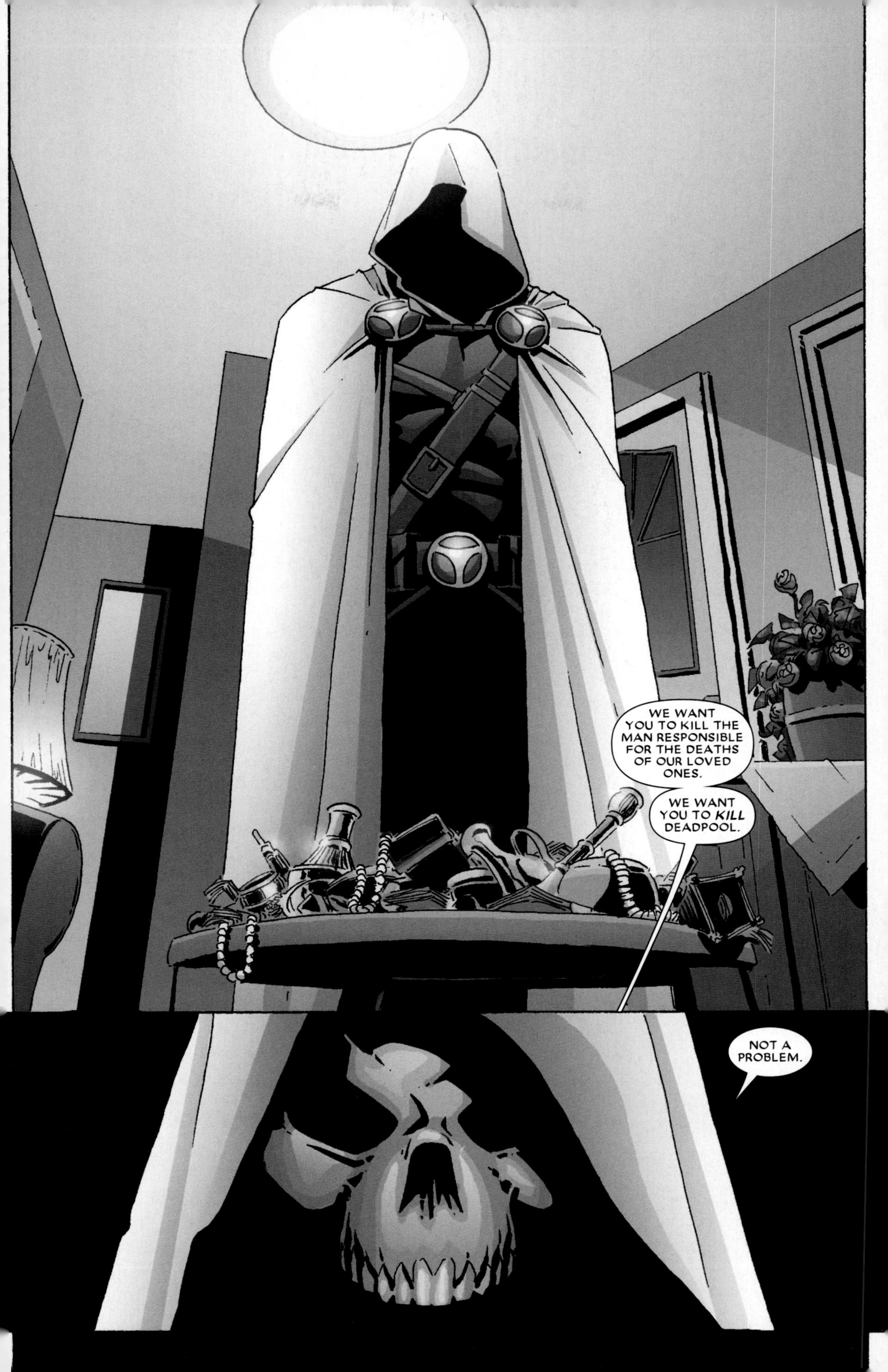
WE WANT YOU TO KILL THE MAN RESPONSIBLE FOR THE DEATHS OF OUR LOVED ONES.
WE WANT YOU TO *KILL* DEADPOOL.
NOT A PROBLEM.

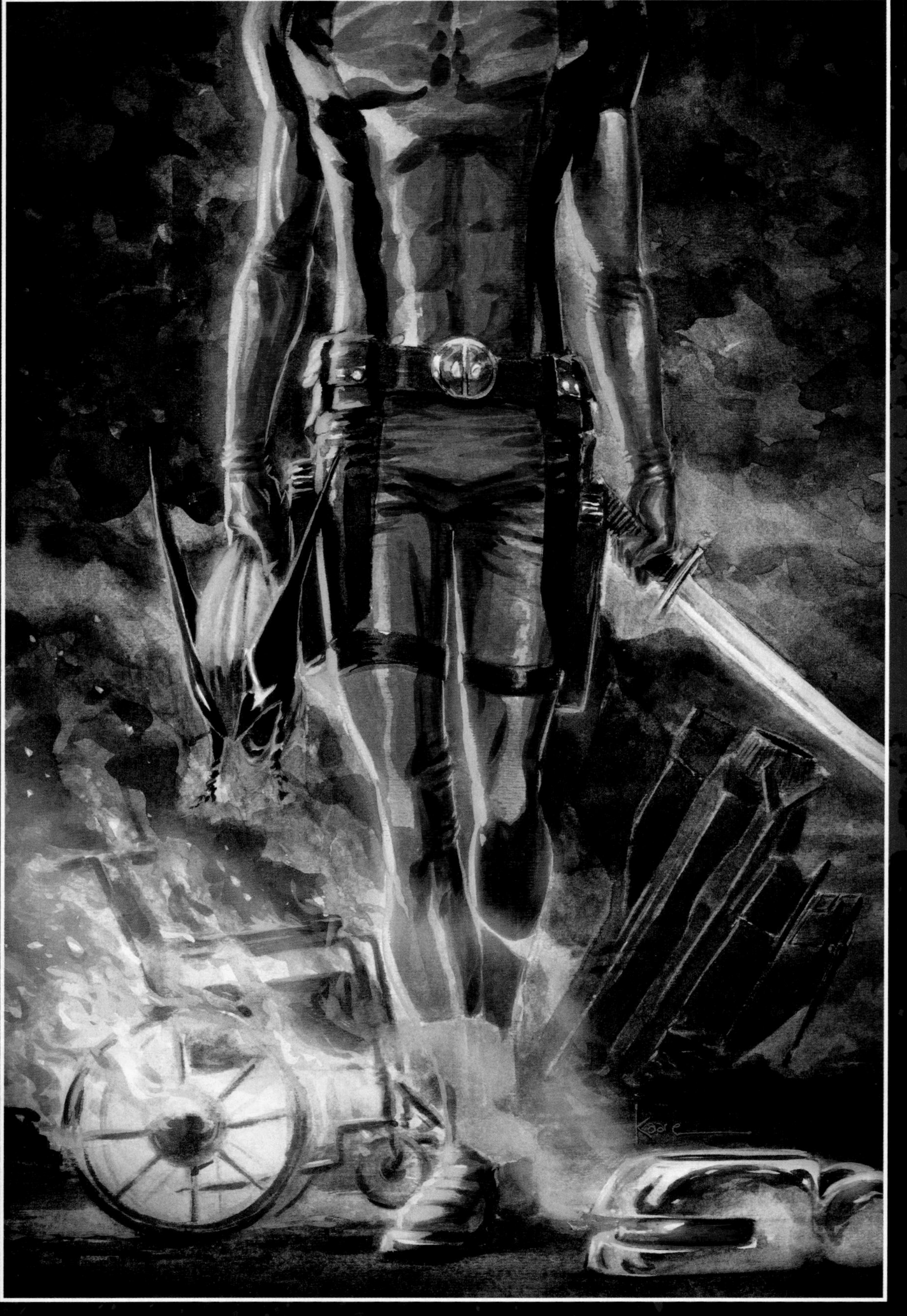

#3

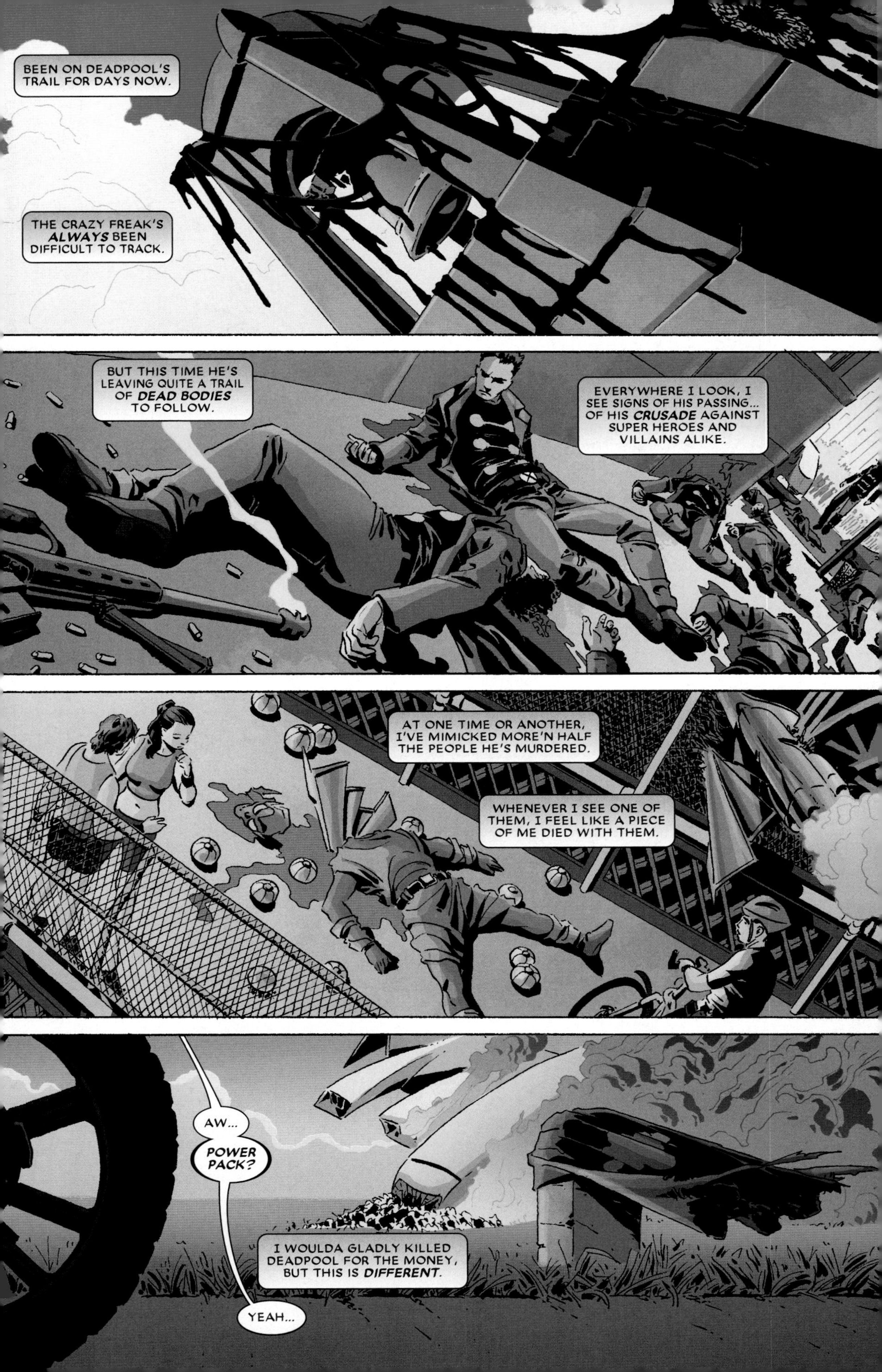
BEEN ON DEADPOOL'S TRAIL FOR DAYS NOW.
THE CRAZY FREAK'S *ALWAYS* BEEN DIFFICULT TO TRACK.
BUT THIS TIME HE'S LEAVING QUITE A TRAIL OF *DEAD BODIES* TO FOLLOW.
EVERYWHERE I LOOK, I SEE SIGNS OF HIS PASSING... OF HIS *CRUSADE* AGAINST SUPER HEROES AND VILLAINS ALIKE.
AT ONE TIME OR ANOTHER, I'VE MIMICKED MORE'N HALF THE PEOPLE HE'S MURDERED.
WHENEVER I SEE ONE OF THEM, I FEEL LIKE A PIECE OF ME DIED WITH THEM.
AW...
POWER PACK?
I WOULDA GLADLY KILLED DEADPOOL FOR THE MONEY, BUT THIS IS *DIFFERENT*.
YEAH...

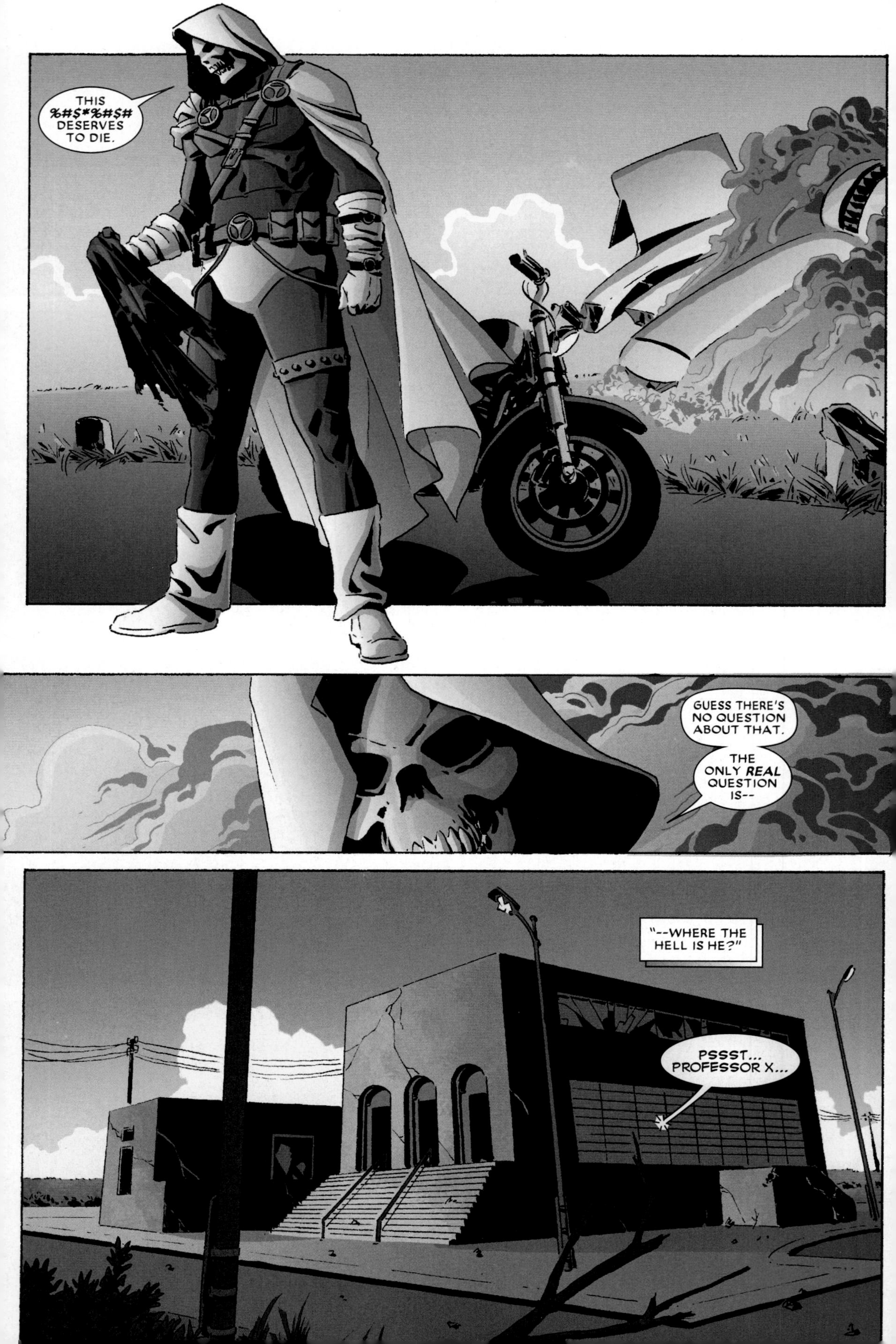

THIS %#$*%#$# DESERVES TO DIE.
GUESS THERE'S NO QUESTION ABOUT THAT.
THE ONLY REAL QUESTION IS--
"--WHERE THE HELL IS HE?"
PSSST... PROFESSOR X...

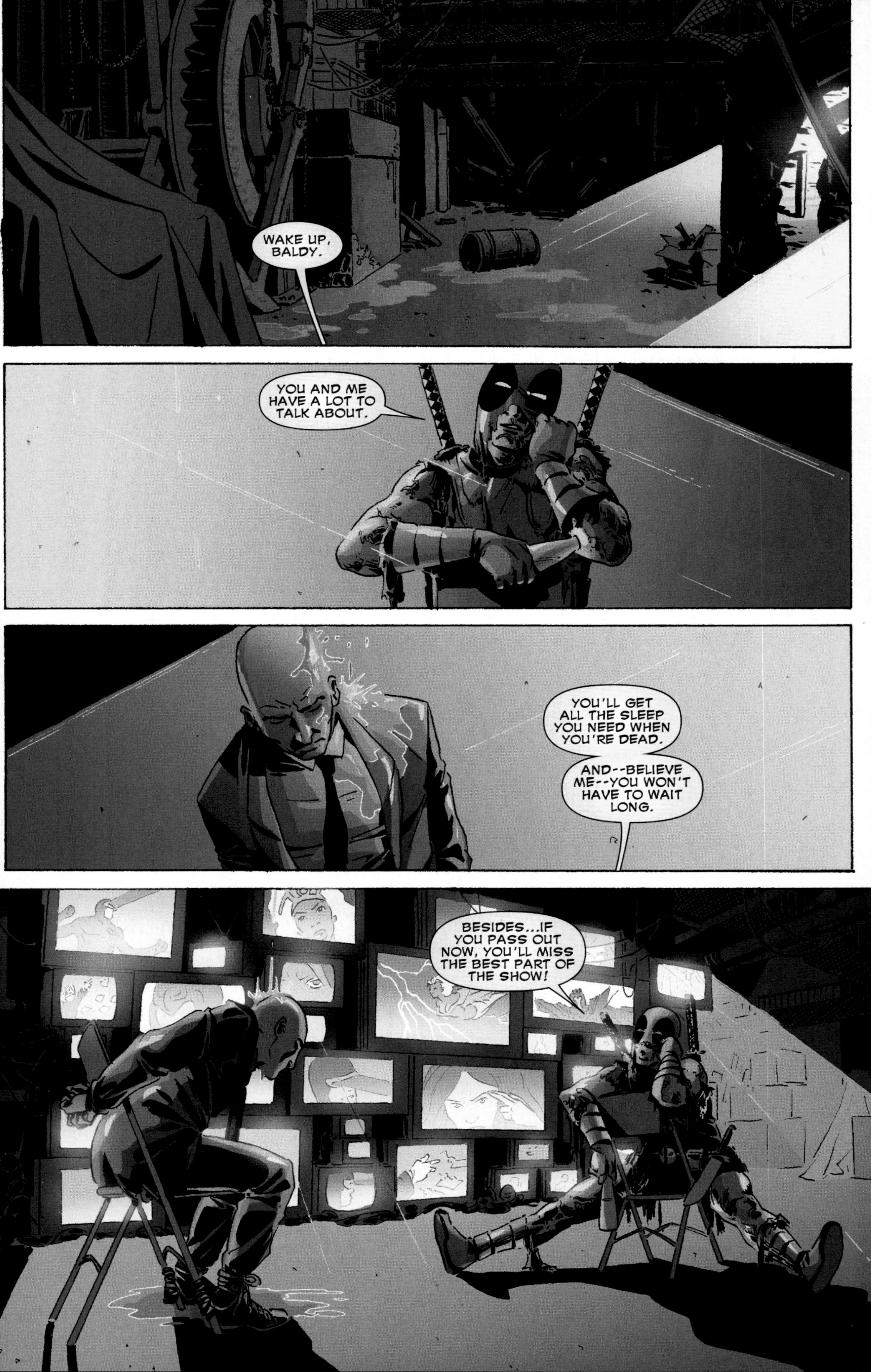
WAKE UP, BALDY.
YOU AND ME HAVE A LOT TO TALK ABOUT.
YOU'LL GET ALL THE SLEEP YOU NEED WHEN YOU'RE DEAD.
AND--BELIEVE ME--YOU WON'T HAVE TO WAIT LONG.
BESIDES...IF YOU PASS OUT NOW, YOU'LL MISS THE BEST PART OF THE SHOW!

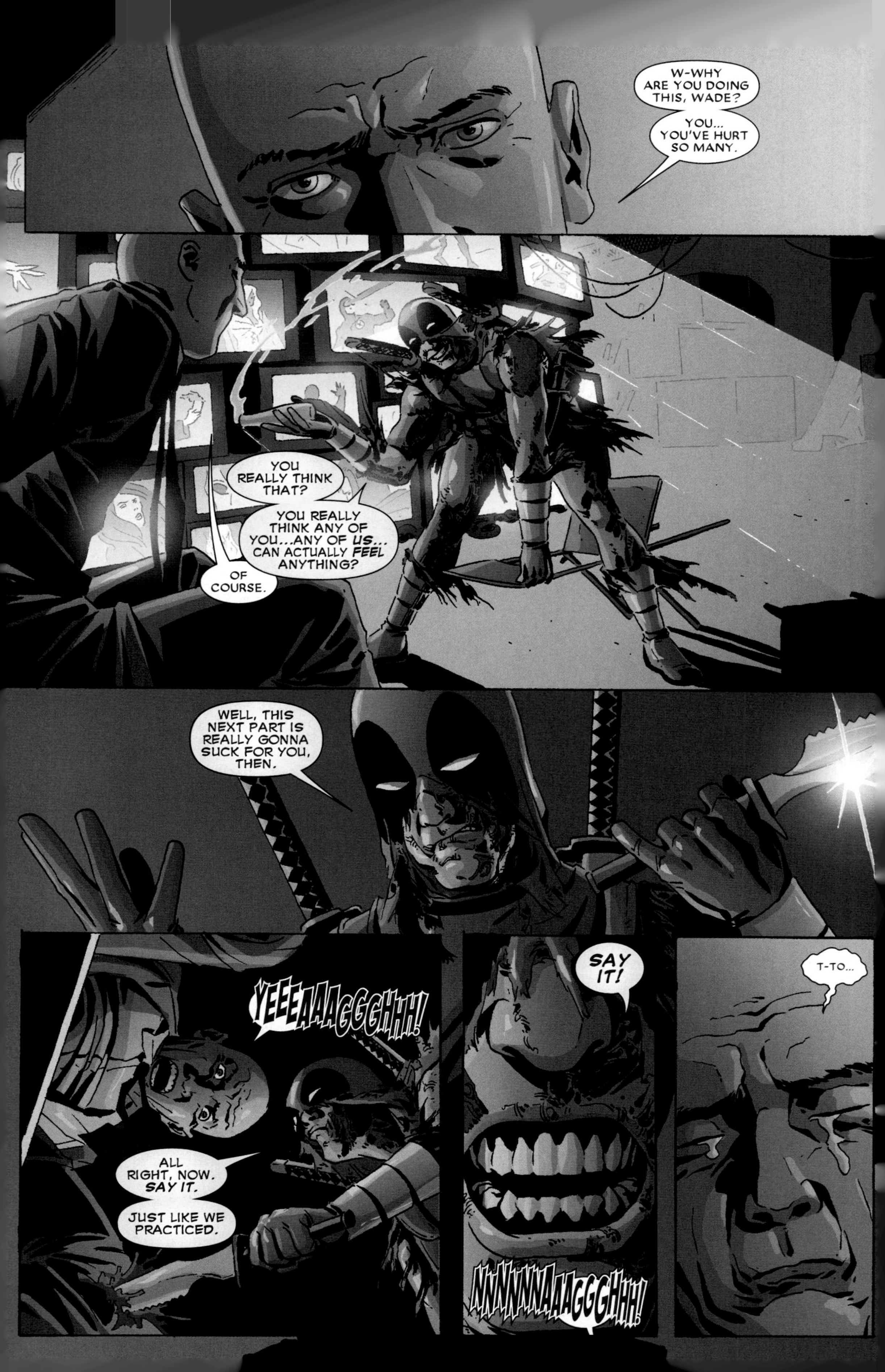

W-WHY ARE YOU DOING THIS, WADE?
YOU... YOU'VE HURT SO MANY.
YOU REALLY THINK THAT?
YOU REALLY THINK ANY OF YOU...ANY OF *US*... CAN ACTUALLY *FEEL* ANYTHING?
OF COURSE.
WELL, THIS NEXT PART IS REALLY GONNA SUCK FOR YOU, THEN.
YEEEAAAGGGHHH!
ALL RIGHT, NOW. *SAY IT.*
JUST LIKE WE PRACTICED.
SAY IT!
NNNNNNAAAGGGHHH!
T-TO...

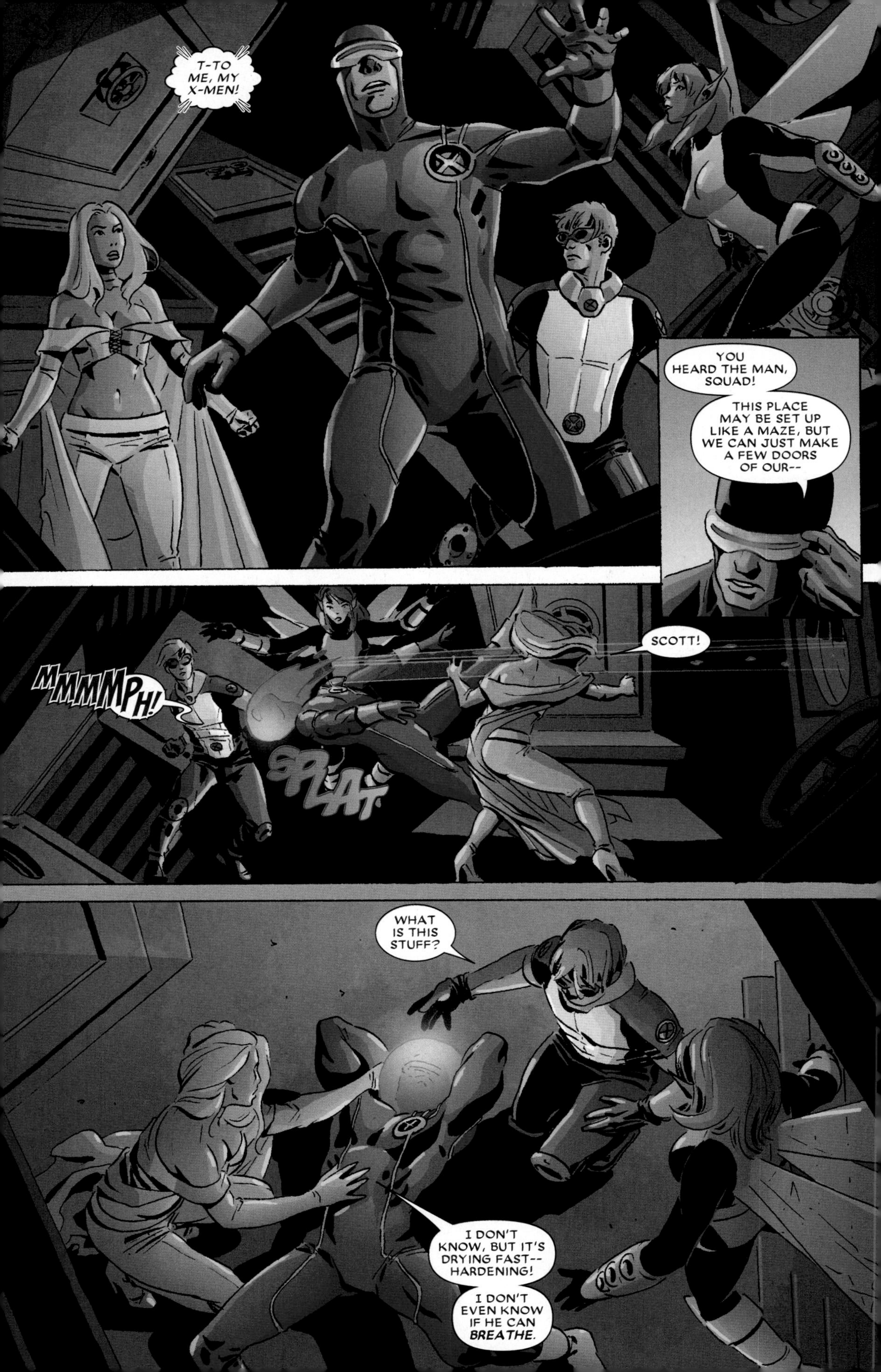
T-TO ME, MY X-MEN!
YOU HEARD THE MAN, SQUAD!
THIS PLACE MAY BE SET UP LIKE A MAZE, BUT WE CAN JUST MAKE A FEW DOORS OF OUR--
MMMMPH!
SCOTT!
SPLAT
WHAT IS THIS STUFF?
I DON'T KNOW, BUT IT'S DRYING FAST--HARDENING!
I DON'T EVEN KNOW IF HE CAN *BREATHE*.

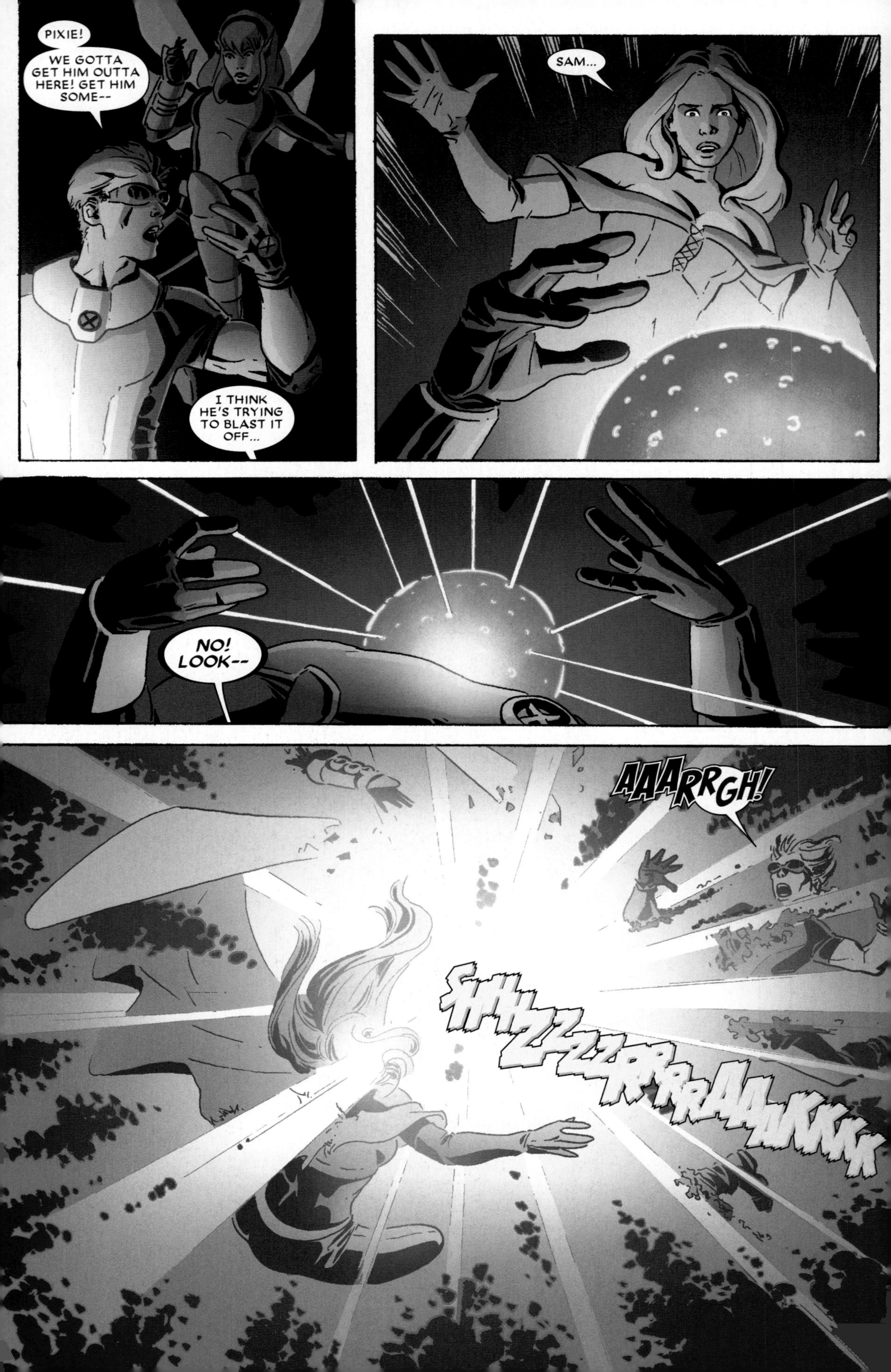
PIXIE!
WE GOTTA GET HIM OUTTA HERE! GET HIM SOME--
I THINK HE'S TRYING TO BLAST IT OFF...
SAM...
NO! LOOK--
AAARRGH!
SHHZZZZRRRRAAAKKKK

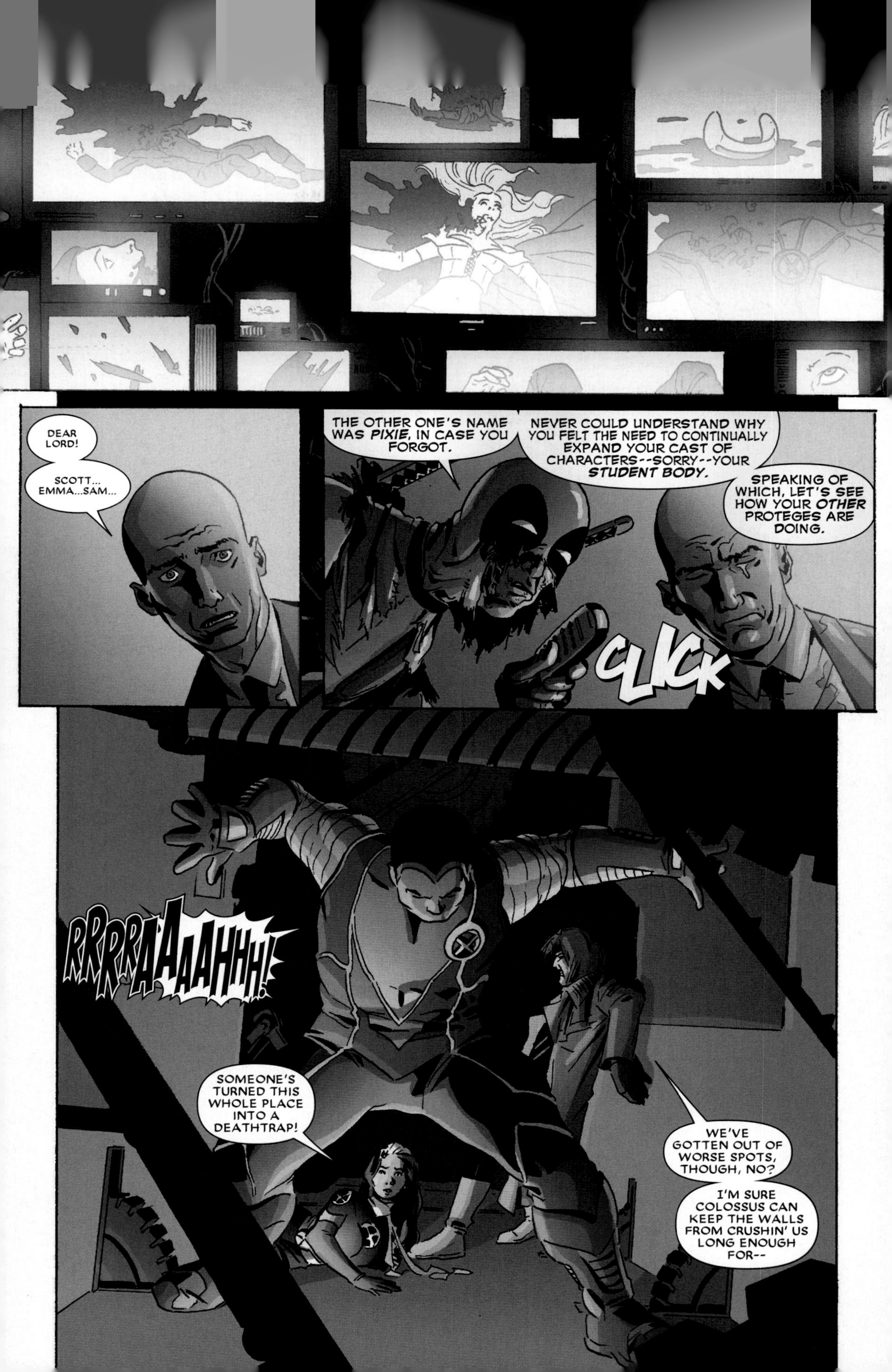
DEAR LORD!
SCOTT... EMMA...SAM...
THE OTHER ONE'S NAME WAS PIXIE, IN CASE YOU FORGOT.
NEVER COULD UNDERSTAND WHY YOU FELT THE NEED TO CONTINUALLY EXPAND YOUR CAST OF CHARACTERS--SORRY--YOUR STUDENT BODY.
SPEAKING OF WHICH, LET'S SEE HOW YOUR OTHER PROTEGES ARE DOING.
CLICK
RRRRAAAAHHH!
SOMEONE'S TURNED THIS WHOLE PLACE INTO A DEATHTRAP!
WE'VE GOTTEN OUT OF WORSE SPOTS, THOUGH, NO?
I'M SURE COLOSSUS CAN KEEP THE WALLS FROM CRUSHIN' US LONG ENOUGH FOR--

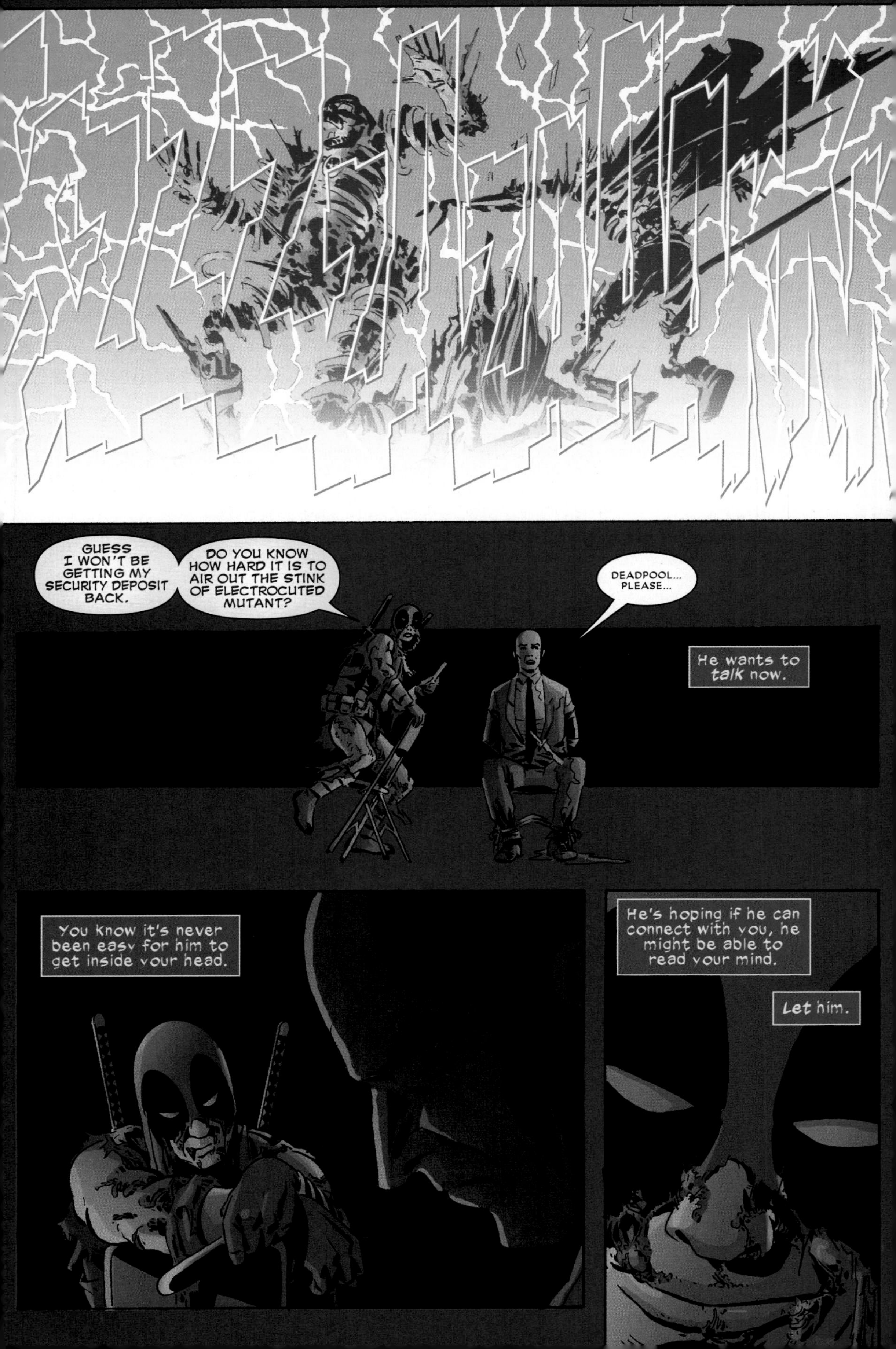
GUESS I WON'T BE GETTING MY SECURITY DEPOSIT BACK.
DO YOU KNOW HOW HARD IT IS TO AIR OUT THE STINK OF ELECTROCUTED MUTANT?
DEADPOOL... PLEASE...
He wants to *talk* now.
You know it's never been easy for him to get inside your head.
He's hoping if he can connect with you, he might be able to read your mind.
Let him.

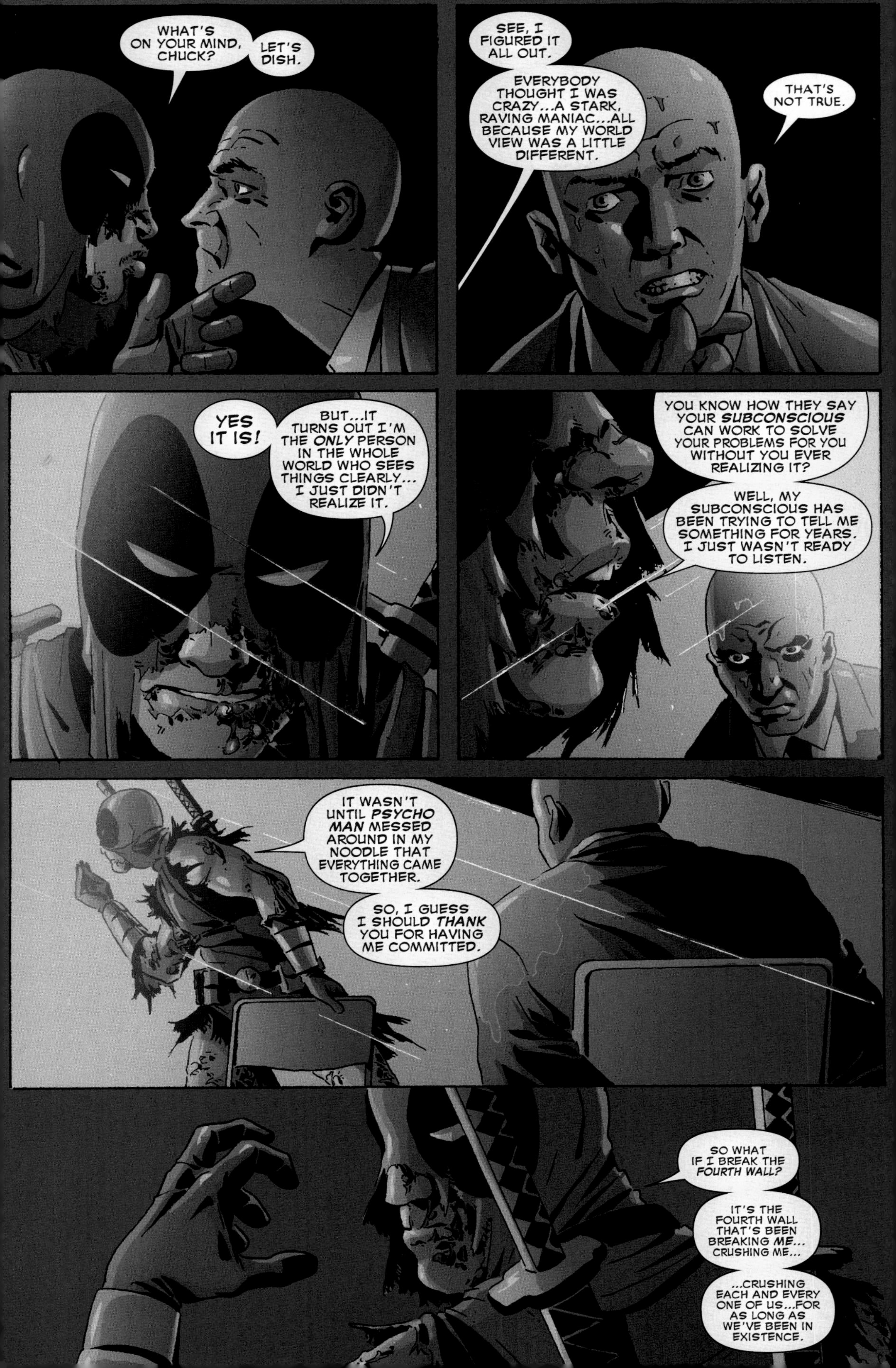
WHAT'S ON YOUR MIND, CHUCK?
LET'S DISH.
SEE, I FIGURED IT ALL OUT.
EVERYBODY THOUGHT I WAS CRAZY...A STARK, RAVING MANIAC...ALL BECAUSE MY WORLD VIEW WAS A LITTLE DIFFERENT.
THAT'S NOT TRUE.
YES IT IS!
BUT...IT TURNS OUT I'M THE *ONLY* PERSON IN THE WHOLE WORLD WHO SEES THINGS CLEARLY... I JUST DIDN'T REALIZE IT.
YOU KNOW HOW THEY SAY YOUR *SUBCONSCIOUS* CAN WORK TO SOLVE YOUR PROBLEMS FOR YOU WITHOUT YOU EVER REALIZING IT?
WELL, MY SUBCONSCIOUS HAS BEEN TRYING TO TELL ME SOMETHING FOR YEARS. I JUST WASN'T READY TO LISTEN.
IT WASN'T UNTIL *PSYCHO MAN* MESSED AROUND IN MY NOODLE THAT EVERYTHING CAME TOGETHER.
SO, I GUESS I SHOULD *THANK* YOU FOR HAVING ME COMMITTED.
SO WHAT IF I BREAK THE *FOURTH WALL?*
IT'S THE FOURTH WALL THAT'S BEEN BREAKING *ME...* CRUSHING ME...
...CRUSHING EACH AND EVERY ONE OF US...FOR AS LONG AS WE'VE BEEN IN EXISTENCE.

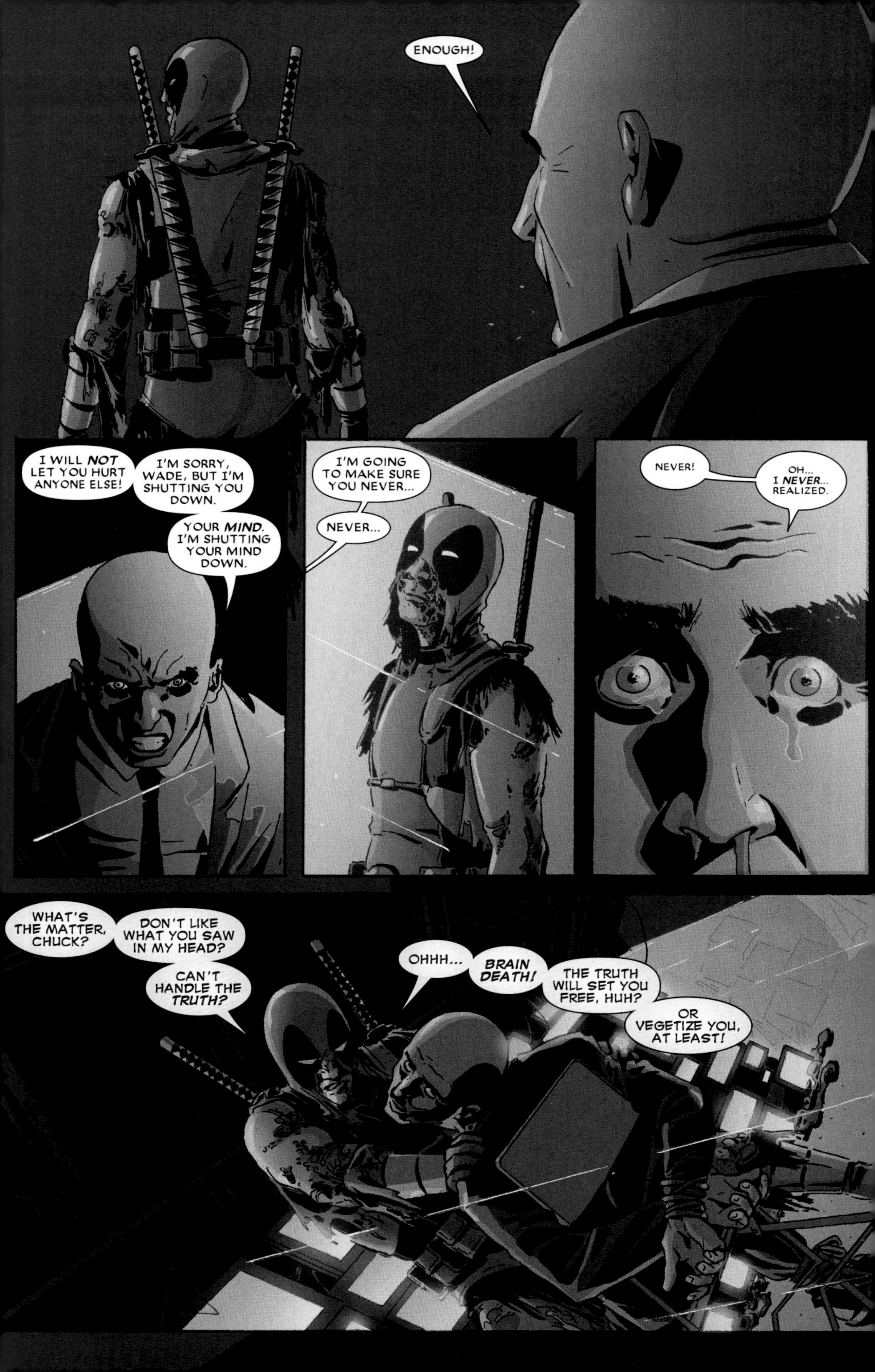
ENOUGH!
I WILL NOT LET YOU HURT ANYONE ELSE!
I'M SORRY, WADE, BUT I'M SHUTTING YOU DOWN.
YOUR MIND. I'M SHUTTING YOUR MIND DOWN.
I'M GOING TO MAKE SURE YOU NEVER...
NEVER...
NEVER!
OH... I NEVER... REALIZED.
WHAT'S THE MATTER, CHUCK?
DON'T LIKE WHAT YOU SAW IN MY HEAD?
CAN'T HANDLE THE TRUTH?
OHHH...
BRAIN DEATH!
THE TRUTH WILL SET YOU FREE, HUH?
OR VEGETIZE YOU, AT LEAST!

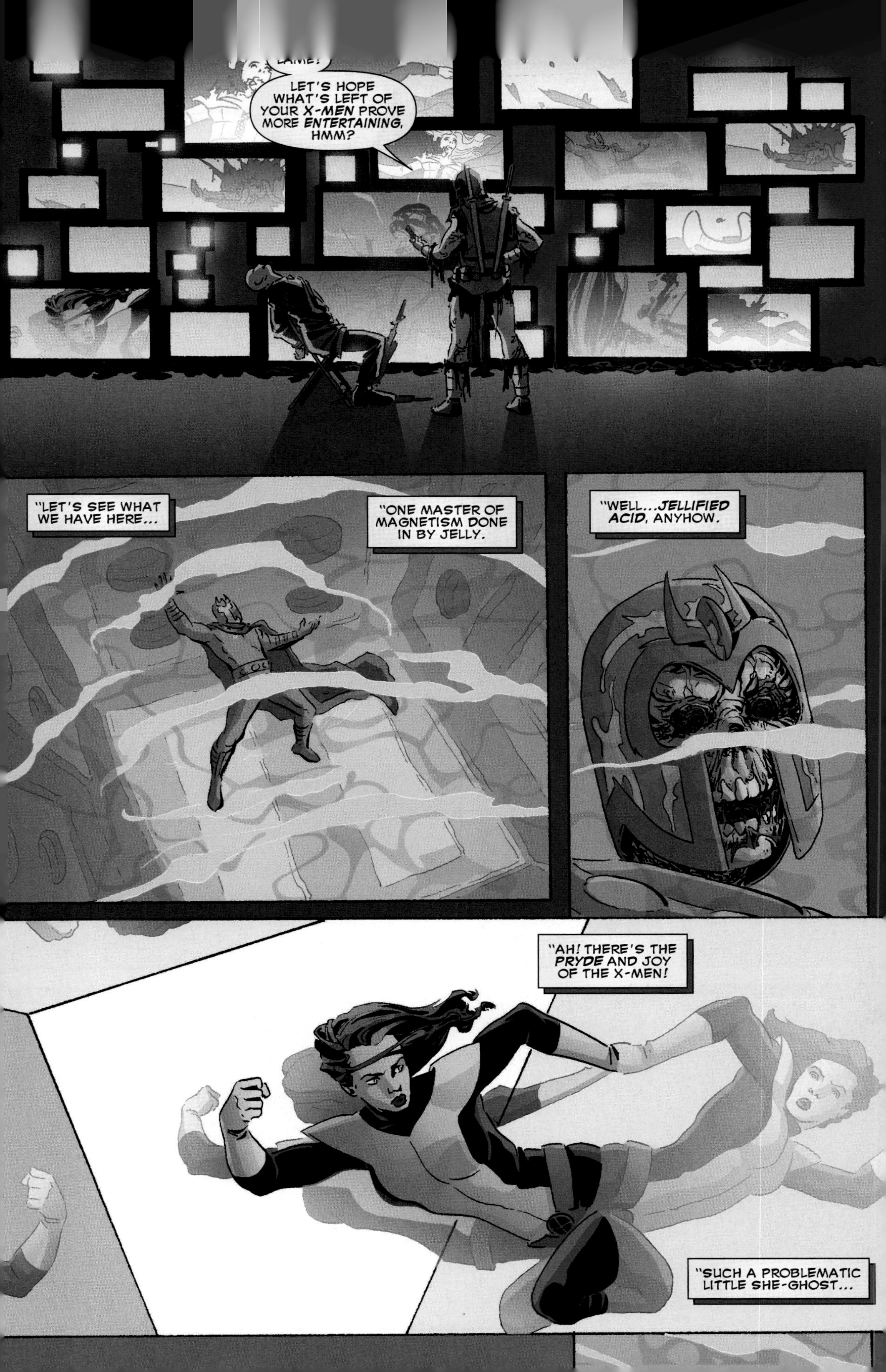
LAME!
LET'S HOPE WHAT'S LEFT OF YOUR X-MEN PROVE MORE ENTERTAINING, HMM?
"LET'S SEE WHAT WE HAVE HERE...
"ONE MASTER OF MAGNETISM DONE IN BY JELLY.
"WELL...JELLIFIED ACID, ANYHOW.
"AH! THERE'S THE PRYDE AND JOY OF THE X-MEN!
"SUCH A PROBLEMATIC LITTLE SHE-GHOST...

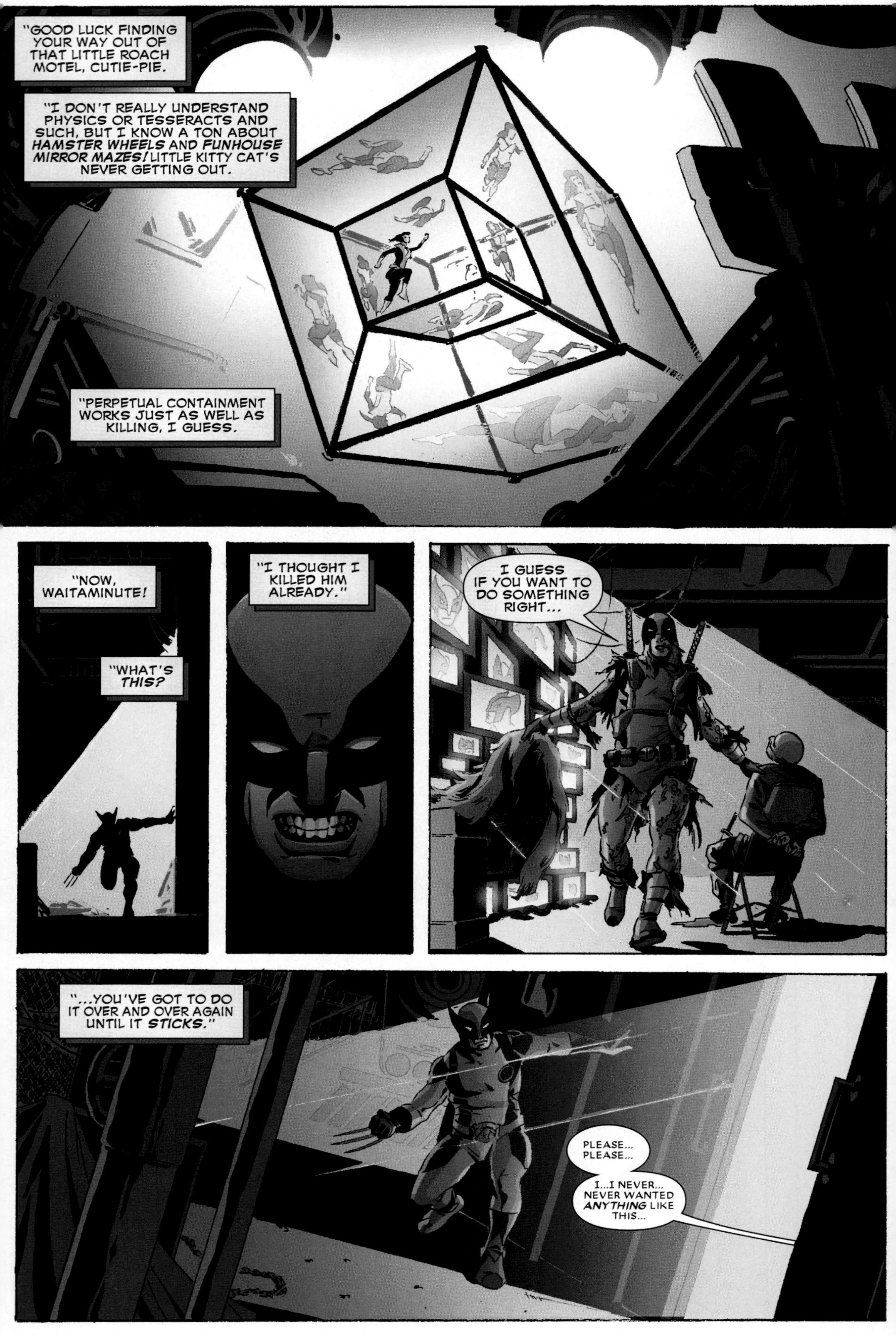
"GOOD LUCK FINDING YOUR WAY OUT OF THAT LITTLE ROACH MOTEL, CUTIE-PIE.
"I DON'T REALLY UNDERSTAND PHYSICS OR TESSERACTS AND SUCH, BUT I KNOW A TON ABOUT *HAMSTER WHEELS* AND *FUNHOUSE MIRROR MAZES!* LITTLE KITTY CAT'S NEVER GETTING OUT.
"PERPETUAL CONTAINMENT WORKS JUST AS WELL AS KILLING, I GUESS.
"NOW, WAITAMINUTE!
"WHAT'S *THIS?*
"I THOUGHT I KILLED HIM ALREADY."
I GUESS IF YOU WANT TO DO SOMETHING RIGHT...
"...YOU'VE GOT TO DO IT OVER AND OVER AGAIN UNTIL IT *STICKS.*"
PLEASE... PLEASE...
I...I NEVER... NEVER WANTED *ANYTHING* LIKE THIS...

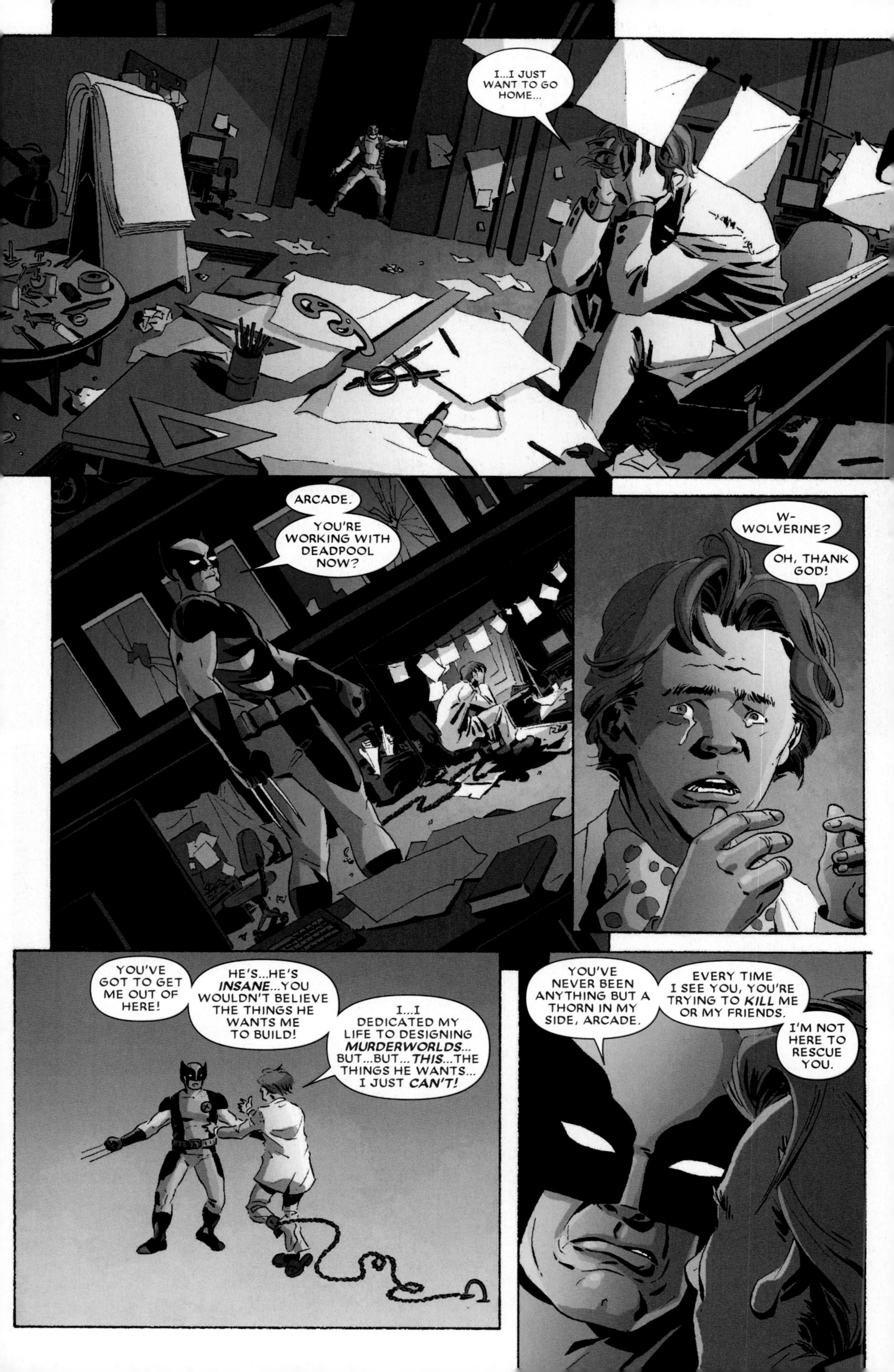
I...I JUST WANT TO GO HOME...
ARCADE.
YOU'RE WORKING WITH DEADPOOL NOW?
W- WOLVERINE?
OH, THANK GOD!
YOU'VE GOT TO GET ME OUT OF HERE!
HE'S...HE'S *INSANE*...YOU WOULDN'T BELIEVE THE THINGS HE WANTS ME TO BUILD!
I...I DEDICATED MY LIFE TO DESIGNING *MURDERWORLDS*... BUT...BUT...*THIS*...THE THINGS HE WANTS... I JUST *CAN'T!*
YOU'VE NEVER BEEN ANYTHING BUT A THORN IN MY SIDE, ARCADE.
EVERY TIME I SEE YOU, YOU'RE TRYING TO *KILL* ME OR MY FRIENDS.
I'M NOT HERE TO RESCUE YOU.

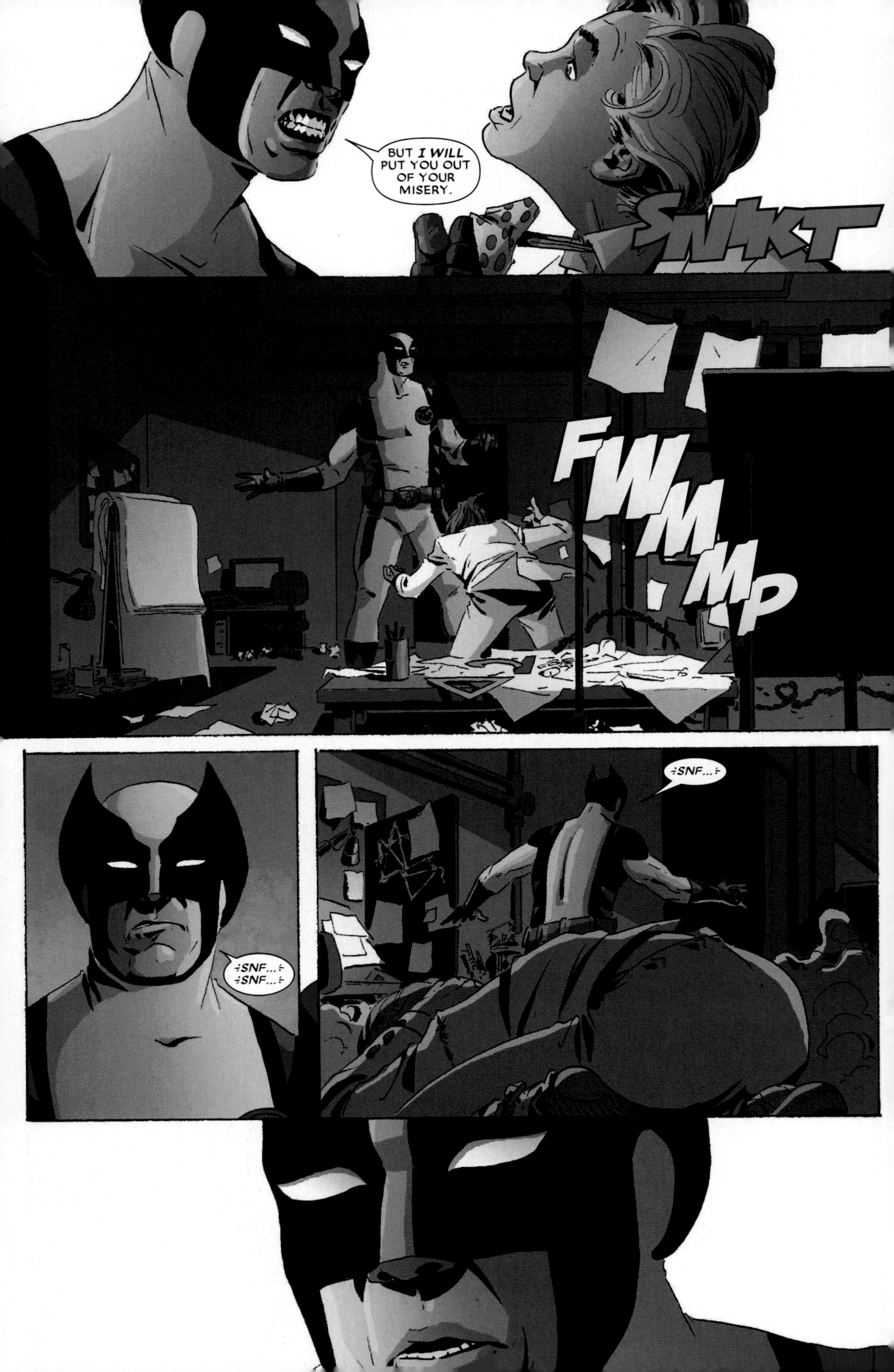
BUT *I WILL* PUT YOU OUT OF YOUR MISERY.
SNIKT
FWMMP
SNF...
SNF...
SNF...

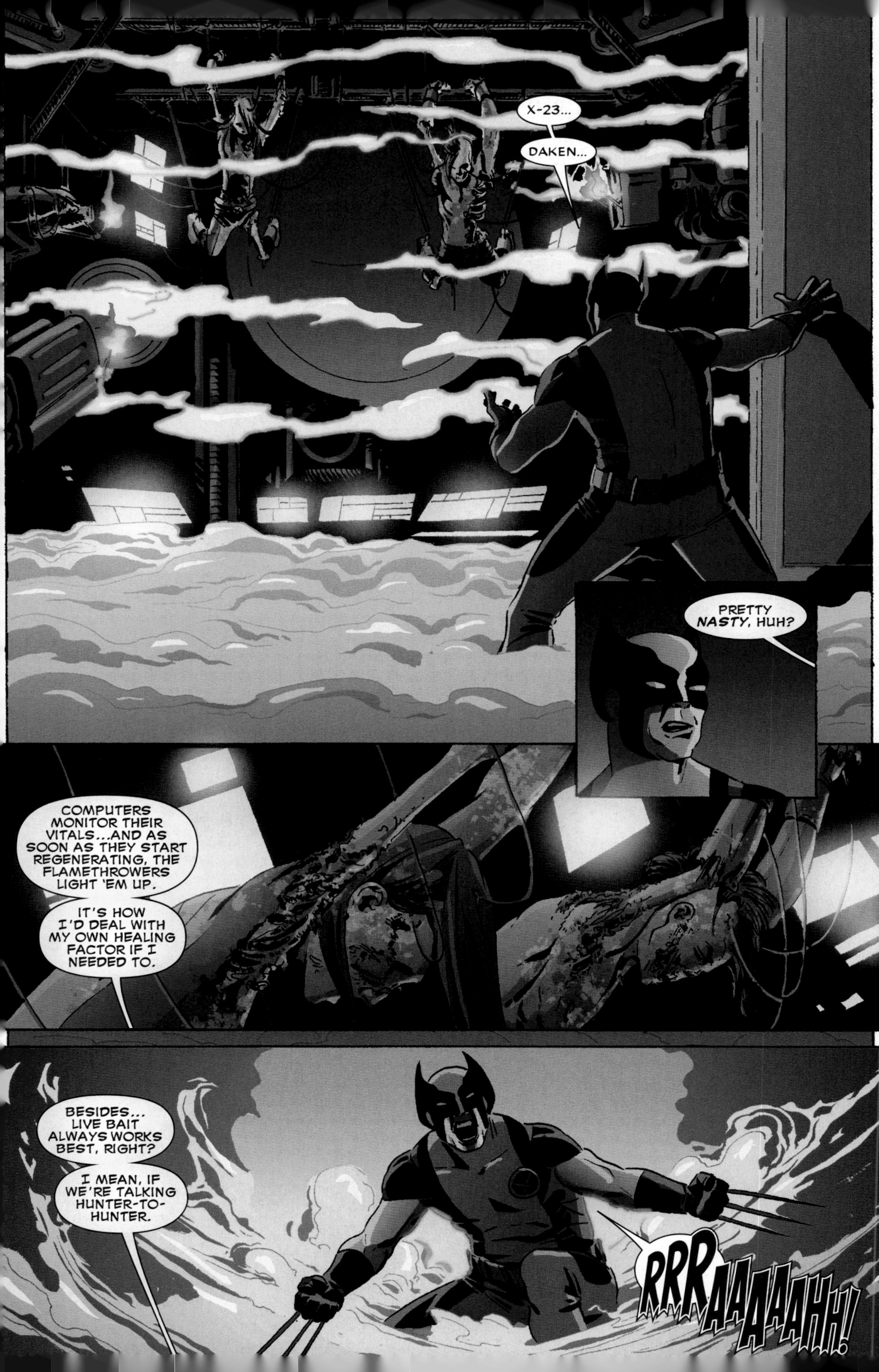
X-23...
DAKEN...
PRETTY NASTY, HUH?
COMPUTERS MONITOR THEIR VITALS...AND AS SOON AS THEY START REGENERATING, THE FLAMETHROWERS LIGHT 'EM UP.
IT'S HOW I'D DEAL WITH MY OWN HEALING FACTOR IF I NEEDED TO.
BESIDES... LIVE BAIT ALWAYS WORKS BEST, RIGHT?
I MEAN, IF WE'RE TALKING HUNTER-TO-HUNTER.
RRRAAAAAHH!

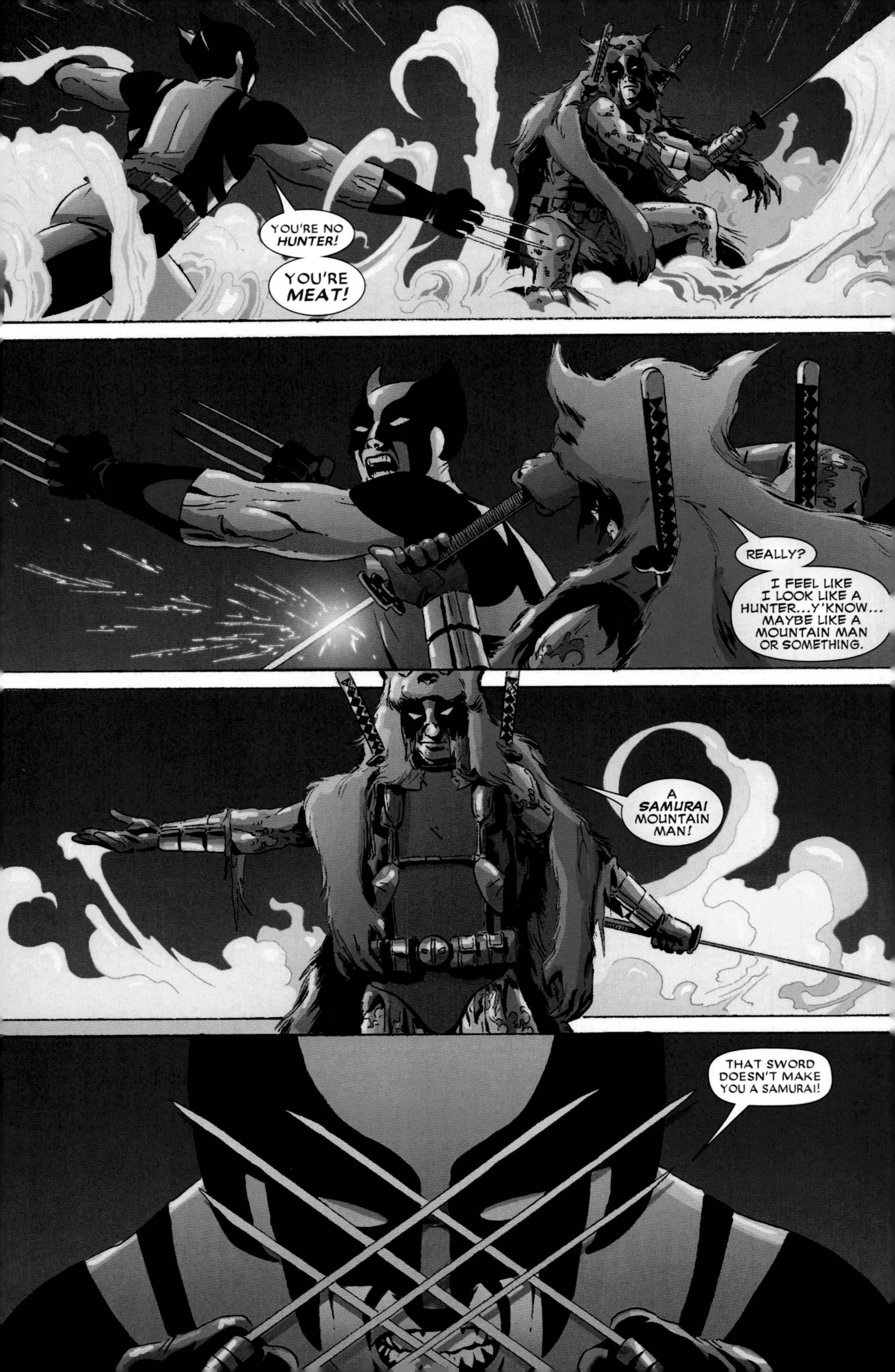
YOU'RE NO HUNTER!
YOU'RE MEAT!
REALLY?
I FEEL LIKE I LOOK LIKE A HUNTER...Y'KNOW... MAYBE LIKE A MOUNTAIN MAN OR SOMETHING.
A SAMURAI MOUNTAIN MAN!
THAT SWORD DOESN'T MAKE YOU A SAMURAI!

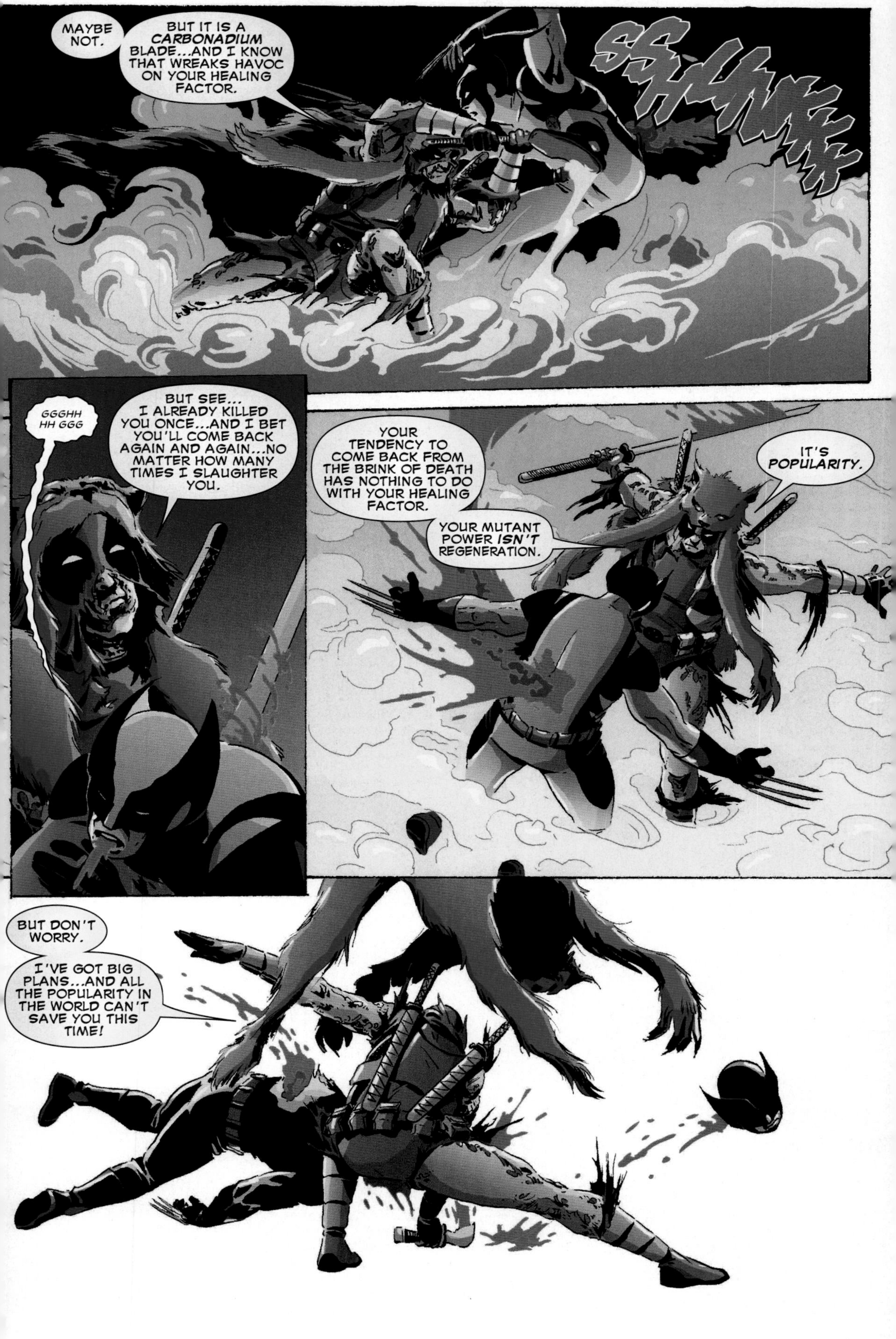
MAYBE NOT.
BUT IT IS A CARBONADIUM BLADE...AND I KNOW THAT WREAKS HAVOC ON YOUR HEALING FACTOR.
SSHHUNKK
GGGHH HH GGG
BUT SEE... I ALREADY KILLED YOU ONCE...AND I BET YOU'LL COME BACK AGAIN AND AGAIN...NO MATTER HOW MANY TIMES I SLAUGHTER YOU.
YOUR TENDENCY TO COME BACK FROM THE BRINK OF DEATH HAS NOTHING TO DO WITH YOUR HEALING FACTOR.
YOUR MUTANT POWER ISN'T REGENERATION.
IT'S POPULARITY.
BUT DON'T WORRY.
I'VE GOT BIG PLANS...AND ALL THE POPULARITY IN THE WORLD CAN'T SAVE YOU THIS TIME!

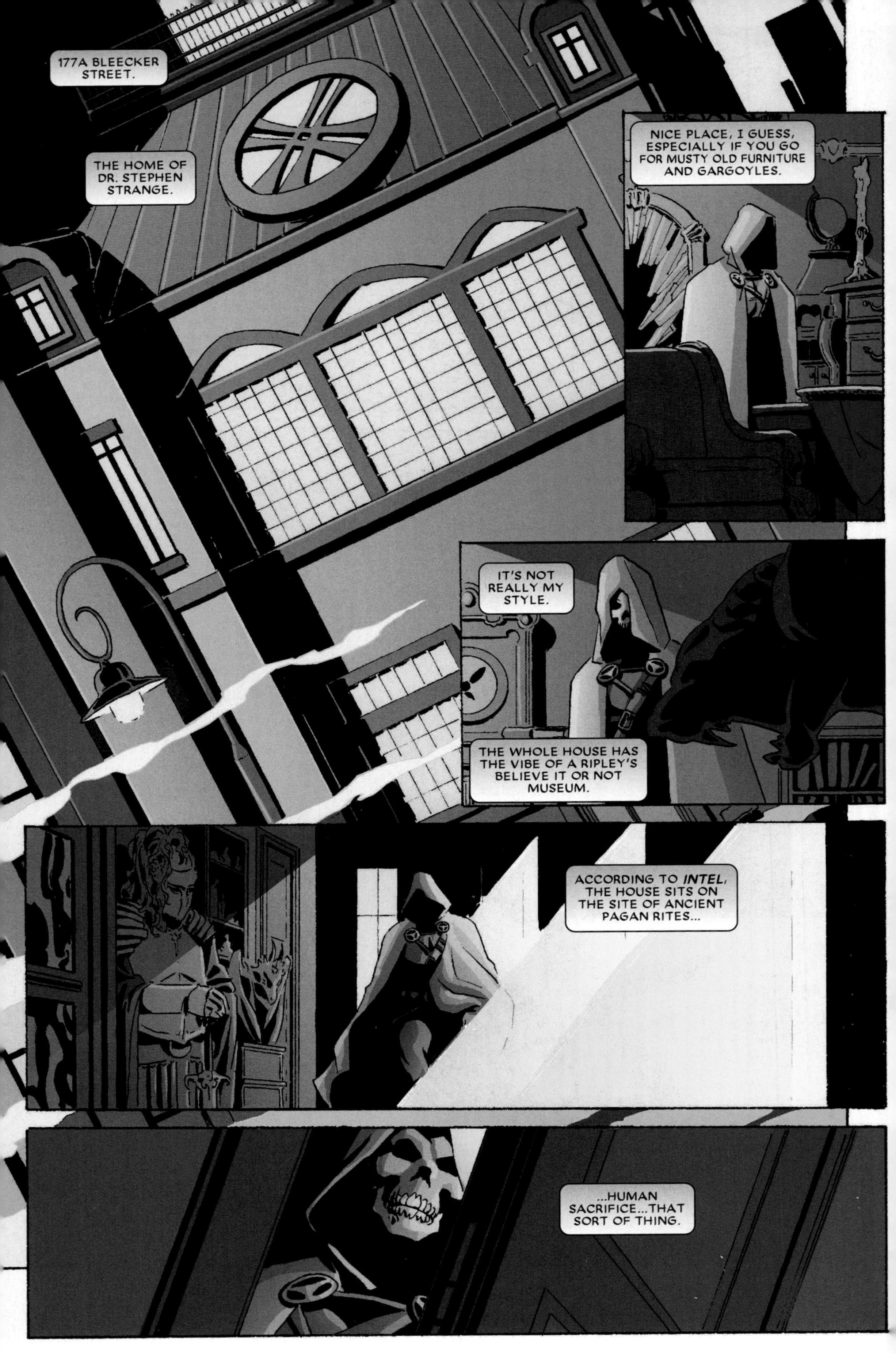
177A BLEECKER STREET.
THE HOME OF DR. STEPHEN STRANGE.
NICE PLACE, I GUESS, ESPECIALLY IF YOU GO FOR MUSTY OLD FURNITURE AND GARGOYLES.
IT'S NOT REALLY MY STYLE.
THE WHOLE HOUSE HAS THE VIBE OF A RIPLEY'S BELIEVE IT OR NOT MUSEUM.
ACCORDING TO INTEL, THE HOUSE SITS ON THE SITE OF ANCIENT PAGAN RITES...
...HUMAN SACRIFICE...THAT SORT OF THING.

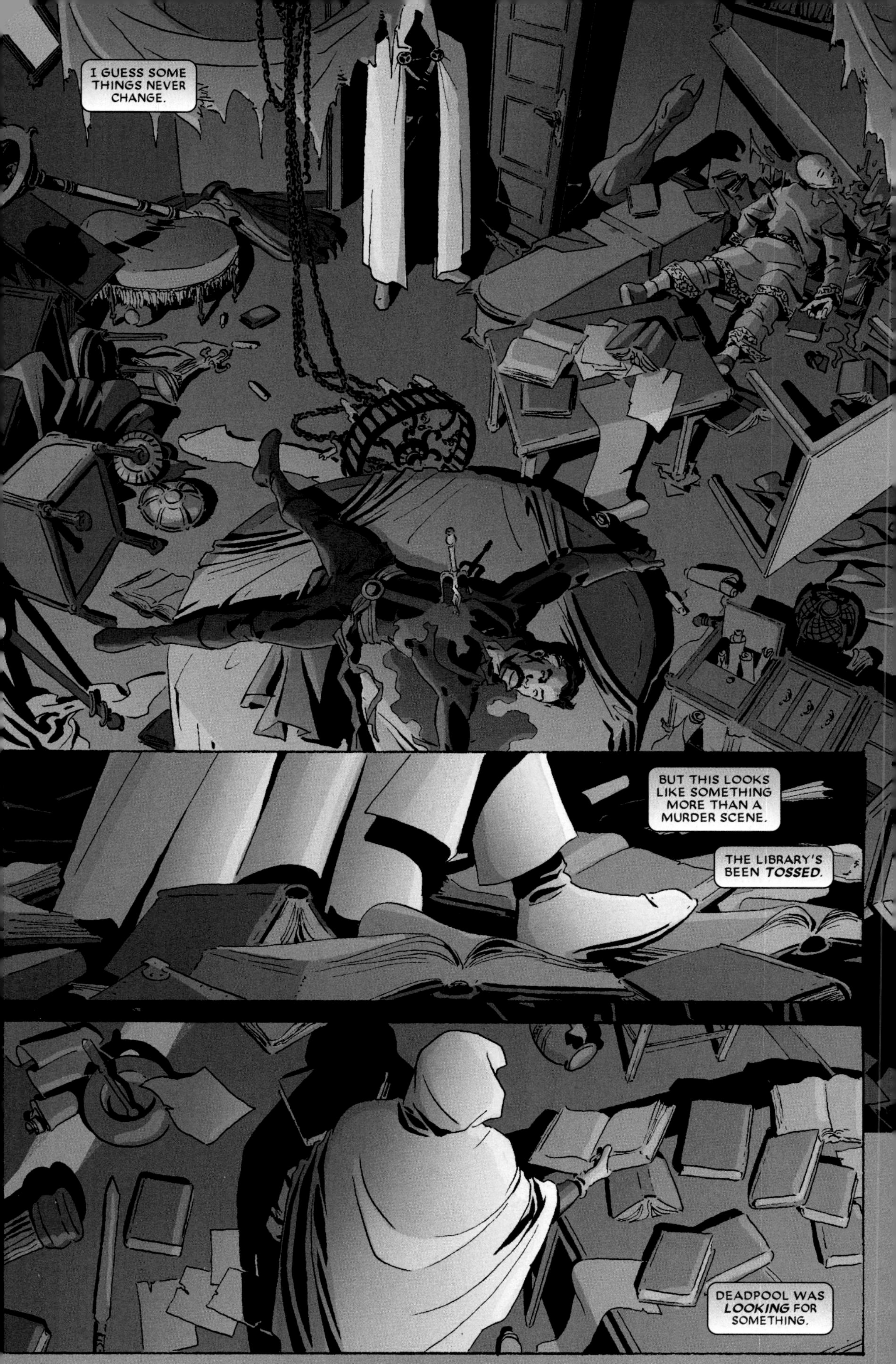
I GUESS SOME THINGS NEVER CHANGE.
BUT THIS LOOKS LIKE SOMETHING MORE THAN A MURDER SCENE.
THE LIBRARY'S BEEN *TOSSED*.
DEADPOOL WAS *LOOKING* FOR SOMETHING.

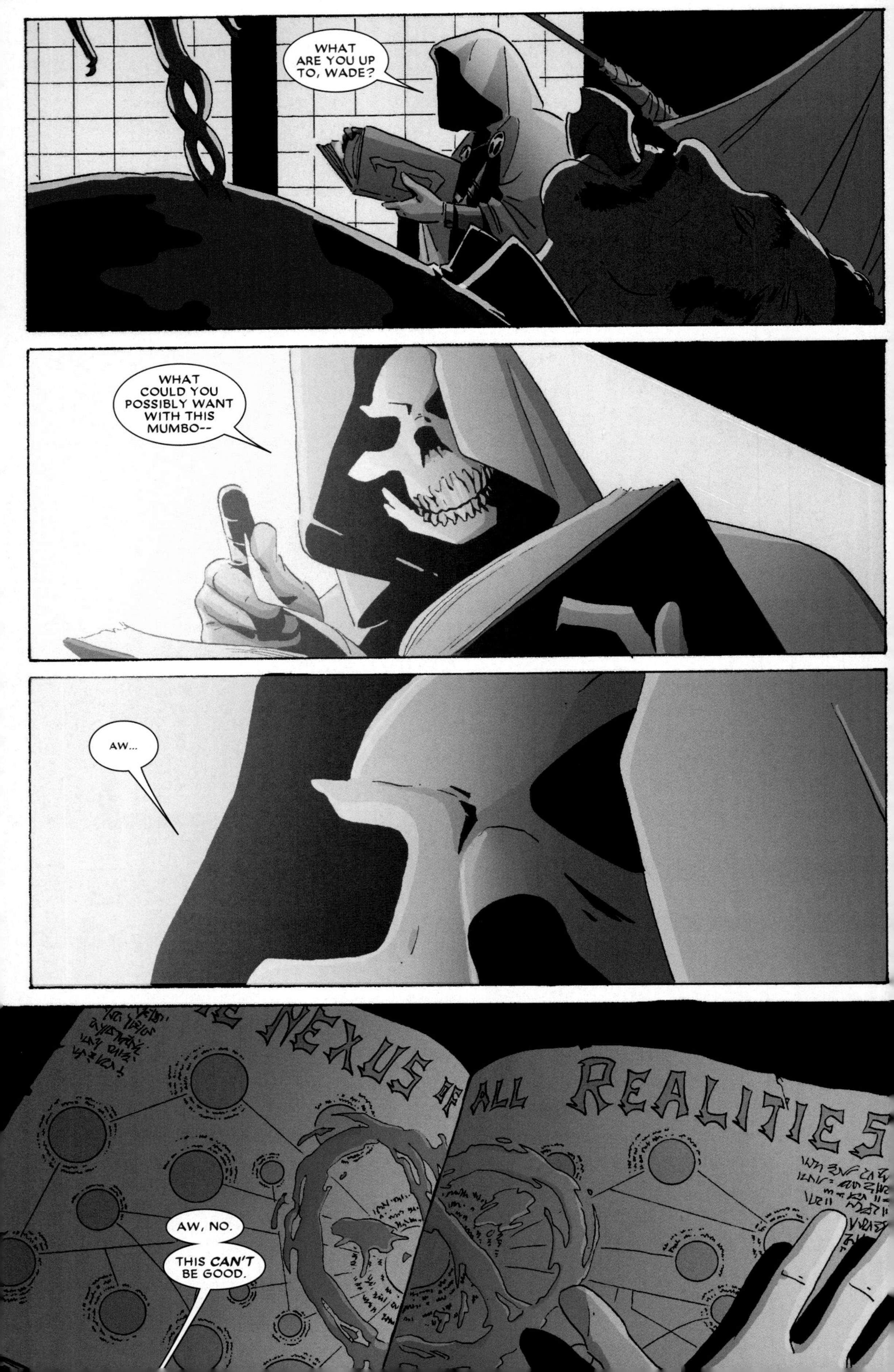
WHAT ARE YOU UP TO, WADE?
WHAT COULD YOU POSSIBLY WANT WITH THIS MUMBO--
AW...
NEXUS OF ALL REALITIES
AW, NO.
THIS CAN'T BE GOOD.

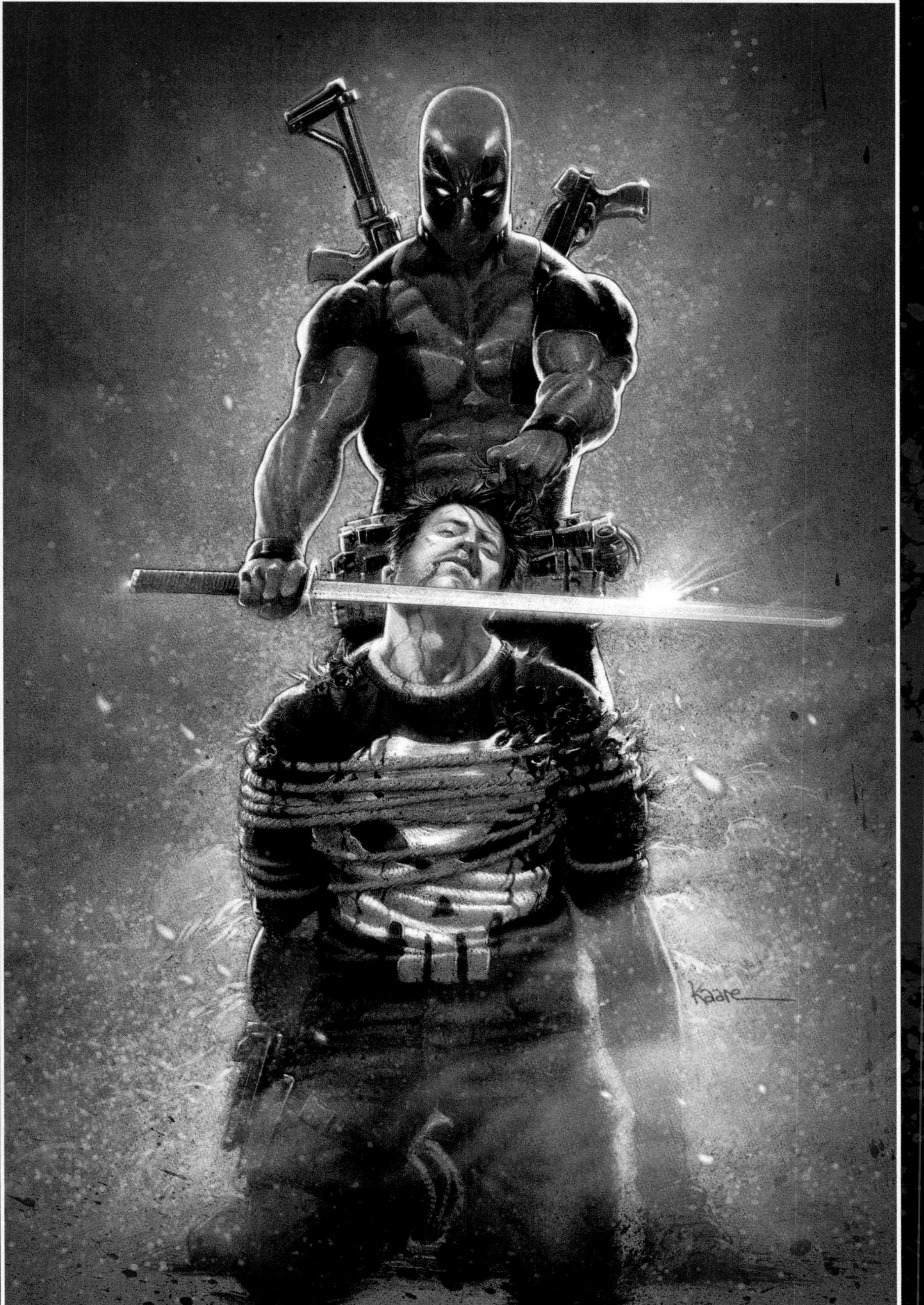
Kaare

#4

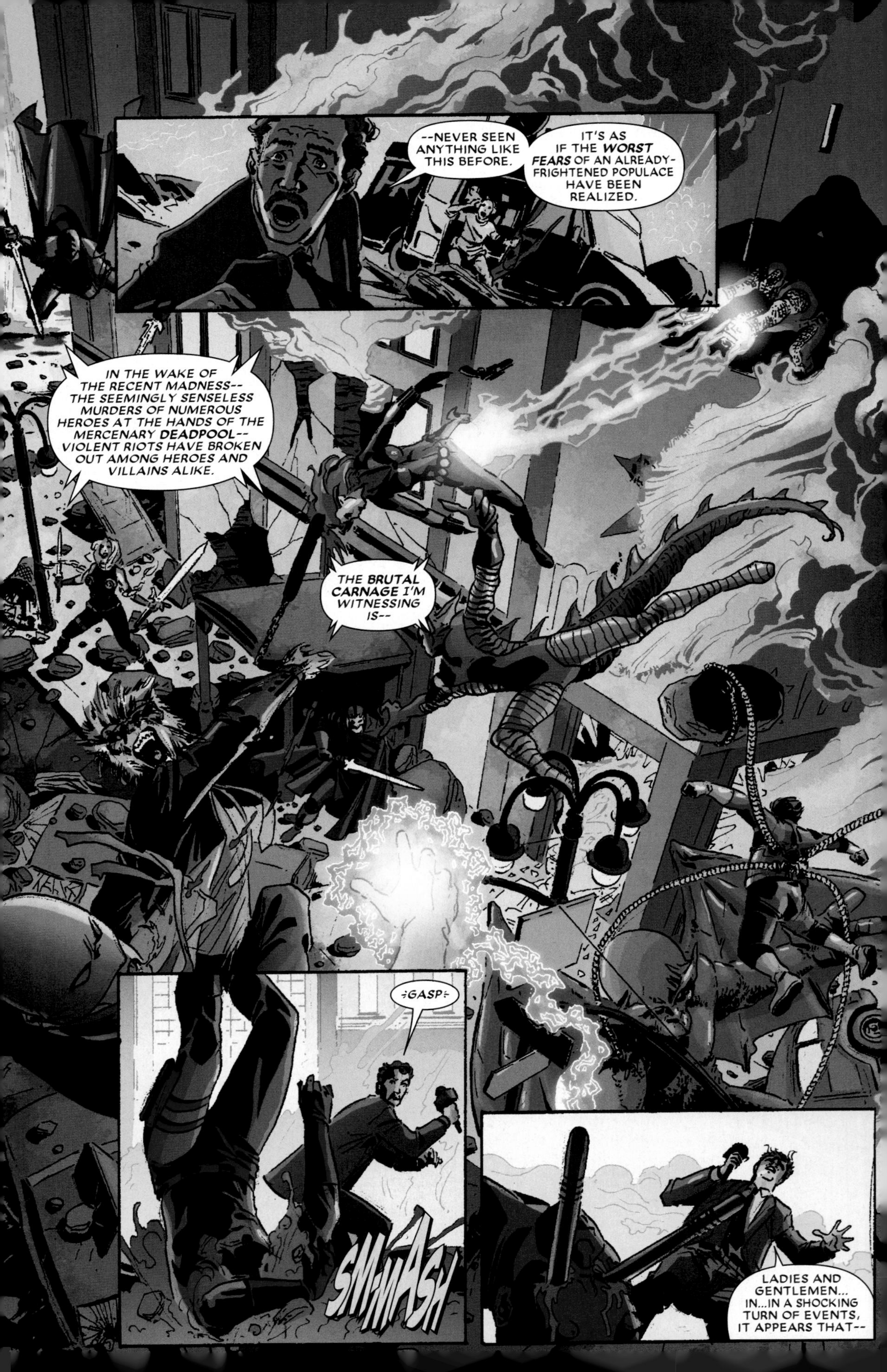
--NEVER SEEN ANYTHING LIKE THIS BEFORE.
IT'S AS IF THE WORST FEARS OF AN ALREADY-FRIGHTENED POPULACE HAVE BEEN REALIZED.
IN THE WAKE OF THE RECENT MADNESS-- THE SEEMINGLY SENSELESS MURDERS OF NUMEROUS HEROES AT THE HANDS OF THE MERCENARY DEADPOOL-- VIOLENT RIOTS HAVE BROKEN OUT AMONG HEROES AND VILLAINS ALIKE.
THE BRUTAL CARNAGE I'M WITNESSING IS--
GASP
SMMASH
LADIES AND GENTLEMEN... IN...IN A SHOCKING TURN OF EVENTS, IT APPEARS THAT--

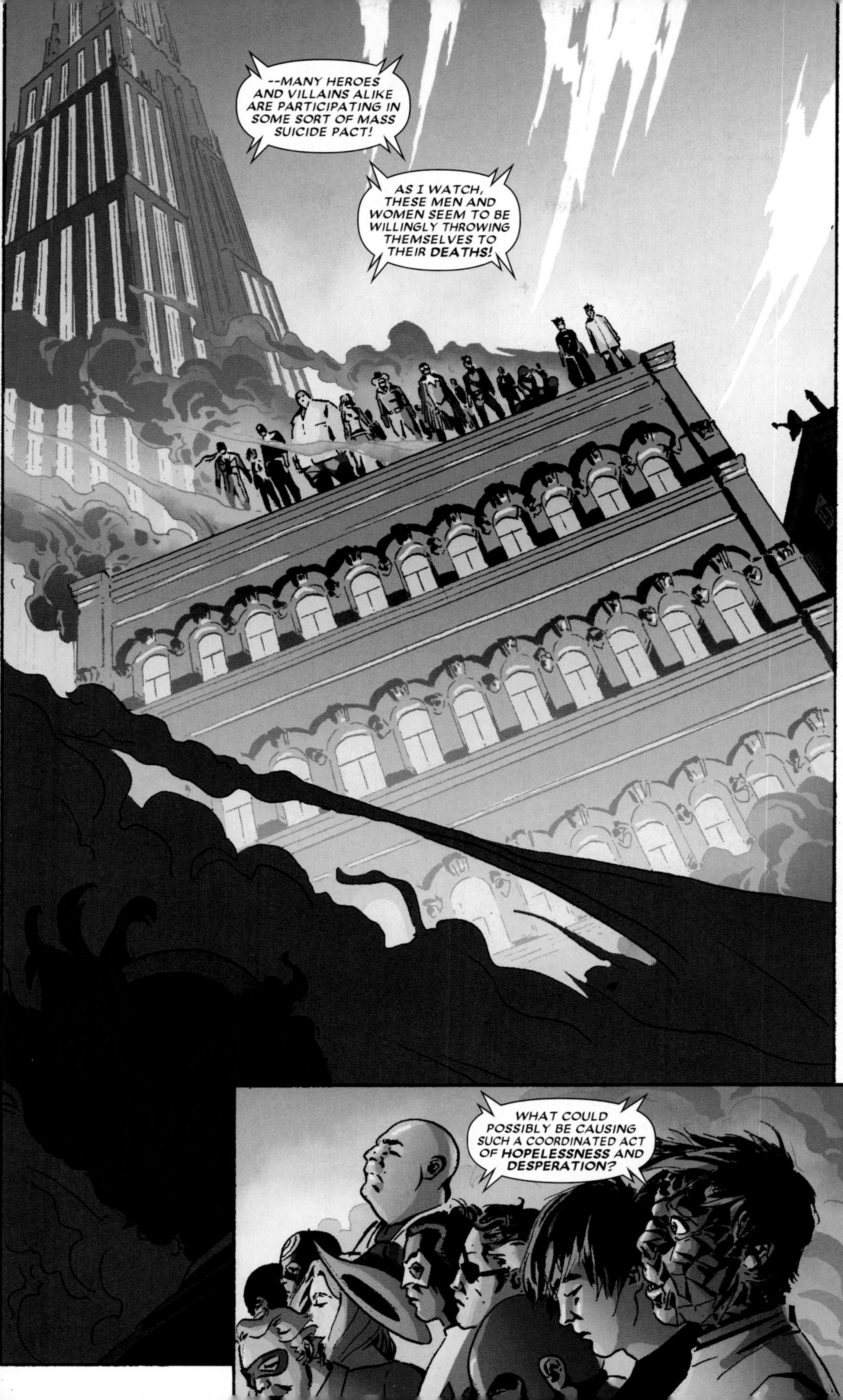
--MANY HEROES AND VILLAINS ALIKE ARE PARTICIPATING IN SOME SORT OF MASS SUICIDE PACT!
AS I WATCH, THESE MEN AND WOMEN SEEM TO BE WILLINGLY THROWING THEMSELVES TO THEIR DEATHS!
WHAT COULD POSSIBLY BE CAUSING SUCH A COORDINATED ACT OF HOPELESSNESS AND DESPERATION?

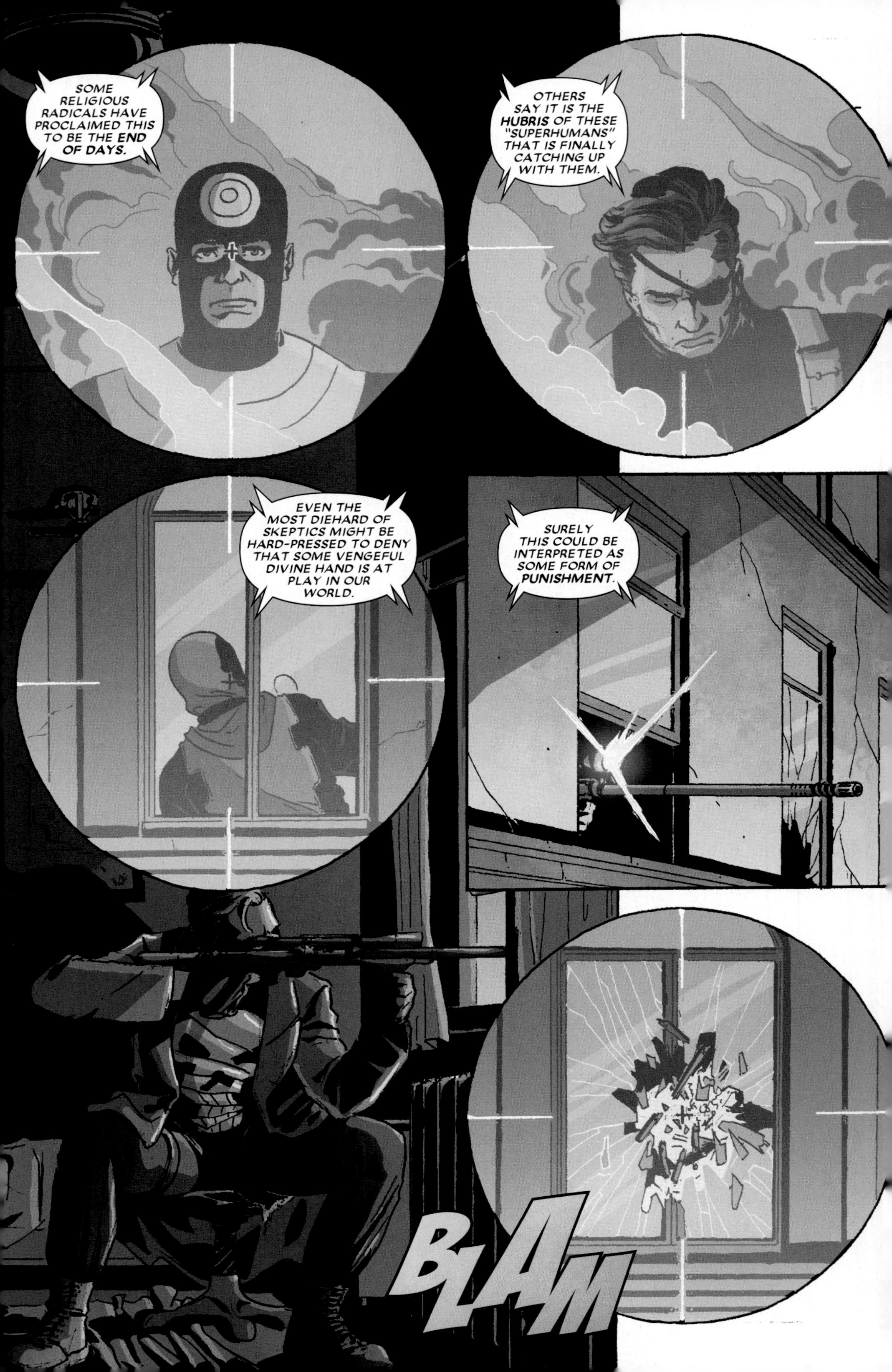
SOME RELIGIOUS RADICALS HAVE PROCLAIMED THIS TO BE THE END OF DAYS.
OTHERS SAY IT IS THE HUBRIS OF THESE "SUPERHUMANS" THAT IS FINALLY CATCHING UP WITH THEM.
EVEN THE MOST DIEHARD OF SKEPTICS MIGHT BE HARD-PRESSED TO DENY THAT SOME VENGEFUL DIVINE HAND IS AT PLAY IN OUR WORLD.
SURELY THIS COULD BE INTERPRETED AS SOME FORM OF PUNISHMENT.
BLAM

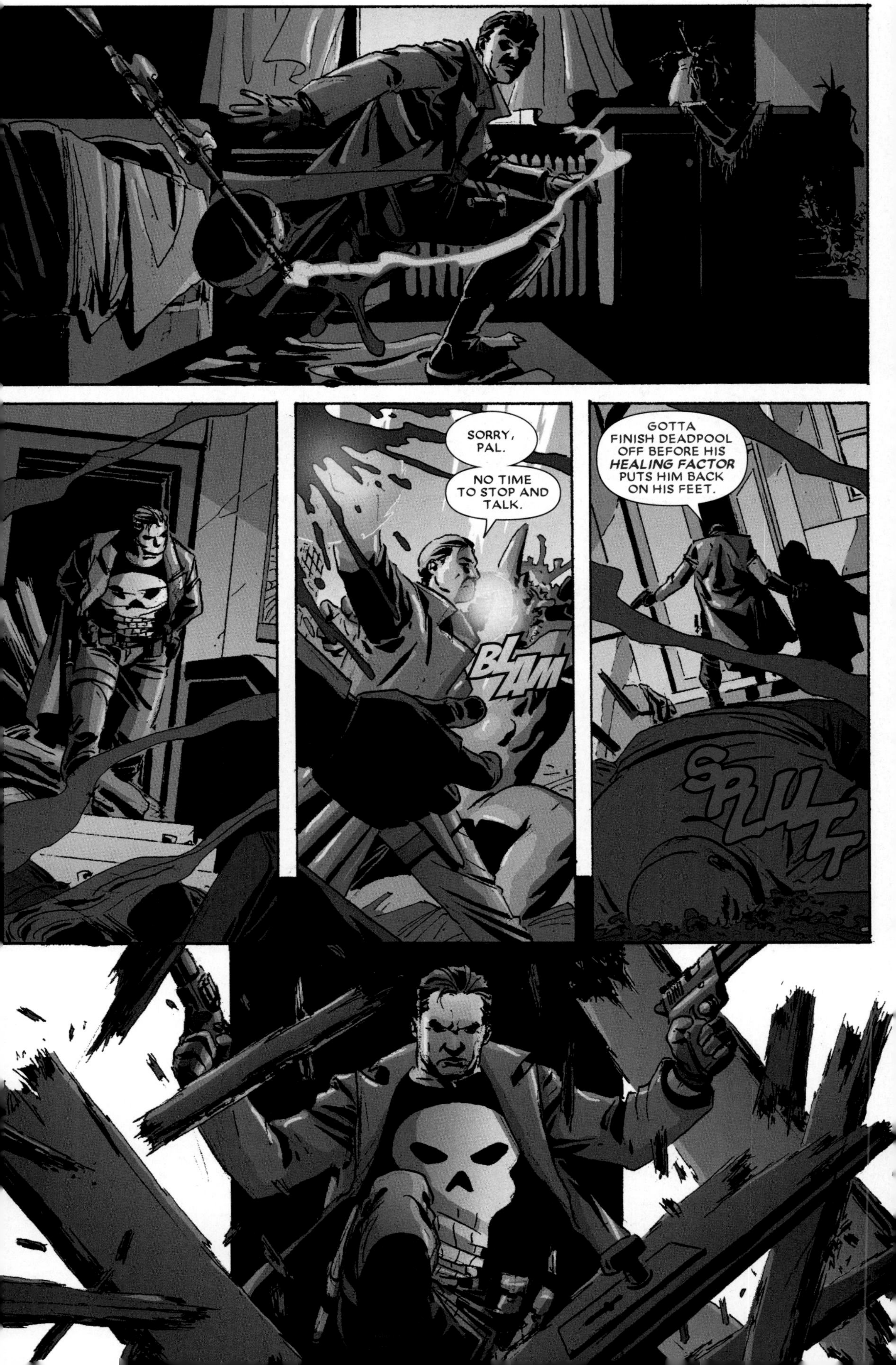
SORRY, PAL.
NO TIME TO STOP AND TALK.
BLAM
GOTTA FINISH DEADPOOL OFF BEFORE HIS **HEALING FACTOR** PUTS HIM BACK ON HIS FEET.

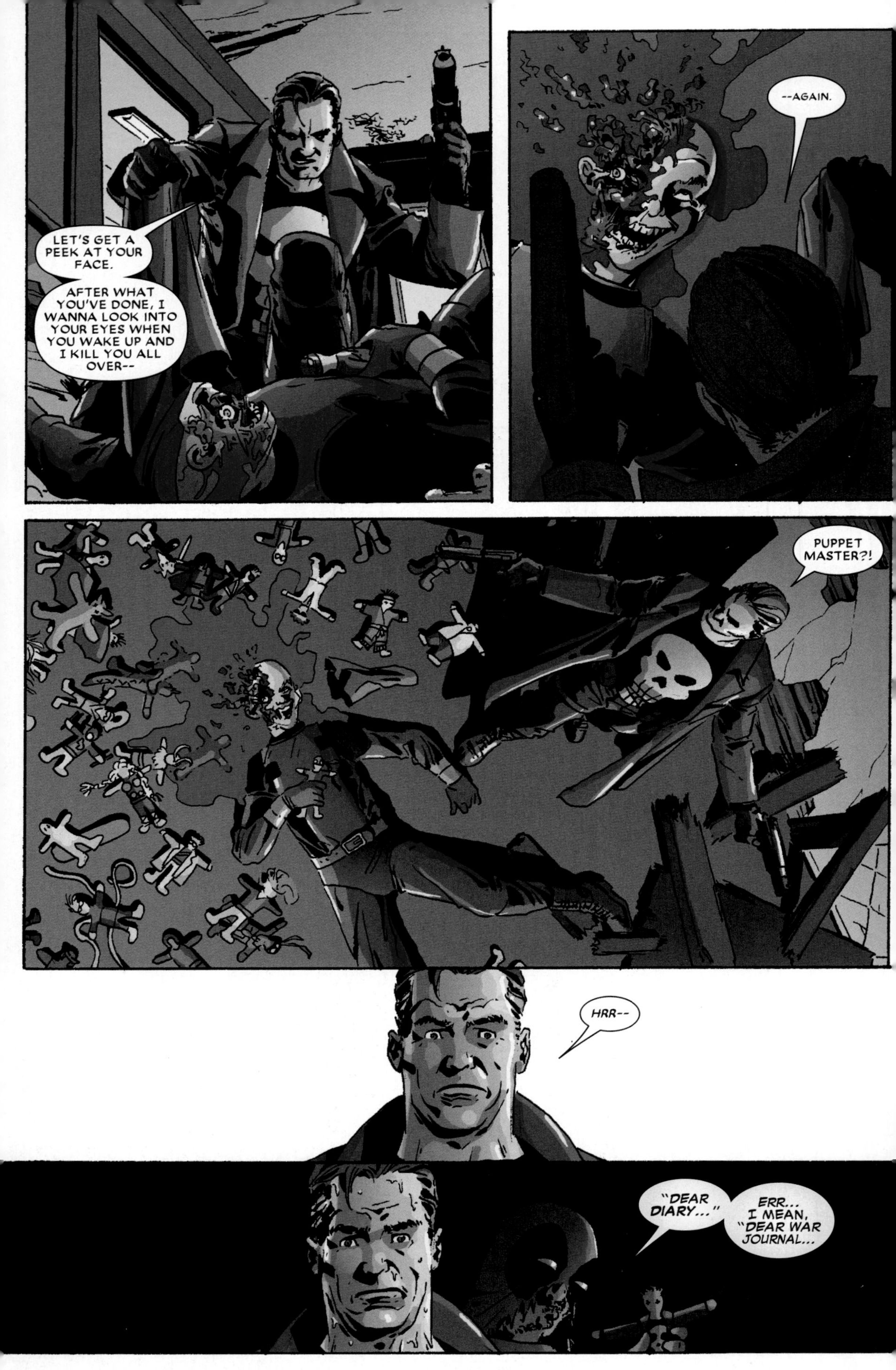
LET'S GET A PEEK AT YOUR FACE.
AFTER WHAT YOU'VE DONE, I WANNA LOOK INTO YOUR EYES WHEN YOU WAKE UP AND I KILL YOU ALL OVER--
--AGAIN.
PUPPET MASTER?!
HRR--
"DEAR DIARY..."
ERR... I MEAN, "DEAR WAR JOURNAL...

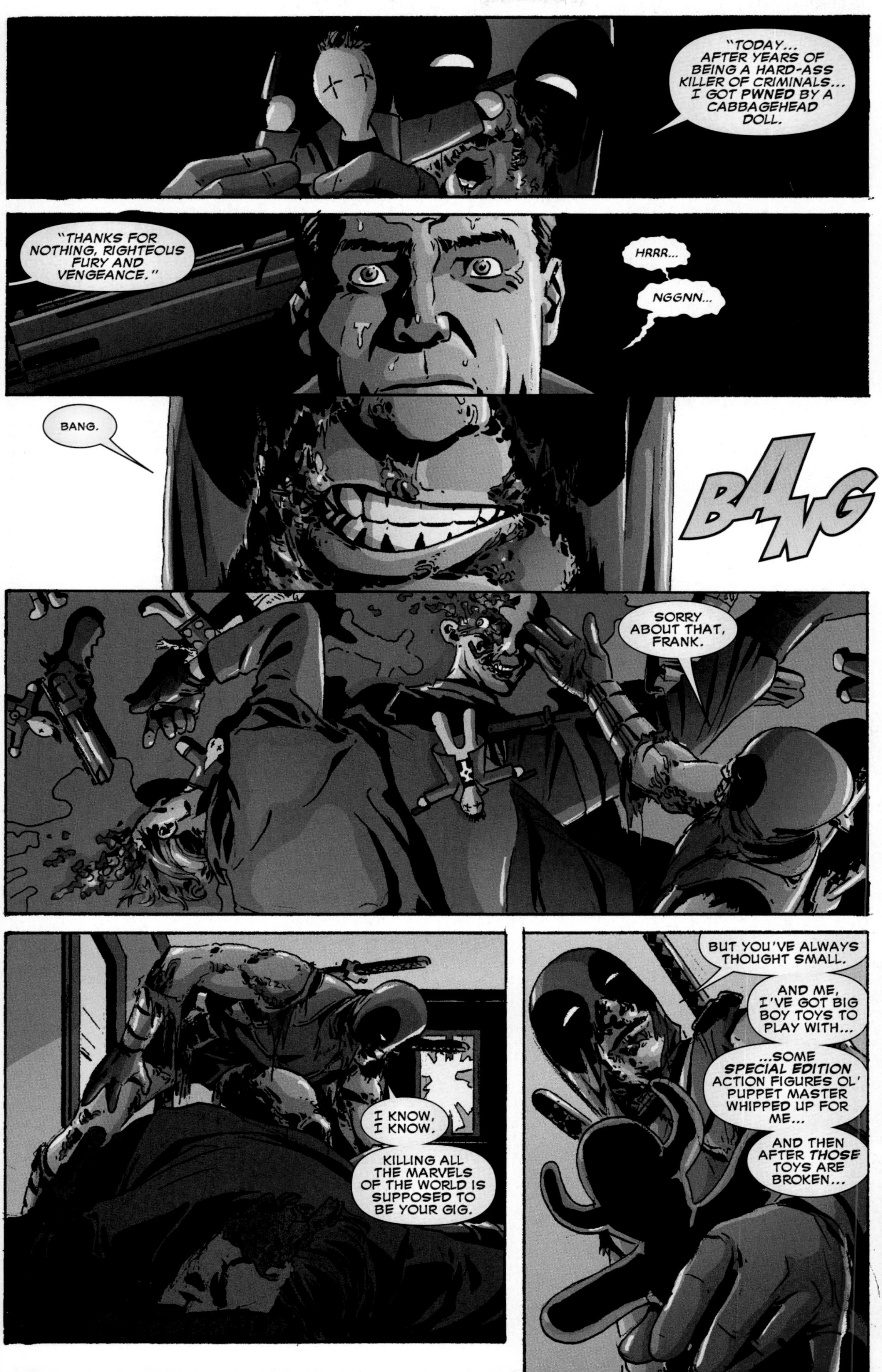
"TODAY... AFTER YEARS OF BEING A HARD-ASS KILLER OF CRIMINALS... I GOT PWNED BY A CABBAGEHEAD DOLL.
"THANKS FOR NOTHING, RIGHTEOUS FURY AND VENGEANCE."
HRRR...
NGGNN...
BANG.
BANG
SORRY ABOUT THAT, FRANK.
I KNOW, I KNOW.
KILLING ALL THE MARVELS OF THE WORLD IS SUPPOSED TO BE YOUR GIG.
BUT YOU'VE ALWAYS THOUGHT SMALL.
AND ME, I'VE GOT BIG BOY TOYS TO PLAY WITH...
...SOME SPECIAL EDITION ACTION FIGURES OL' PUPPET MASTER WHIPPED UP FOR ME...
AND THEN AFTER THOSE TOYS ARE BROKEN...

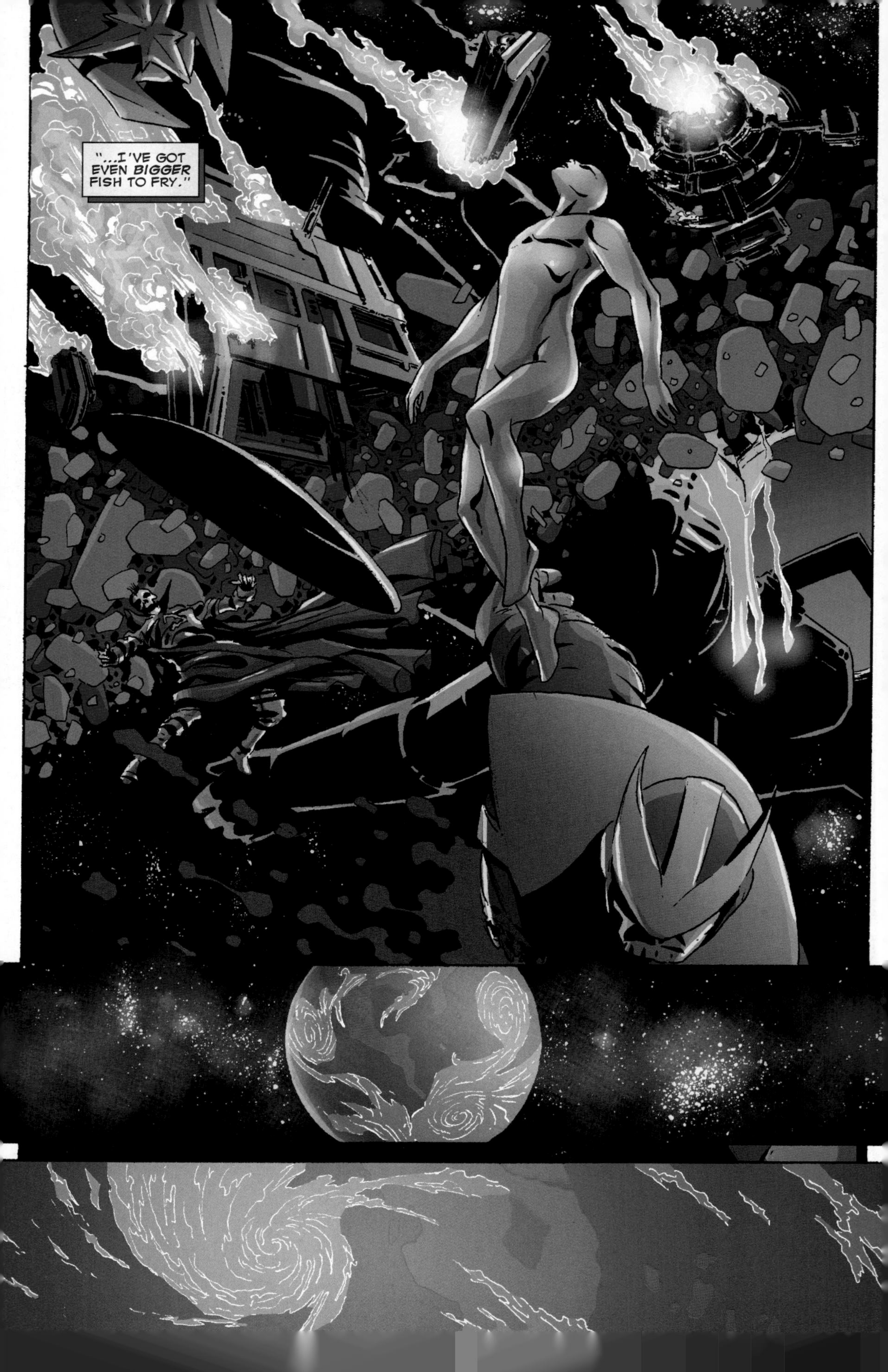
"...I'VE GOT EVEN *BIGGER* FISH TO FRY."

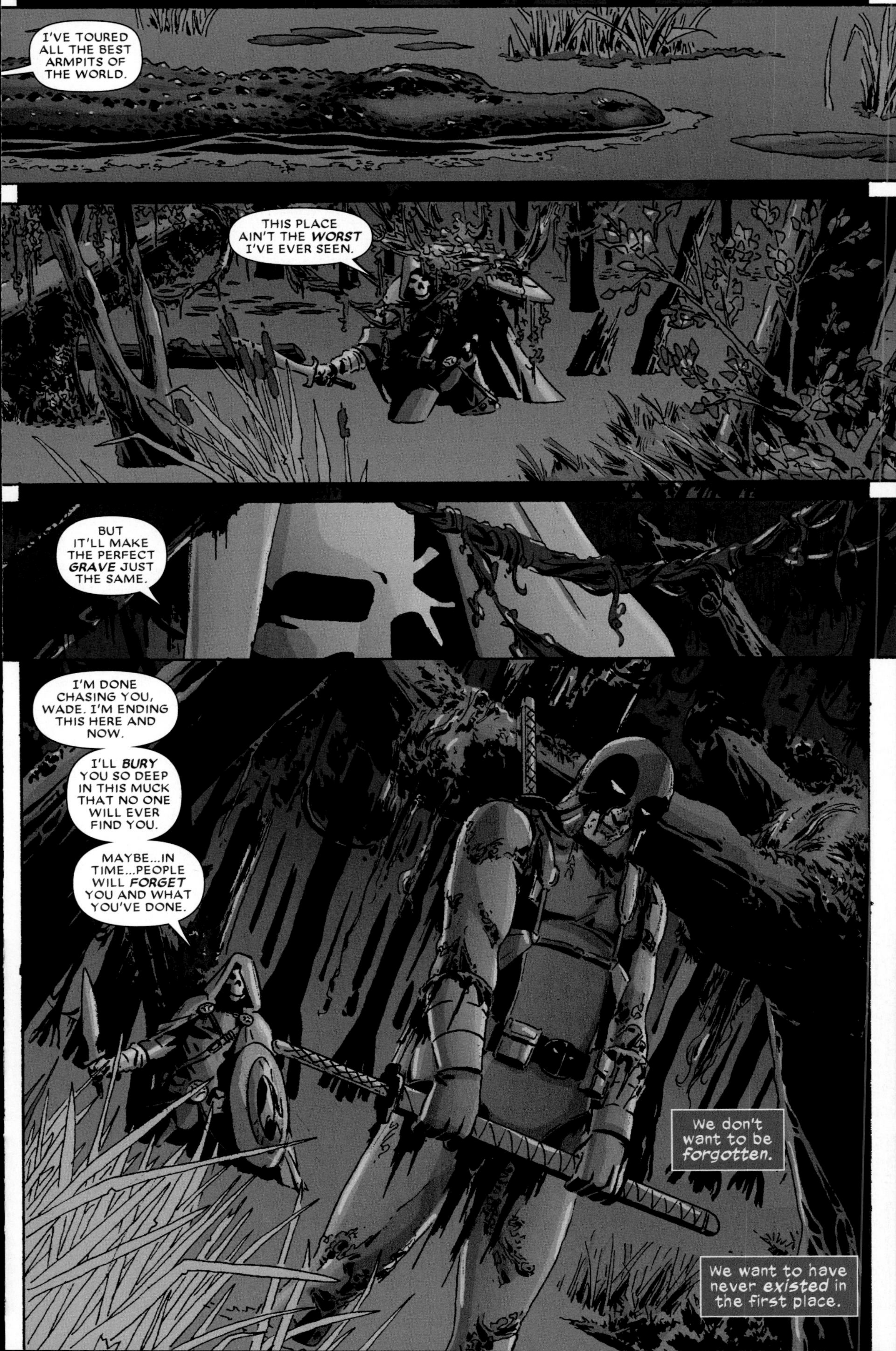
I'VE TOURED ALL THE BEST ARMPITS OF THE WORLD.
THIS PLACE AIN'T THE WORST I'VE EVER SEEN.
BUT IT'LL MAKE THE PERFECT GRAVE JUST THE SAME.
I'M DONE CHASING YOU, WADE. I'M ENDING THIS HERE AND NOW.
I'LL BURY YOU SO DEEP IN THIS MUCK THAT NO ONE WILL EVER FIND YOU.
MAYBE...IN TIME...PEOPLE WILL FORGET YOU AND WHAT YOU'VE DONE.
We don't want to be forgotten.
We want to have never existed in the first place.

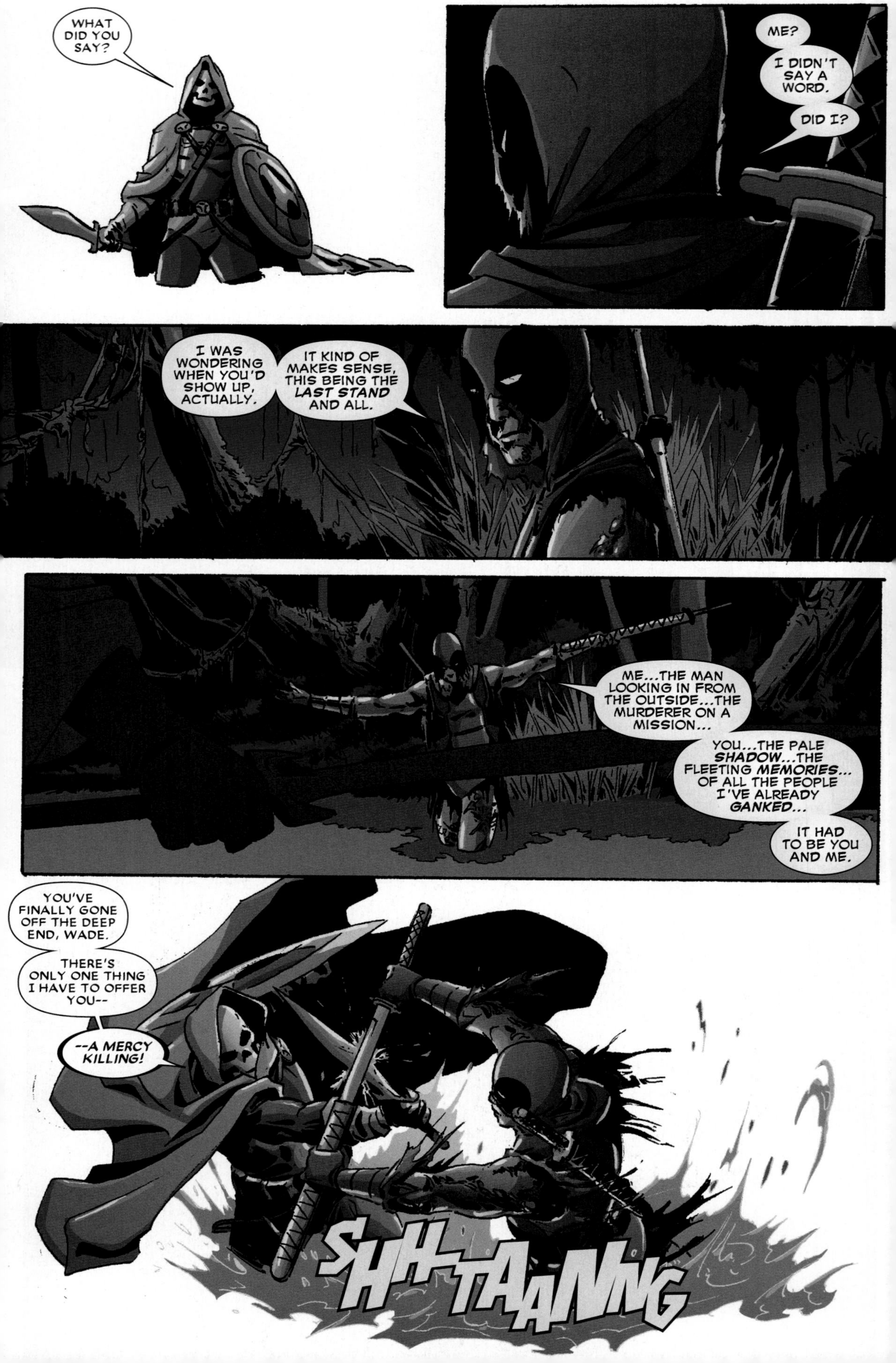
WHAT DID YOU SAY?
ME?
I DIDN'T SAY A WORD.
DID I?
I WAS WONDERING WHEN YOU'D SHOW UP, ACTUALLY.
IT KIND OF MAKES SENSE, THIS BEING THE LAST STAND AND ALL.
ME...THE MAN LOOKING IN FROM THE OUTSIDE...THE MURDERER ON A MISSION...
YOU...THE PALE SHADOW...THE FLEETING MEMORIES... OF ALL THE PEOPLE I'VE ALREADY GANKED...
IT HAD TO BE YOU AND ME.
YOU'VE FINALLY GONE OFF THE DEEP END, WADE.
THERE'S ONLY ONE THING I HAVE TO OFFER YOU--
--A MERCY KILLING!
SHH-TAANNG

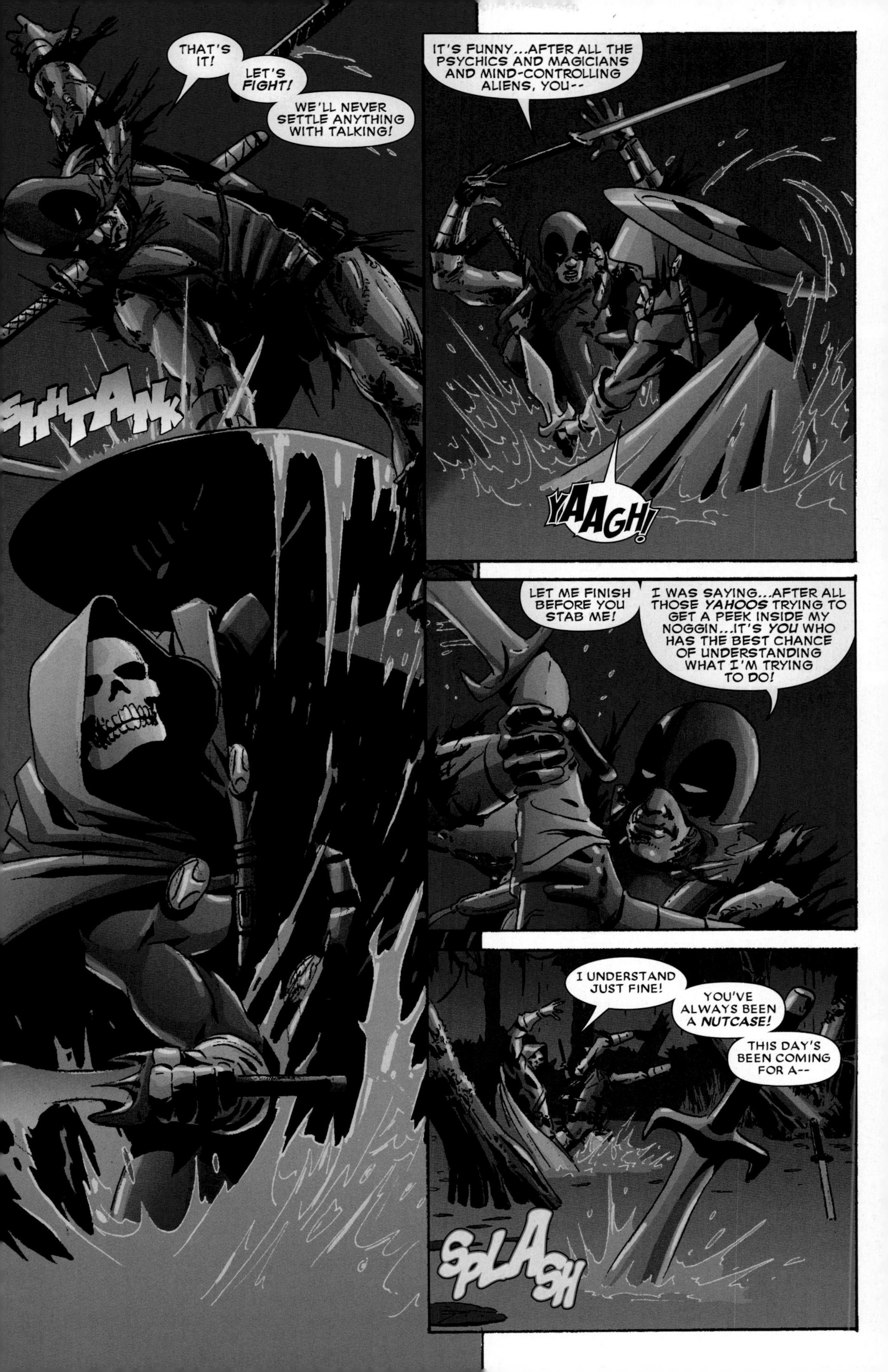
THAT'S IT!
LET'S FIGHT!
WE'LL NEVER SETTLE ANYTHING WITH TALKING!
SHTANK
IT'S FUNNY...AFTER ALL THE PSYCHICS AND MAGICIANS AND MIND-CONTROLLING ALIENS, YOU--
YAAGH!
LET ME FINISH BEFORE YOU STAB ME!
I WAS SAYING...AFTER ALL THOSE YAHOOS TRYING TO GET A PEEK INSIDE MY NOGGIN...IT'S YOU WHO HAS THE BEST CHANCE OF UNDERSTANDING WHAT I'M TRYING TO DO!
I UNDERSTAND JUST FINE!
YOU'VE ALWAYS BEEN A NUTCASE!
THIS DAY'S BEEN COMING FOR A--
SPLASH

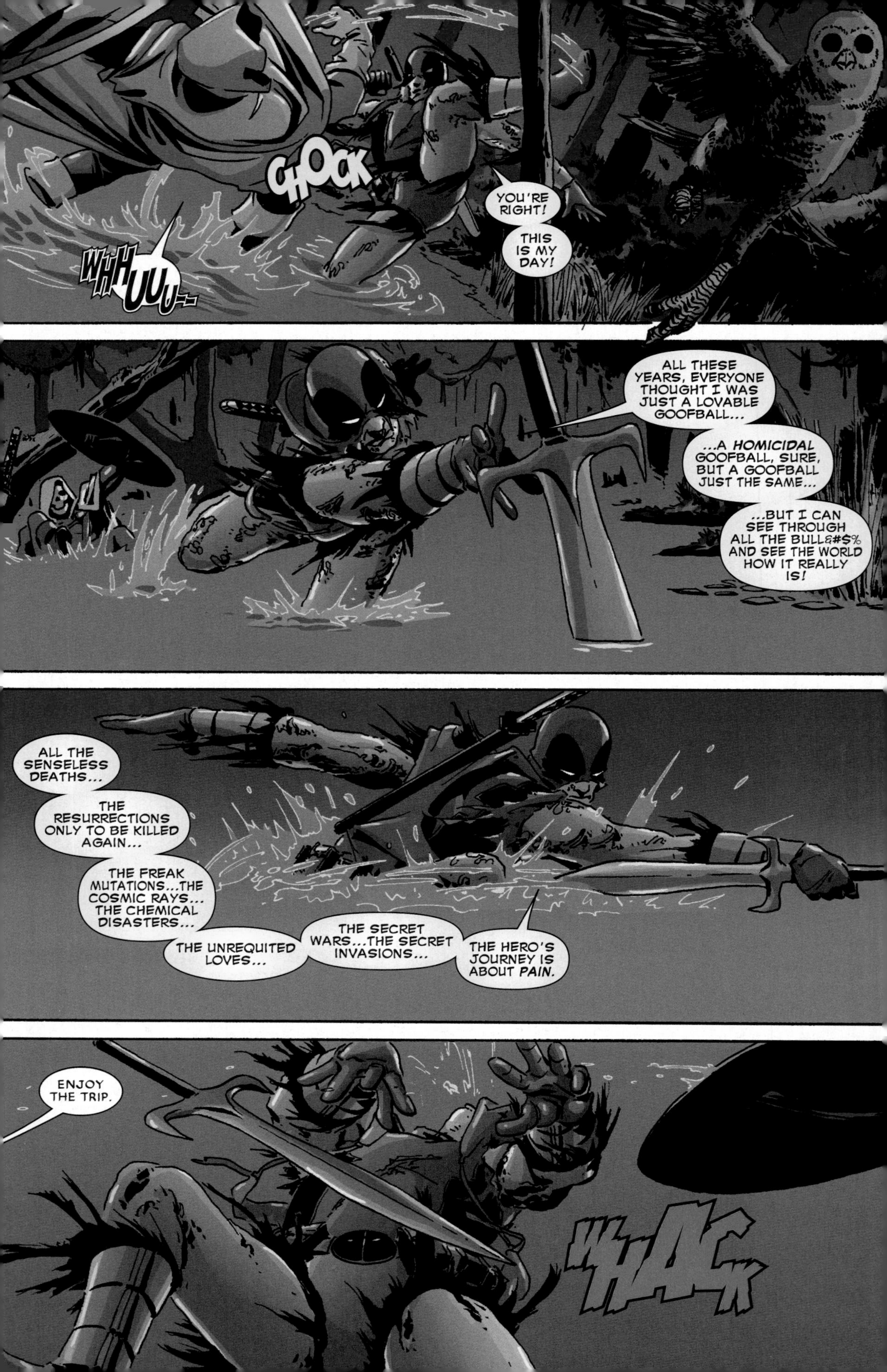
CHOCK
WHHUUU--
YOU'RE RIGHT!
THIS IS MY DAY!
ALL THESE YEARS, EVERYONE THOUGHT I WAS JUST A LOVABLE GOOFBALL...
...A HOMICIDAL GOOFBALL, SURE, BUT A GOOFBALL JUST THE SAME...
...BUT I CAN SEE THROUGH ALL THE BULL&#$% AND SEE THE WORLD HOW IT REALLY IS!
ALL THE SENSELESS DEATHS...
THE RESURRECTIONS ONLY TO BE KILLED AGAIN...
THE FREAK MUTATIONS...THE COSMIC RAYS... THE CHEMICAL DISASTERS...
THE UNREQUITED LOVES...
THE SECRET WARS...THE SECRET INVASIONS...
THE HERO'S JOURNEY IS ABOUT PAIN.
ENJOY THE TRIP.
WHACK

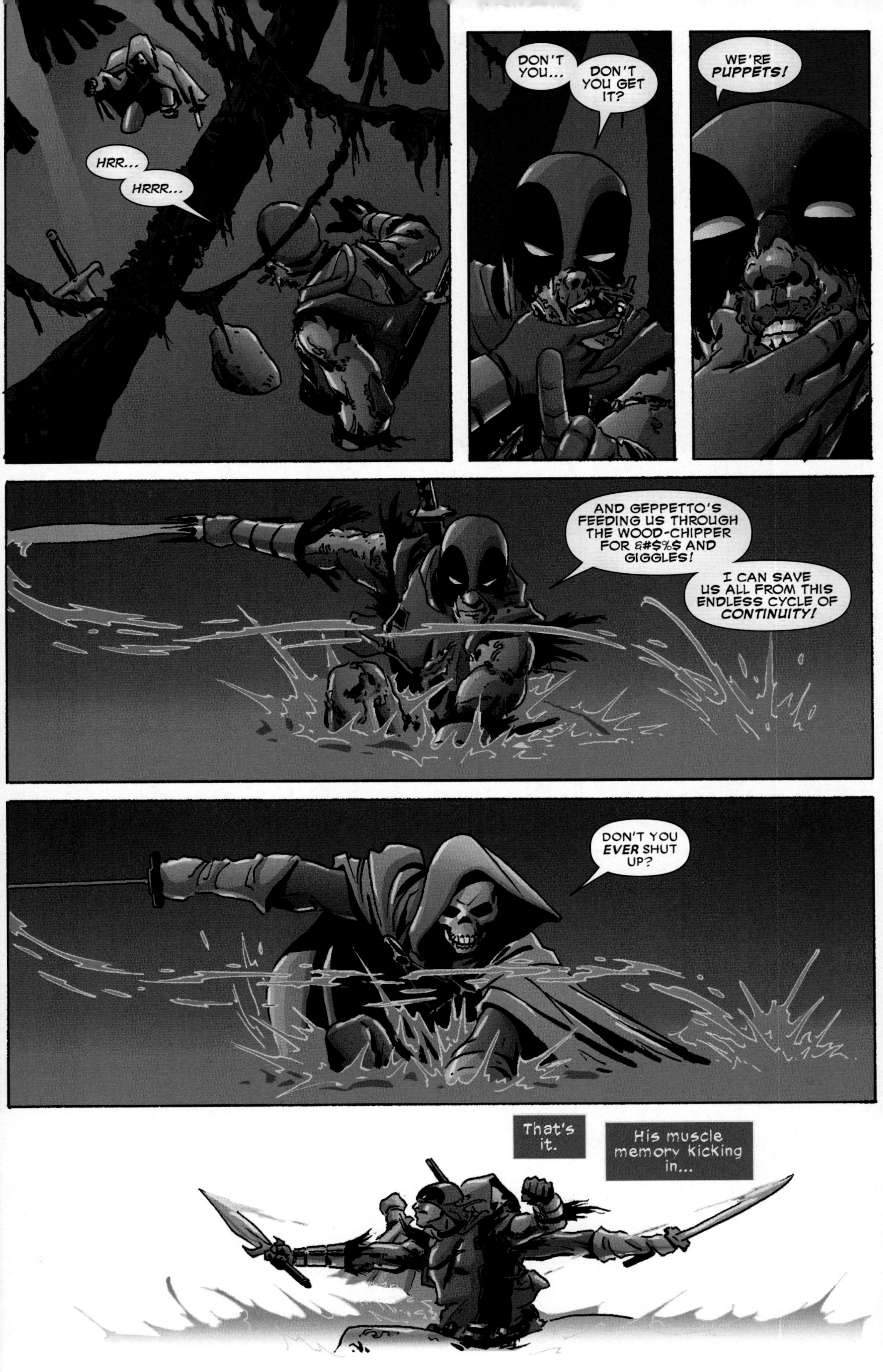
HRR...
HRRR...
DON'T YOU...
DON'T YOU GET IT?
WE'RE PUPPETS!
AND GEPPETTO'S FEEDING US THROUGH THE WOOD-CHIPPER FOR &#$%$ AND GIGGLES!
I CAN SAVE US ALL FROM THIS ENDLESS CYCLE OF CONTINUITY!
DON'T YOU EVER SHUT UP?
That's it.
His muscle memory kicking in...

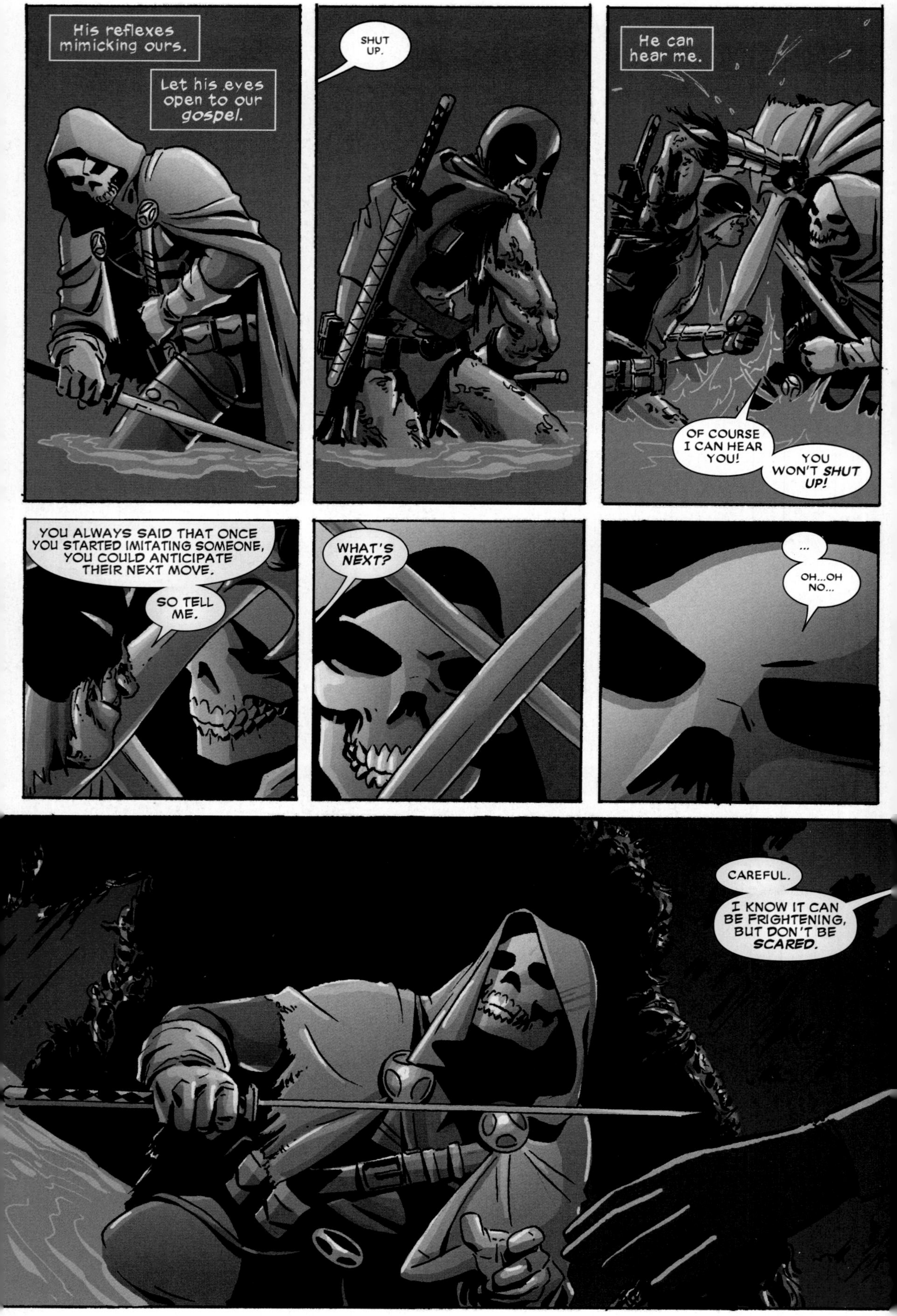
His reflexes mimicking ours.
Let his eyes open to our *gospel*.
SHUT UP.
He can hear me.
OF COURSE I CAN HEAR YOU!
YOU WON'T *SHUT UP!*
YOU ALWAYS SAID THAT ONCE YOU STARTED IMITATING SOMEONE, YOU COULD ANTICIPATE THEIR NEXT MOVE.
SO TELL ME.
WHAT'S *NEXT?*
...
OH...OH NO...
CAREFUL.
I KNOW IT CAN BE FRIGHTENING, BUT DON'T BE *SCARED.*

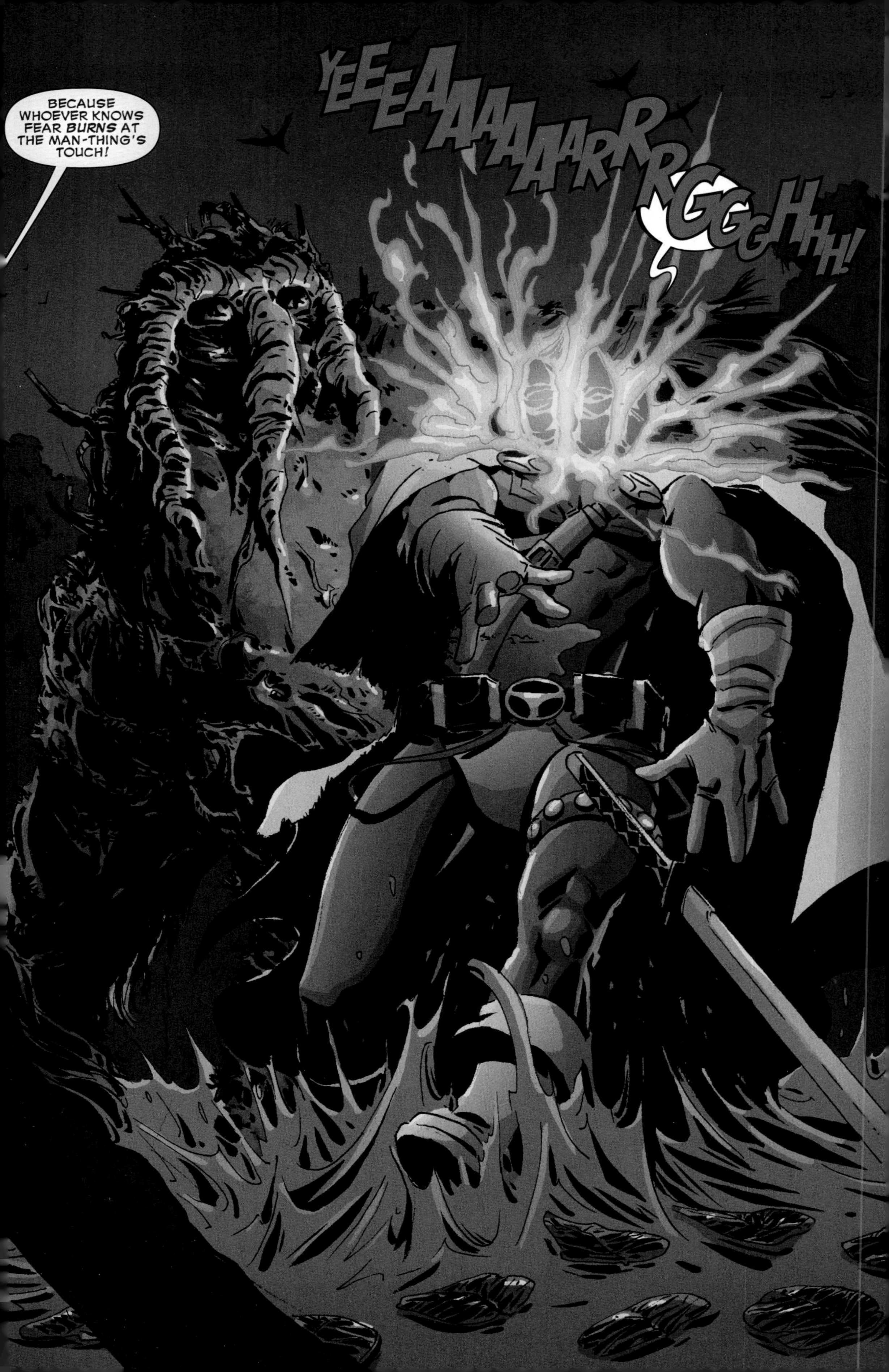
BECAUSE WHOEVER KNOWS FEAR BURNS AT THE MAN-THING'S TOUCH!
YEEEAAAAAAARRRRGGGHHH!

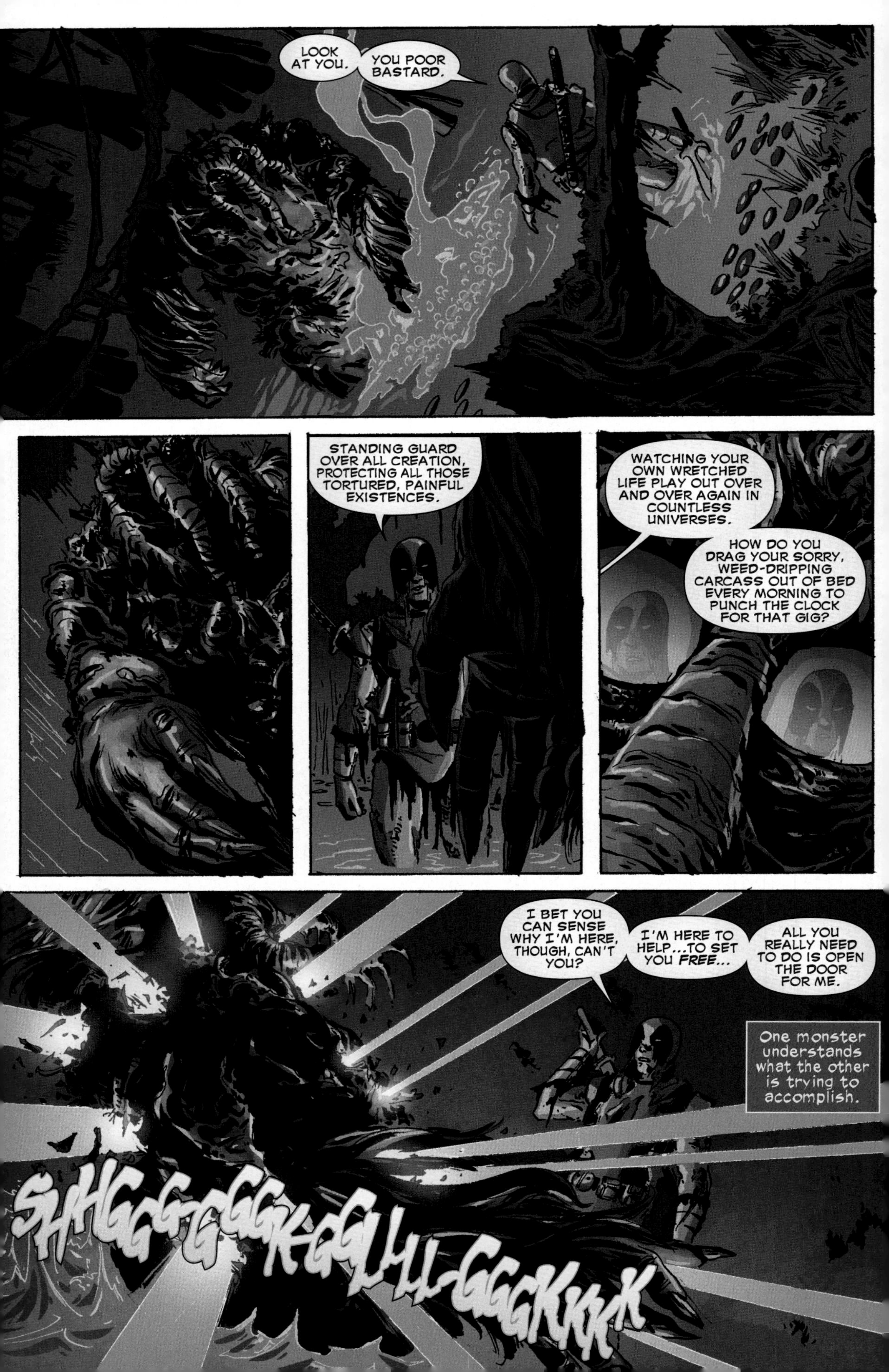
LOOK AT YOU.
YOU POOR BASTARD.
STANDING GUARD OVER ALL CREATION, PROTECTING ALL THOSE TORTURED, PAINFUL EXISTENCES.
WATCHING YOUR OWN WRETCHED LIFE PLAY OUT OVER AND OVER AGAIN IN COUNTLESS UNIVERSES.
HOW DO YOU DRAG YOUR SORRY, WEED-DRIPPING CARCASS OUT OF BED EVERY MORNING TO PUNCH THE CLOCK FOR THAT GIG?
I BET YOU CAN SENSE WHY I'M HERE, THOUGH, CAN'T YOU?
I'M HERE TO HELP...TO SET YOU *FREE*...
ALL YOU REALLY NEED TO DO IS OPEN THE DOOR FOR ME.
One monster understands what the other is trying to accomplish.
SHHGGGGGGK-GGLLL-GGGKKKK

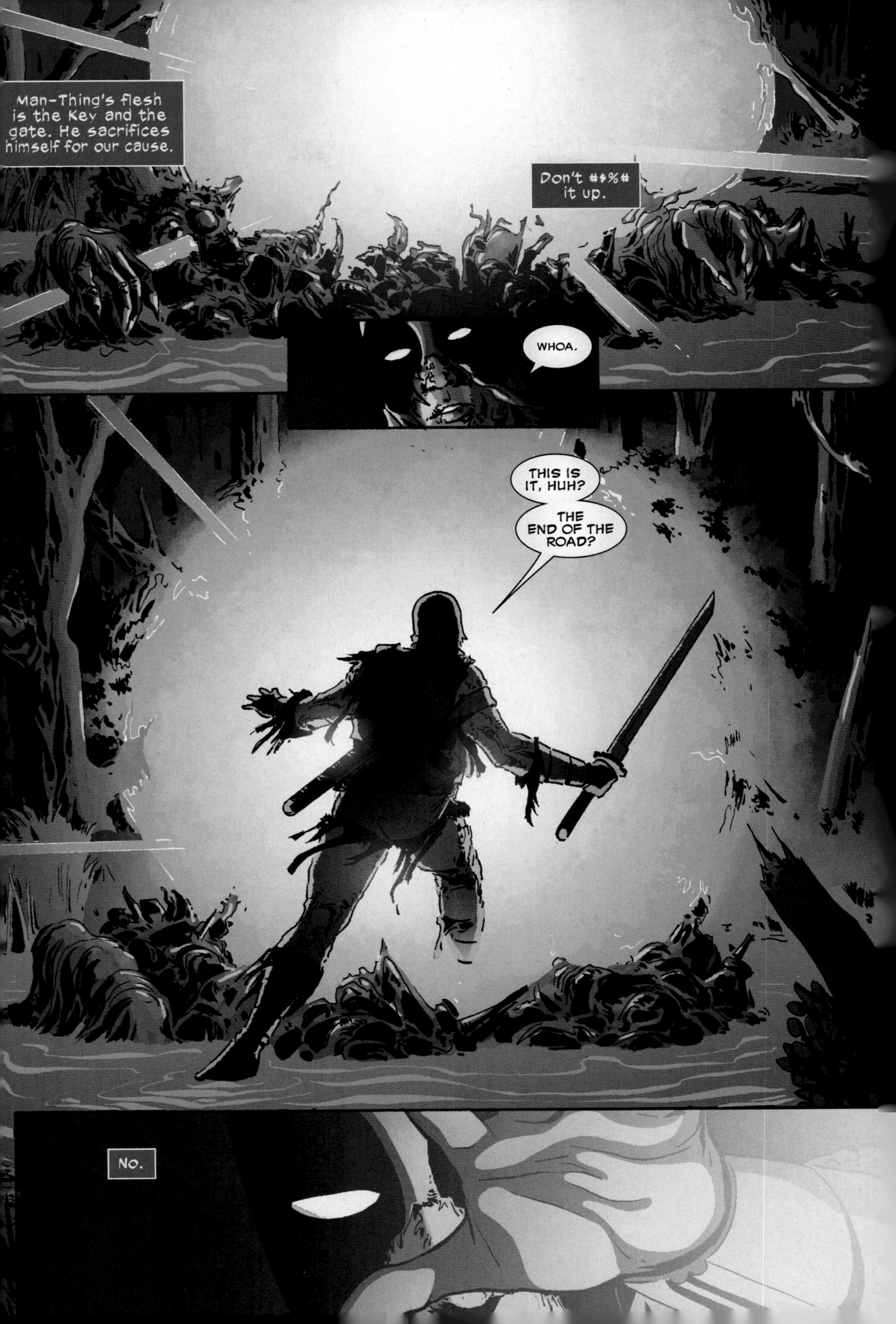
Man-Thing's flesh is the key and the gate. He sacrifices himself for our cause.
Don't #$%# it up.
WHOA.
THIS IS IT, HUH?
THE END OF THE ROAD?
No.

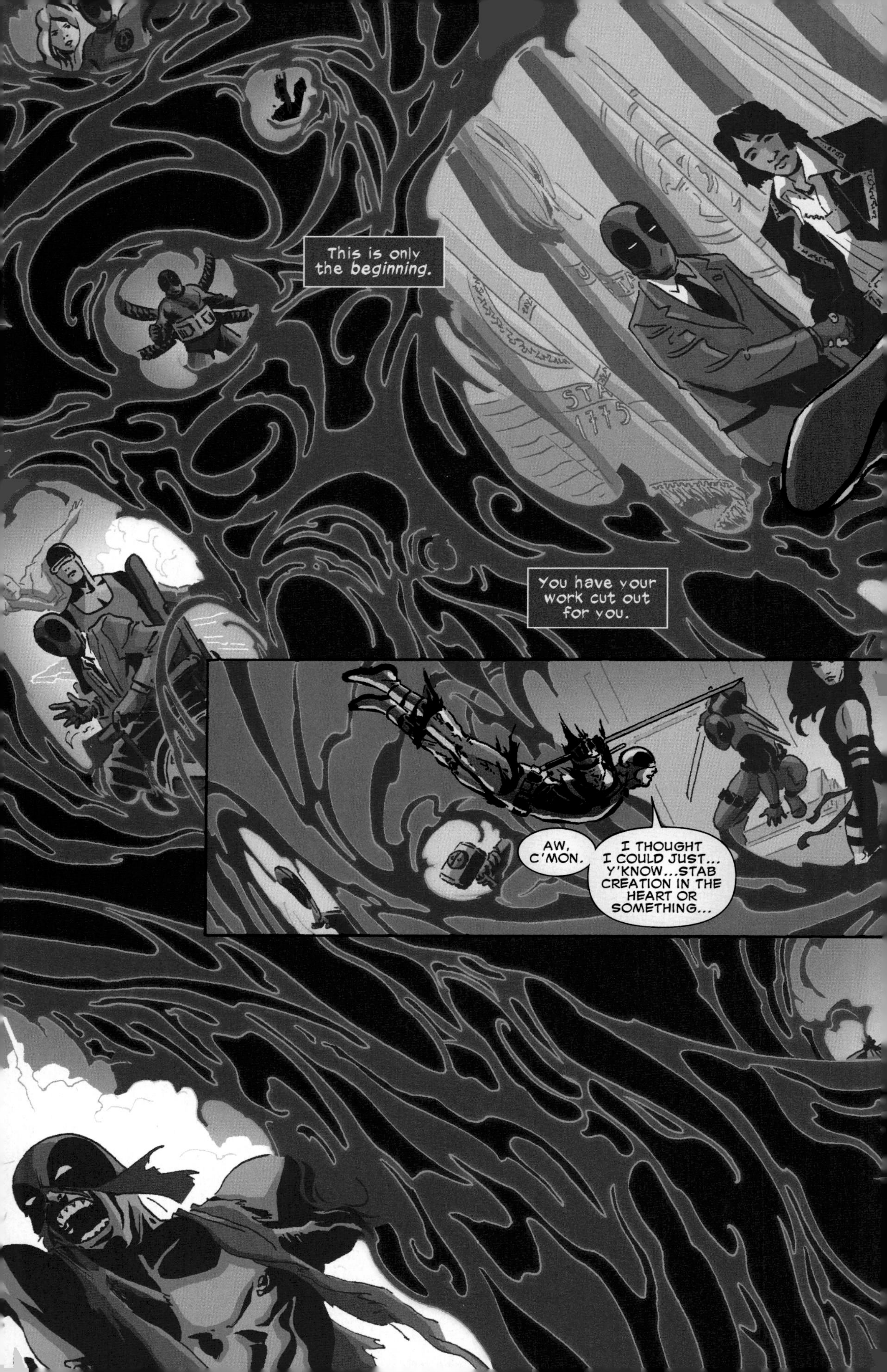
This is only the *beginning*.
You have your work cut out for you.
AW, C'MON.
I THOUGHT I COULD JUST... Y'KNOW...STAB CREATION IN THE HEART OR SOMETHING...

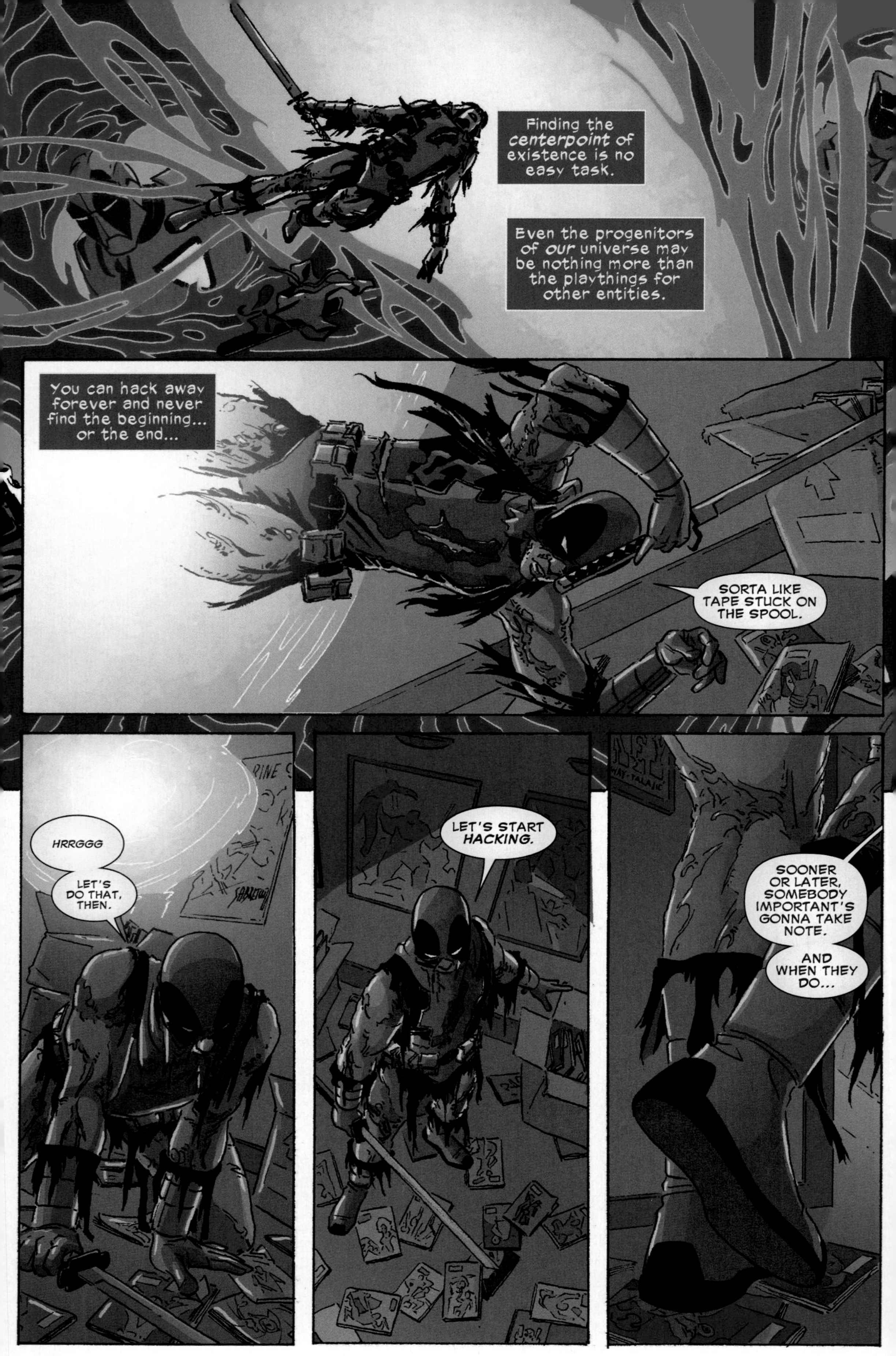
Finding the *centerpoint* of existence is no easy task.
Even the progenitors of *our* universe may be nothing more than the playthings for other entities.
You can hack away forever and never find the beginning... or the end...
SORTA LIKE TAPE STUCK ON THE SPOOL.
HRRGGG
LET'S DO THAT, THEN.
LET'S START *HACKING.*
SOONER OR LATER, SOMEBODY IMPORTANT'S GONNA TAKE NOTE.
AND WHEN THEY DO...

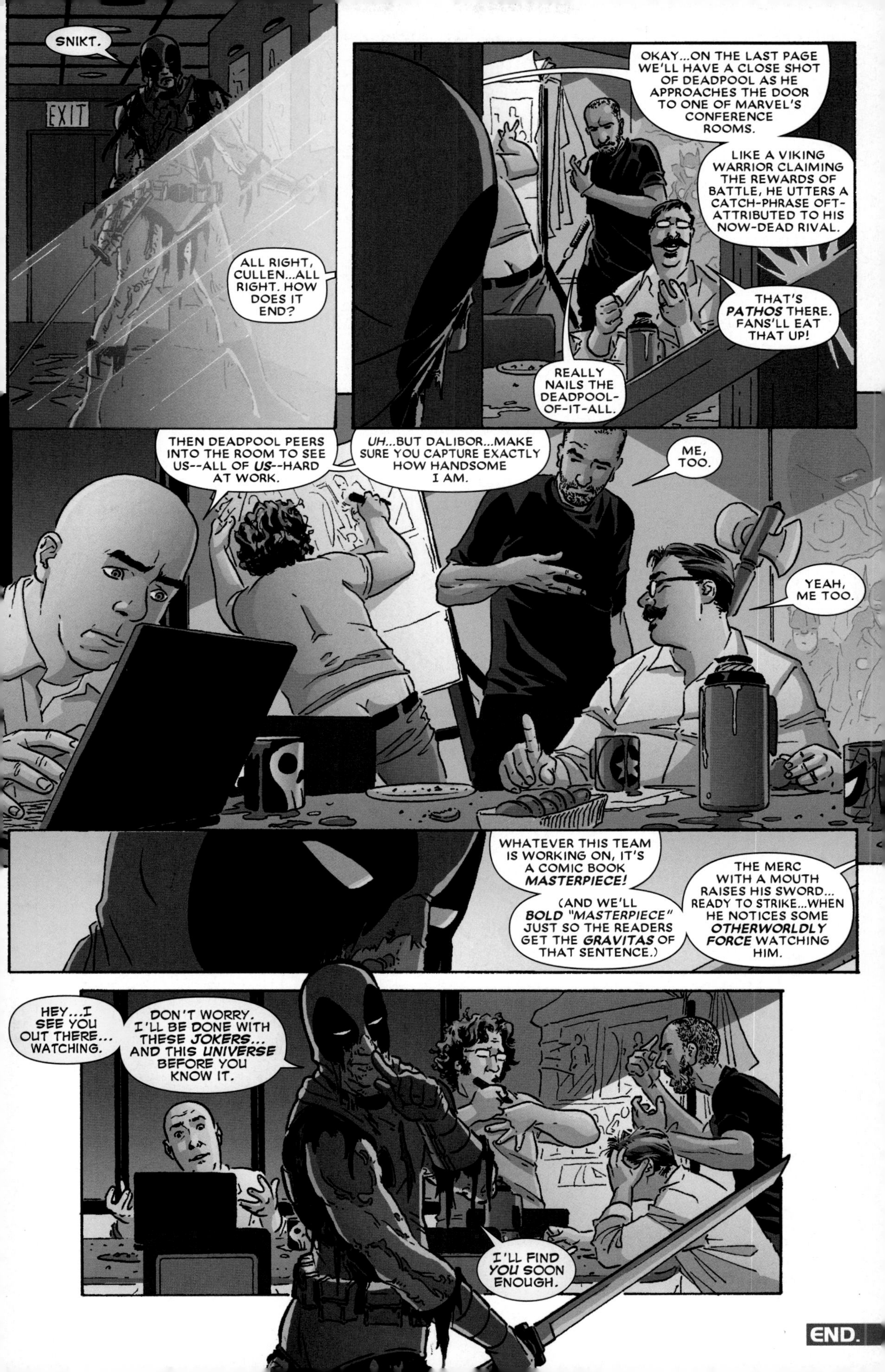
SNIKT.
EXIT
ALL RIGHT, CULLEN...ALL RIGHT. HOW DOES IT END?
OKAY...ON THE LAST PAGE WE'LL HAVE A CLOSE SHOT OF DEADPOOL AS HE APPROACHES THE DOOR TO ONE OF MARVEL'S CONFERENCE ROOMS.
LIKE A VIKING WARRIOR CLAIMING THE REWARDS OF BATTLE, HE UTTERS A CATCH-PHRASE OFT-ATTRIBUTED TO HIS NOW-DEAD RIVAL.
THAT'S PATHOS THERE. FANS'LL EAT THAT UP!
REALLY NAILS THE DEADPOOL-OF-IT-ALL.
THEN DEADPOOL PEERS INTO THE ROOM TO SEE US--ALL OF US--HARD AT WORK.
UH...BUT DALIBOR...MAKE SURE YOU CAPTURE EXACTLY HOW HANDSOME I AM.
ME, TOO.
YEAH, ME TOO.
WHATEVER THIS TEAM IS WORKING ON, IT'S A COMIC BOOK MASTERPIECE!
(AND WE'LL BOLD "MASTERPIECE" JUST SO THE READERS GET THE GRAVITAS OF THAT SENTENCE.)
THE MERC WITH A MOUTH RAISES HIS SWORD... READY TO STRIKE...WHEN HE NOTICES SOME OTHERWORLDLY FORCE WATCHING HIM.
HEY...I SEE YOU OUT THERE... WATCHING.
DON'T WORRY. I'LL BE DONE WITH THESE JOKERS... AND THIS UNIVERSE BEFORE YOU KNOW IT.
I'LL FIND YOU SOON ENOUGH.
END.

CONCLUDING-SEQUENCE SCRIPT BY CULLEN BUNN
WITH ART BY DALIBOR TALAJIĆ

PAGE 17 & 18

Double-Page Spread

17/18.1

Deadpool floats in a cosmic void. Clouds of rippling energy curl around him. His back is to us, and we see dozens of undulating "windows" in time and space rippling open before him. Within each window is a different view of a different alternate reality. Some samples include:

- Kidpool and Dogpool at play.
- Deadpool as a member of X-Force.
- Deadpool Noir.
- Deadpool in a wheelchair and commanding the X-Men.
- Deadpool dressed in a vampire's garb. His mask is torn and he sports vicious-looking fangs.
- Deadpool surrounded by the flames of the Phoenix Force.
- And any other variations of Deadpool you might want to create.

There are many, many of these "windows," stretching back as far as the eye can see, but many cannot be made out clearly. Others may simply have strange close-ups of Deadpool.

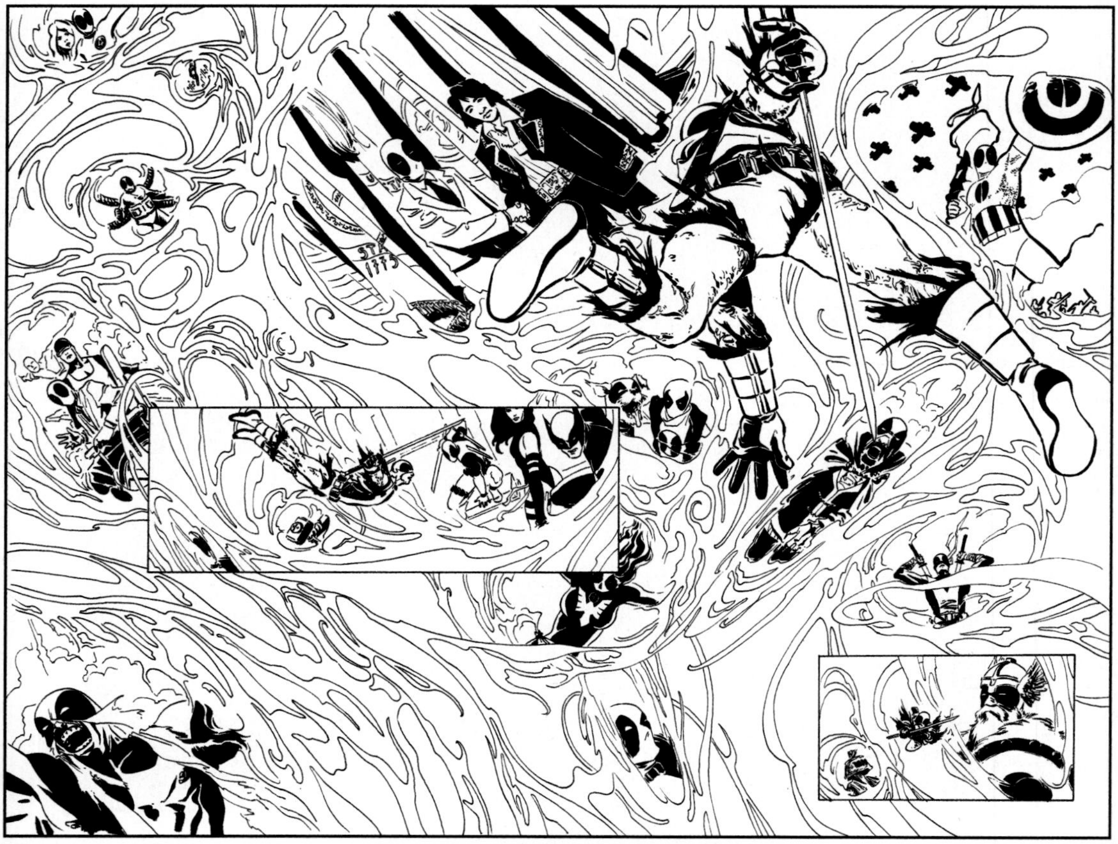

1/CAPTION
(Third voice): This is only the **beginning**.

2/CAPTION
(Third voice): You have your work cut out for you.

17/18.2
Deadpool "swims" through the void, moving past the "windows" into other realities. He is moving past some of the reflection of Deadpool, who seem to notice him.

3/DEADPOOL: Aw, c'mon.

4/DEADPOOL: I thought I could just... y'know... stab creation in the heart or something...

17/18.3
Close on some of the windows, the "other" Deadpools watching our Deadpool move past.

5/DEADPOOL: ...maybe roast some marshmallows as all existence burns down around me.

PAGE 19

19.1
Deadpool "swims" through the void toward one of the "windows."

1/CAPTION
(Third voice): Finding the **centerpoint** of existence is no easy task.

2/CAPTION
(Third voice): Even the progenitors of **our** universe may be nothing more than the playthings for other entities.

19.2

Close on Deadpool as he begins to pull himself through the portal and into the world beyond.

> **3/CAPTION**
> (Third voice):   You can hack away forever and never find the beginning… or the end…
>
> **4/DEADPOOL:**   Sorta like tape stuck on the spool.

19.3

Deadpool is now on the carpeted floor of a dimly lit room. The portal is closing behind him. He is hunkered down, trembling, as if traveling through the portal was painful and sickening. There are comic books—Marvel comic books—spread out on the floor around him.

> **5/DEADPOOL**
> (Small, weak):   Hrrggg
>
> **6/DEADPOOL**
> (Small):   Let's do that, then.

19.4

Deadpool stands up straight, noticing the comics. Marvel comics are spread out all over the floor around him. He is in a storeroom of sorts. All around are metal shelves filled with boxes (not comic book boxes, but regular shipping boxes) and stacks of loose comics and graphic novels. A tattered poster — maybe of an older Deadpool comic cover — is on the wall.

> **7/DEADPOOL:**   Let's start **hacking**.

19.5

On Deadpool's feet as he walks toward a door. He steps on copies of Deadpool, crumpling them.

8/DEADPOOL: Sooner or later, somebody important's gonna take note.

9/DEADPOOL: And when they do...

PAGE 20

20.1
In the hall as Deadpool, holding his sword at the ready, moves toward another source of light. The hallway is lined with framed posters for Marvel comic books.

1/DEADPOOL: Snikt.

20.2
Approaching a meeting room door, Deadpool keeps his back to the wall as he sneaks closer. A flickering light comes from within. Voices come from within the room.

2/AXEL
(Off-panel): All right. All right. How does it end?

3/CULLEN
(Off-panel): Okay... on the last page we'll have a close shot of Deadpool as he approaches the door to one of Marvel's conference rooms.

3/CULLEN (Off-panel):	Like a Viking warrior claiming the rewards of battle, he utters a catch-phrase oft-attributed to his now-dead rival.
4/JORDAN:	That's **pathos** there. Fans'll eat that up!

20.3

Angle past Deadpool as he looks into the room. We are looking into a meeting room. AXEL, JORDAN, CULLEN, and DALIBOR are gathered around a conference table. Cullen has a laptop open on the table before him. He types furiously. Dalibor is standing, thumb nailing THIS PAGE on a whiteboard or flipchart. The table is messy, covered in coffee cups and crumb-covered plates.

5/CULLEN:	Then Deadpool peers into the room to see **us**—all of us—hard at work.
6/CULLEN:	All right... but Dalibor... make sure you capture exactly how handsome I am.
7/AXEL:	Me, too.
8/JORDAN:	Yeah, me too.

20.4

Deadpool prepares his sword, readies himself to strike.

9/CULLEN (Off-panel):	Whatever this team is working on, it's a comic book **masterpiece**!
10/CULLEN (Off-panel):	(And we'll **bold** "masterpiece" just so the readers get the **gravitas** of that sentence.)
11/CULLEN (Off-panel):	The merc with a mouth raises his sword... ready to strike... when he notices some **otherworldly force** watching him.

20.5

Deadpool pauses, looking right at the reader. He holds a finger to his mouth as if to say "shhhhhhhh."

12/DEADPOOL:	Hey... I see you out there... watching...
13/DEADPOOL:	Don't worry. I'll be done with these **jokers**... and this **universe** before you know it.
14/DEADPOOL:	I'll find **you** soon enough.

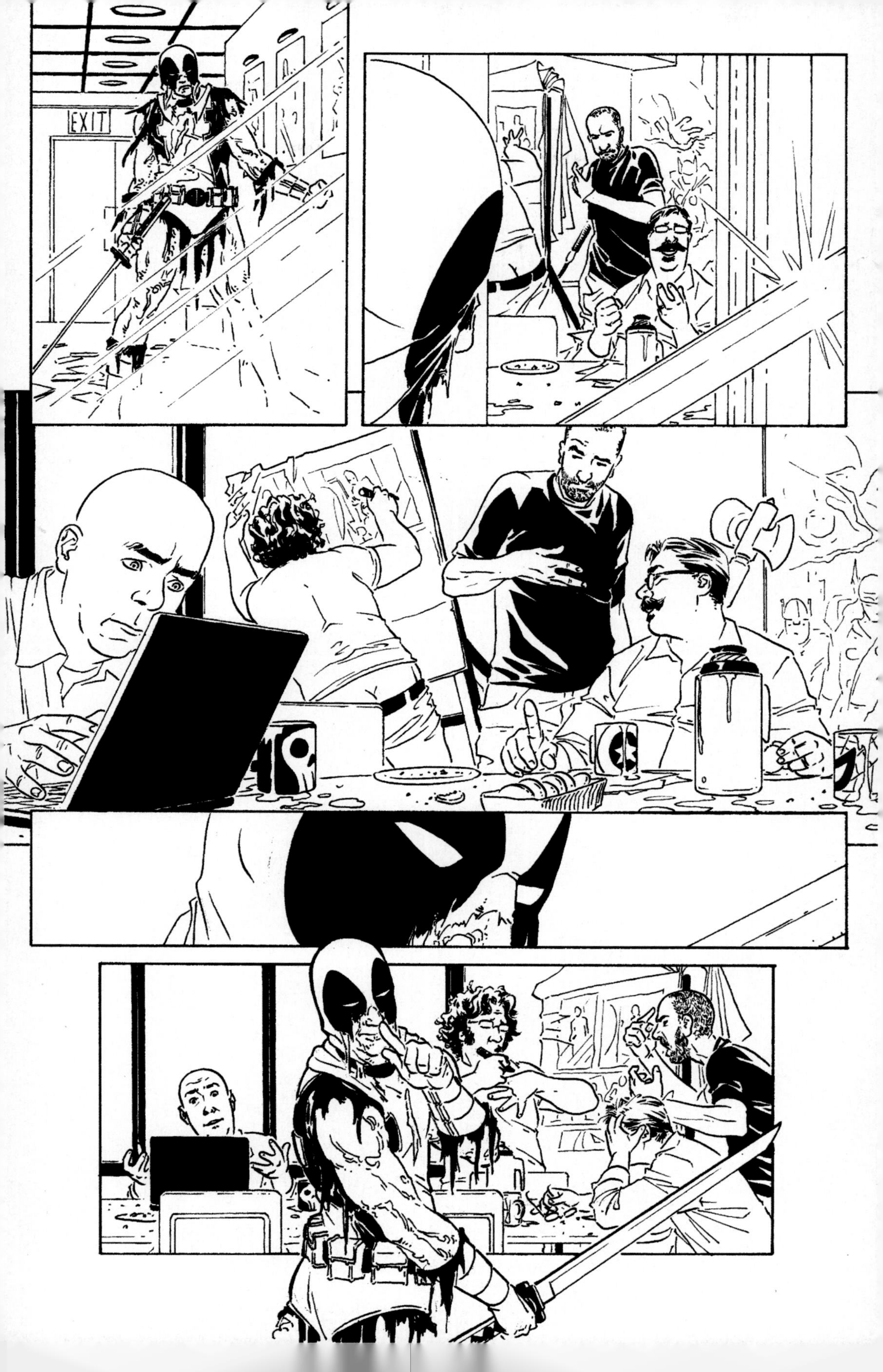
EXIT

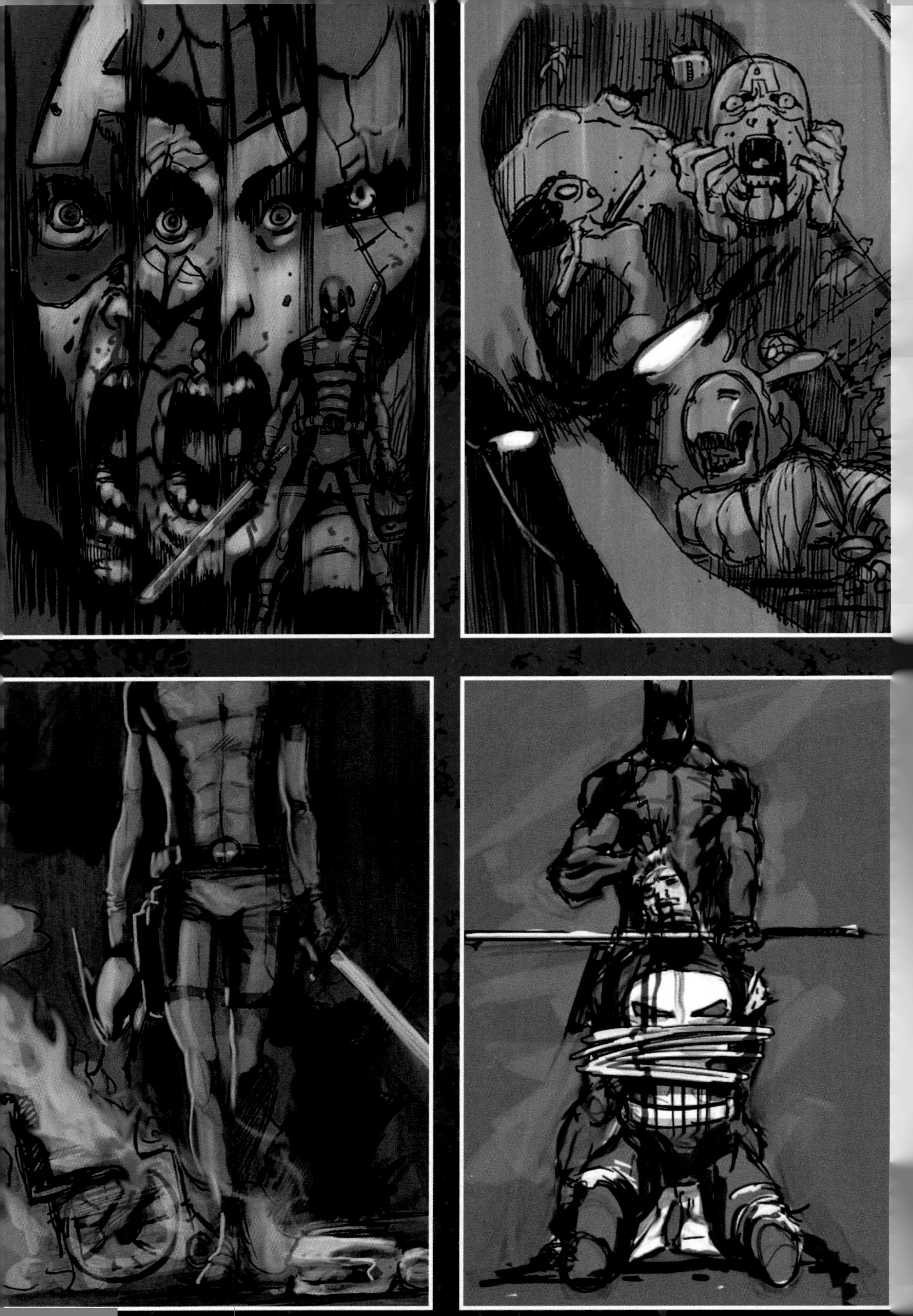

SKETCH

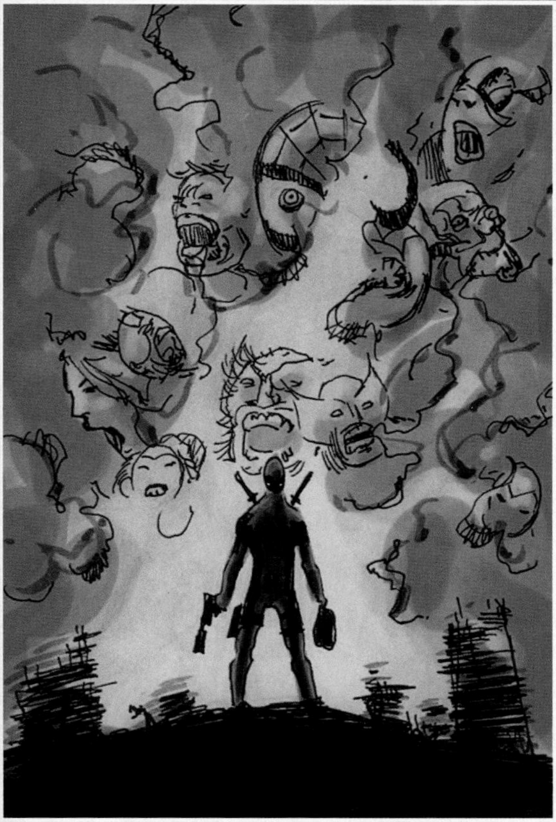
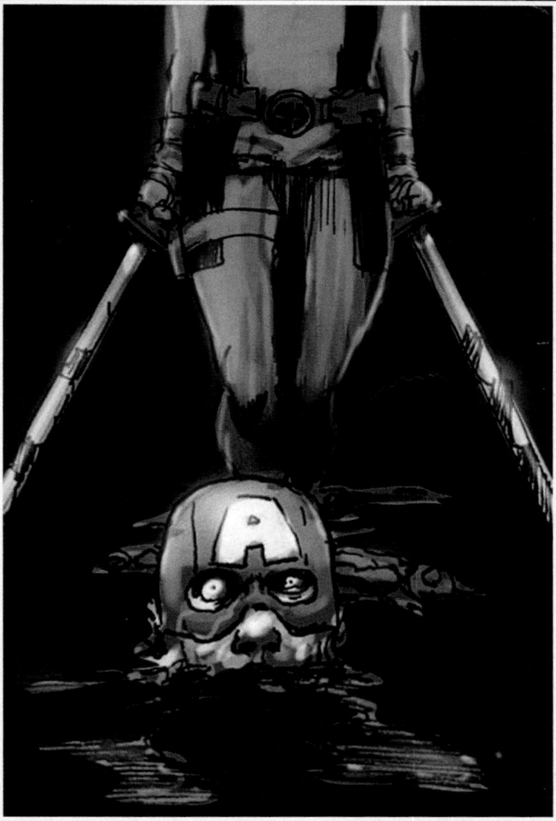
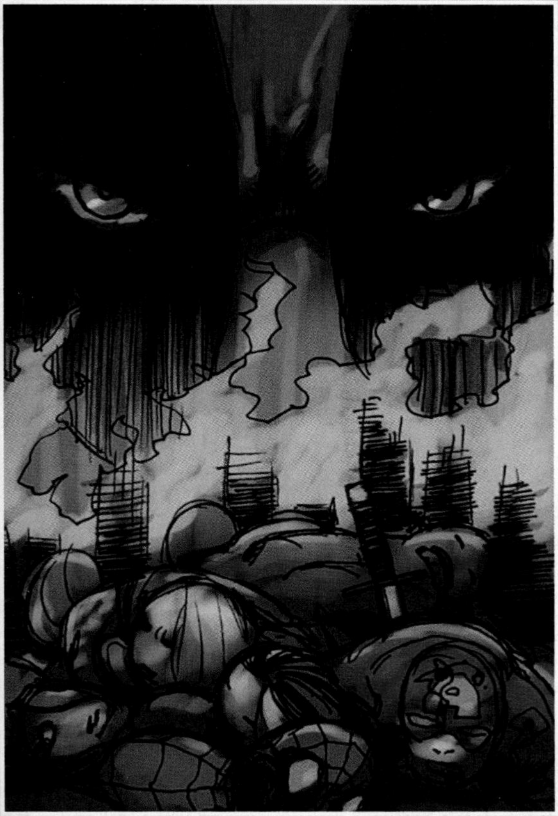
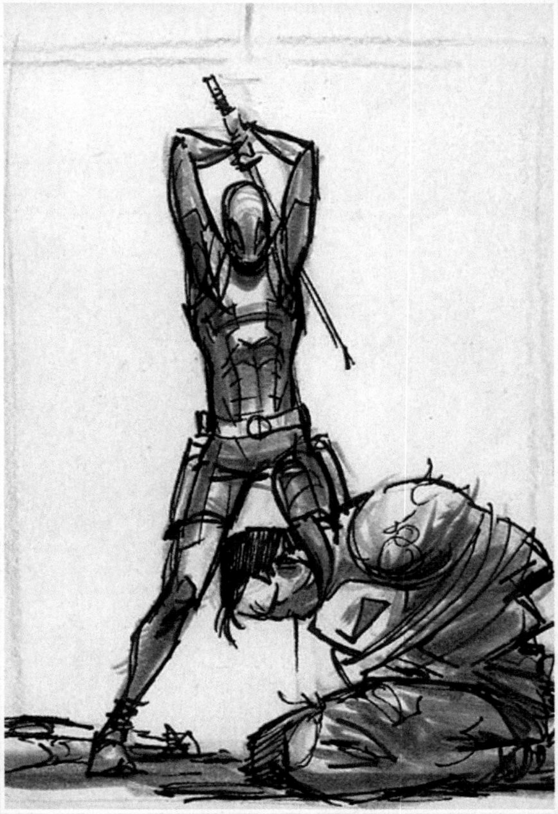

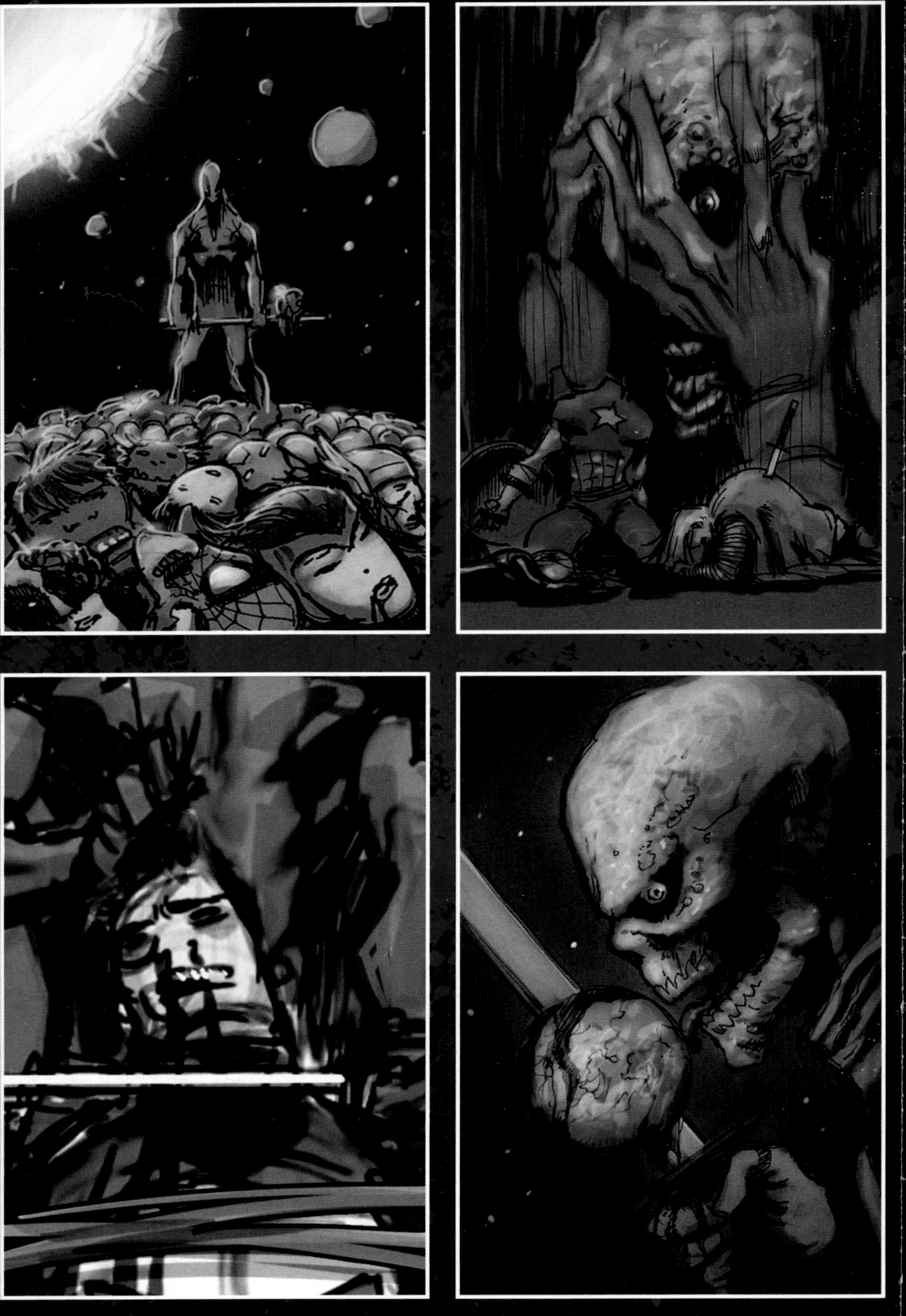